THINKING ABOUT GOD

JOHN MACQUARRIE

Thinking about God

1817

HARPER & ROW, PUBLISHERS
New York, Evanston, San Francisco, London

FIRST U.S. EDITION

ISBN: 0–06–065367–1

LIBRARY OF CONGRESS CATALOG CARD NUMBER: 74–25704

In Memoriam
Daniel Day Williams
1910-1973

Contents

Acknowledgments

Earlier versions of some of the chapters have appeared in various theological journals. I am especially indebted to the Editor and Publishers of *The Expository Times*, in which several pieces have appeared. Single items have been published in *The Anglican Theological Review, Christianity and Crisis, The International Journal of Philosophy of Religion, The Modern Churchman, Perspective, Theology* and *Theology Today.*

Preface

The chapters of this book originated for the most part as lectures, but they are held together by the common theme announced in the title, and I have revised and arranged them in such a way that as a whole they present an ordered discussion of the question of God and how we may think of him today.

The first seven chapters deal with problems of theological method, the nature of language about God, criteria for truth, types of theological approach and so on. The next six chapters are concerned directly with the meaning of belief in God and the grounds for such belief, and especially with the question of God's relation to the world. The final seven chapters discuss some representative religious thinkers, beginning with Schleiermacher, the father of modern theology, and ending with representatives of existential theology, process theology and the theology of hope.

Christ Church,   John Macquarrie
Oxford

PART ONE

Concepts and Method

1

The Nature of Theological Language

Probably the most important and distinctive characteristic of man is his use of language. He has been defined as *zoon logon echon* – 'the living being that has the word'. Whatever man does beyond the most elementary biological reactions, he makes use of language. Even when he is doing nothing overtly, his thoughts are formed by language.

Just as there are innumerable activities in which human beings engage, so, it would seem, there are innumerable kinds of language. These languages are appropriate to different activities and different situations, and each of them has its own rules – its 'logic', as we call it. Some logics are more clearly formulated than others, but we have to be careful not to set up one single pattern of logic and expect that all the different kinds of language will conform to it. The mathematician, the chemist, the poet, the historian, the politician, these all use language, but they use it in such different ways and for such different purposes that one could not expect that their different kinds of talk would conform to a single pattern. The differences arise on the one hand from the different subject-matters; language about mathematical entities is bound to be different from language about chemical substances, and this in turn will be different from language about such human phenomena as the state. The differences arise on the other hand from the different ways in which the speaker is related to what he is talking about; he may be a detached observer describing as objectively as possible phenomena that can be seen by anyone who looks, or he may be an active participant in what he is talking about, so that his words are also a report on his own attitudes. Clearly, too, there are many intermediate positions between that of the observer who is determined simply to report the objective facts of the case and that of a poet, let us say, who desires to communicate his own feelings and evaluations as these have been evoked by some state of affairs.

Yet while it can be acknowledged that there are many kinds of language and many logics, this in itself is not very helpful or informative. We want to know what these different logics are, how they are related to one another and whether they are all compatible with one another. We sometimes hear it said that every language has its logic. No doubt this broadminded assertion is preferable to the restrictive outlook of the logical positivists of an earlier time, and to their attempt to set up a single type of logic to which every language had to conform or else be dismissed as meaningless. But to allow that every language has its logic is not to say that all kinds of language are equally valuable or useful, or that some languages may not be illusory and misleading. Rather, the user of each kind of language is being invited to tell us what the logic of his particular language is. He is being asked to explain his procedures, to show where he gets his data, to say how he interprets the data, to specify what truth claims he is making and what criteria he has for testing them. The need to give this kind of explanation becomes especially urgent in certain border clashes, as it were, between disciplines, when different accounts of the same phenomenon are offered. In Gilbert Ryle's words, 'There often arise quarrels between theories, or, more generally, between lines of thought, which are not rival solutions of the same problem and which, none the less, seem to be irreconcilable with each other.'[1] For instance, a theologian might give an account of revelation in terms of the action of the Holy Spirit, while a psychologist might account for the same pheomenon in terms of factors immanent in the human psyche. These are not rival theories in the same sense in which two psychologists, working within the terms of their discipline, might produce different accounts of the matter. The theologian and the psychologist have come to the phenomenon along different lines of thought. But would it be enough to say that because of their different approaches, the two investigators perceive aspects of the matter which differ in each case? Or that the theologian is paying attention to factors which the psychologist, because of his method, leaves out? It would be too simple just to claim that the two approaches are different and that each is valid. There may be a real tension between the findings, especially if the psychologist claims that his account is exhaustive and that nothing of importance has been left out. The theologian is then required to produce his logical credentials and to show reasons for believing that his approach does indeed stand alongside the psychologist's and takes account of factors which the psychologist excludes.

To put the matter differently, although it may be said that every language has its logic, it does not follow that all these logics are equally coherent. And even if every language has its logic, all languages (I am referring here to the 'languages' of the various disciplines) use, aside from the specialist terminology belonging to each, the same basic vocabulary, and they employ the same basic syntax. Thus every language, if it is to be taken seriously, ought to be backed up by logical credentials commensurate with the importance of its truth claims and showing that it is entitled to its place in the whole family of meaningful languages.

It is perhaps unfortunate that so much has been made of Ludwig Wittgenstein's expression, 'language-game', for this might be taken to suggest a lack of seriousness, as if one could devise any language whatsoever as a matter of indifference. To quote a perceptive comment of James Alfred Martin: 'There may be reason to regret Wittgenstein's use of the idea of "games" in relation to language. Subsequent discussion reveals that what he meant is far from clear. Perhaps a more productive, though no less complex, idea is found in his suggestion that "to imagine a language means to imagine a form of life". Languages *can* be "imagined", and the contemplation of an imaginary language may remind one of certain basic characteristics of all languages as such. But men operate in the world with real, not imaginary, languages, and to say that they are "forms of life" is to say that they are living expressions of the knowledge, convictions, hopes, fears and visions of human beings engaged in the business of life.'[2] Still more unfortunately, the very expression 'form of life' seems to be afflicted with some ambiguity in Wittgenstein. Martin takes it that a language is itself a form of life, and his interpretation would seem to be correct on the basis of the passage that he quotes from Wittgenstein.[3] But elsewhere Wittgenstein uses the expression 'form of life' not simply for the language but for the whole activity with which the language is associated, so that he can say that 'the speaking of a language is *part* of an activity or of a form of life'.[4]

Some German philosophers are accustomed to make a useful distinction between 'language' (*Sprache*) and 'talk' (*Rede*). Language, in the restricted sense in which they understand it, consists of words and sentences, and these may be assessed in terms of their own logic, by considering their internal consistency and whether they abide by the rules of the game. Talk, on the other hand, is understood as living discourse; it is a human or existential phenomenon, a form of life. One could imagine a language which, though abiding by a logic of its own, did not articulate any actual form of life. Also, one could imagine a form of life which could not be articulated in a language governed by a conventional logic. The utterance of a poet, for instance, may be quite 'illogical' by formal standards – we are frequently puzzled to know what a poet means, as we say. Yet when seen in the context of the living discourse where the utterance originated, it may make very good sense and convey a definite insight; and the fact that it brings an insight shows that it is not merely an emotive utterance.

Up till now, my remarks have been applicable to language in general. But what has been said will be helpful in clarifying our particular problem, the nature of theological language. Since theology claims to deal with some of the most important matters affecting human existence, it is not very appropriate to talk of it as a 'language-game'. Certainly, theology has its logic, its own fairly complex 'rules of play' and these make it an internally coherent language. For instance, the logic of theology allows me to say 'God is loving', but if I say 'God weighs a billion tons', I am at once aware that this is inappropriate language, for I have broken one of the rules which says that a particular class of predicates may not be applied to God. (Incidentally, this also shows that the logic of God-language is not identical with that of person-language, for it is entirely appropriate to say both that Mary is loving and that Mary weighs fifty kilos.) Perhaps the later Wittgenstein did hold that the very fact that a game is played according to its own rules is a sufficient justification of that game; or that a form of life exists is just a fact to be accepted. He does indeed say: 'What has to be accepted, the given, is – so one could say – forms of life.'[5] This seems to lead in the direction of a theological fideism. One is reminded of the remark of existentialist Unamuno: 'The fact that faith exists, and only that, proves its truth.'[6]

But can God-talk be so lightly vindicated? I do not think so. Theology makes such large truth claims and carries such implications for all aspects of human life that neither its advocates nor its critics could be content to leave the question here. Its advocates will refuse to accept that God-talk is adequately represented as a self-justifying linguistic phenomenon, whether we call it a 'language-game' or a 'form of life'. They consider it *part* of a form of life which is more than linguistic, so that the language which articulates and expresses this form of life points to realities beyond the language itself. They would have to part company with Wittgenstein if indeed, as David Pears says, 'it is Wittgenstein's later doctrine that outside human thought and speech there are no independent objective points of support, and meaning and necessity are preserved only in the linguistic practices which embody them'.[7] And surely the critics of theology would be equally unwilling to accept it as a 'given' linguistic practice, for they think it is a thoroughly misleading one.

If the theologian is to stay with his truth claims, he cannot escape giving an account of the credentials of his subject, and showing how it is related to and where it differs from psychology, sociology, history and so on. Especially at a time when theology is suspect and some people want to classify it with such pseudo-sciences as astrology and alchemy, it is necessary that the theologian should show that he is in a legitimate line of business.

Several preliminary points may be made about the nature of theological language.

1. The form of life which this language articulates is the life of faith or religion. That is to say, it is in the life of faith or religion that concrete theological discourse has its home, so to speak. It is in this life setting that one must attempt 'the empirical placing of theological phrases', to borrow the late Ian Ramsey's expression.[8] Religious language includes prayer, confession, recital and many other forms, and is therefore much wider than theology, which is only one part of religious language. Theology is a reflective and sophisticated kind of religious language, yet any attempt to explain its logic must have regard to its connection with religious language as a whole and to the life of faith in which religious discourse takes place.

2. The key-word of theology is the word 'God' – indeed, etymologically, theology is 'God-talk' or discourse about God. This word (or some more or less equivalent word) lies behind everything that the theologian says, and integrates all the separate areas into which his investigations may lead him. Whether the theologian talks of revelation or grace or justification or the last things, these are all understood as acts or manifestations of God, so that if one could give an account of the logic of the word 'God' one would have gone far towards giving an account of the logic of theology as a whole. Here again we see the necessity and the urgency of our task, for it is precisely this word 'God' that seems to have become elusive in the contemporary secularized world, and some

people even tell us that the word has become meaningless or at least that any talk employing this word is hopelessly incoherent.

3. If theology is on the one side related to the language of religion, it is related on the other to the language of science. I use the word 'science' here in the widest sense, to stand for an ordered intellectual discipline. It is obvious that theology is not a science in the same way that chemistry is. Neither of them are sciences in the same way that history is a science. It is a gain to recognize the difference of theology from both the natural and the social sciences, and we may readily accept Pears' claim that 'by refusing to locate the truths of religion and morality within factual discourse, Wittgenstein was not rejecting them but trying to preserve them'.[9] But it is significant that he speaks of the *'truths* of religion'. Theology is no doubt a different kind of science, but it does claim to be an intellectual discipline and to aim at truth. Its business is to explain and interpret, to make intelligible and credible, and these are characteristics that it has in common with all other intellectual disciplines. This implies that theology must have its own standards of methodological integrity, different no doubt, yet no less strict, than the standards accepted by the historian or the chemist in their fields.

These three preliminary points already indicate how complex is our problem. Theological language is one into which many strands have entered and become interwoven. It is even doubtful if we may speak of theological language in the singular, as if it were a unitary phenomenon. What is there in common between, let us say, the language of St Thomas Aquinas with its objective affirmations, and the language of Schleiermacher with its subjective ponderings? Or between the language of Barth with its kerygmatic and biblical style, and the language of Tillich with its apologetic and philosophical approach? Perhaps all that they have in common is that they represent attempts to talk reflectively about God and his action. Yet it can be argued that these styles of theological language do belong together within the general framework of discoures about God, and that the differences which they exhibit arise from differences in the weighting which each of these theologians assigns to the various strands that go to make up theological discourse. There are certain poles within which theological discourse is conducted, but quite naturally we find different theologians swinging out toward opposite poles. Let me now try to say what some of the polarities are, and in that way we shall map out the boundaries of theological talk. It will be noted however that each polarity tends to overlap with the others.

We begin with the *confessional-critical polarity*. The language of theology, as distinct, let us say, from the language of a consciously disinterested philosophy of religion, speaks from within faith. It arises within the community of faith, and strives to bring the form of life that it finds there to clearer verbal expression. All theology therefore has an element of confessional language. It brings to expression the confession of the community as it acknowledges its experience of God. Statements of theological belief put out by religious bodies are appropriately known as 'confessions of faith'.

Here we may take note of a sub-polarity that arises in theology – that between the experience of the individual and the history of the community. Theology is usually produced by individuals. Unless the individual did have in his own experience some acquaintance with the phenomena designated by the names 'sin', 'grace', 'the presence of God' and the like, he could hardly know what such expressions mean and he might not believe that there are such experiences at all. Yet he also sets his own experiences in the total history of the community, and allows them to be judged and interpreted according to the common understanding of the community. In the case of the Christian theologian, this means that he sets his own experiences of sin, grace and the rest in the context of what the Bible and the traditional teaching of the church have to say on these matters. There is always a reciprocal process of interpretation going on between the individual's experience and the community's tradition. In some cases, this may be experienced as a very acute tension, for inevitably some theologians will find a discrepancy between their own experience and the tradition. The theologian has to avoid the danger of setting up his individual peculiarities as universal norms (and this has been a common defect in so-called 'empirical' theologies) and yet he has equally to avoid the danger of passively accepting a tradition that may seem to have little affinity with his own experience or the experience of his generation. This tension is one of the factors that operates in the development of theology.

However this sub-polarity is resolved, the first strand in theological language is undoubtedly the confessional one, the acknowledgment of what God has done in the experience of the faithful community or faithful individual. This confessional element is clearly seen in the order of almost any textbook of dogmatic theology, for although such a book is arranged systematically and follows the logical connections of the several doctrines, it still reflects the narrative order of the Bible and of the confession or recital of the believing community – creation, fall, redemption, expectation.

But theological language is always more than confessional. It must show something of the other pole also, the critical pole. When Peter acknowledged the Lord with the words, 'You are the Christ' (Mark 8.29), or Thomas with the words, 'My Lord and my God!' (John 20.28), this was confession, but it was not yet theology. Such utterances of faith provide the raw material for theology, but they become theology only as they are subjected to a critical process of reflection, interpretation, comparison, correction. It is this critical aspect of theology that constitutes it an intellectual discipline. The theologian will seek to explicate the meaning of the faith of the confessing community as clearly as he can in the language of his day. He will compare this faith with other convictions that men hold, and ask whether it is compatible with them. He will compare his own interpretation with those offered by such secular investigators of religion as the anthropologist and the psychologist, and again he will ask about the compatibility of the different accounts. He will probe into the foundations of faith and ask whether it is well founded or whether it seems more likely to be illusion. At least in some of his investigations, notably those into historical events, the methods of the theologian will not differ from those of any other investigator into such matters.

Yet, so long as theology remains theology, it will show both its confessional and critical aspects. In a kerygmatic type of theology, such as that of Barth, the confessional language preponderates, while in an answering or apologetic type of theology, such as that of Tillich, the critical language is more in evidence. But Barth is not uncritical, and Tillich is not non-confessional.

A second polarity to be noted is the *existential-ontological*. By this expression I mean that a genuine theology speaks always of God and man together, and not of either of them in isolation. In the later phase of his thinking, Barth went so far as to say that theology would be better called 'theanthropology'.[10] We do not talk of God in isolation, as if we could stand back and observe him, as we might do in the case of a natural phenomenon. We speak of him only on the basis of his self-communication to us, and this points us again to the confession of the community of faith and its belief that God has made himself known in certain revelatory experiences. But this does not mean that talk of God is merely subjective, or that it has to do only with describing our states of mind and attitudes. This language talks also of 'the way things are', for it is a fundamental conviction of faith that the whole initiative in the life of faith comes from beyond man, and that his life is touched by a reality beyond himself and prior to himself. This reality he calls God; it constitutes the objective pole of the relation, and theological discourse is conducted in the tension between these two poles.

Let us begin with the existential side. Theological language is not neutrally descriptive. It is a language which involves the speaker's own being and which expresses his attitudes and evaluations. Such language can therefore be interpreted existentially, as setting before us a style of existence. Especially Rudolf Bultmann, in recent decades, has shown the importance of the existential dimension of theology. The doctrine of creation, for instance, would be misunderstood if it were taken to be simply a report about how the world got started in the remote past. The doctrine is theologically significant because it tells us who we are.

But once again theology has to employ a dialectical language that will not be absorbed in only one pole but will move in the field of tension between two poles. There can be little doubt that much contemporary theology has swung towards an almost complete subjectivizing, so that theology comes near to being swallowed up in anthropology. Extreme versions of 'secular theology' and 'death of god theology' illustrate this, though it should be noted that even in them some kind of 'ultimate concern' remains as a surrogate for God.

But theology does not confine itself to talking of what it feels like to have faith. Emotive, conative and purely existential theories of religious language short-change faith itself, in the sense that they do not exhaust the meaning of faith and ignore faith's own basic conviction that it is faith *in* some reality beyond faith itself. Faith is intentional. It seems to make no sense to talk of faith in isolation, a kind of faith for faith's sake. One must also be prepared to say something about the ground of faith, about that which makes faith possible and evokes it. But to do this means that we have to talk not just of our own attitudes, but of 'the way things are'. God is certainly our 'ultimate concern', to take up Tillich's expression, quoted in the preceding paragraph, that is to say, God has profound existential significance. But Tillich saw that God must also be recognized as 'being itself' if he is properly an ultimate concern and not an idol. More generally, we might say that anyone who seriously ponders the human condition and the goals that claim man's ultimate allegiance is led inevitably to ask about the wider context of being within which man's being has its setting. He is led to the ontological question. This is especially true in the perplexing times in which we live, and it seems likely that positivism is less common today than it was a generation ago.

A third polarity is the *particular-universal*, and this is one that is experienced with special acuteness in Christian theology. For Christianity is not a body of timeless truths of reason but claims to be founded on historical events that took place at a particular time in history and at a particular place on the face of the earth. Yet these events are at the same time invested with a universal significance.

At times when rationalist and idealist philosophies have been in the ascendant, the concrete historical aspects of Christianity have been devalued, and the figure of Jesus Christ himself made merely the exemplar of a life pleasing to God (Kant) or the union of the divine and the human (Hegel). For these philosophers and for much of the theology which they influenced, it is the universal essence or idea which matters, not its instantiation in a particular historical person. But surely this does less than justice to the Christian affirmation, which is not merely that there is a Logos or idea, but that the Logos has become flesh in a particular man at a particular time in a particular place. Without this concreteness, Christianity becomes another gnosis. So in opposition to the philosophies of essence, there arises the philosophy of existence, and we find Kierkegaard stressing the unique concrete incarnation of the Logos in Jesus Christ, however much of a paradox or even an offence such an incarnation may be. Yet even if we agree that Kierkegaard had an important point as against idealism, the universal significance of the Christ remains, and Christian theology has to find a language which will preserve the tension between the particular and the universal and will not be entirely determined by either pole in isolation from the other.

We come to a fourth polarity, the *symbolic-conceptual*. We have seen that if theology is to be true to its aim and to the intention of faith, it must talk about God as well as of man. But how can we talk of God? Our language seems to be adapted for talking about the finite beings we encounter in the world, whether material things or other persons. We have left far behind the mythological mentality, which supposed that the gods too appeared in sensible shape among the phenomena of space and time. For a long time too, men have been aware that if anything affirmative can be said about God, it can be said only in an oblique way, in which we use the finite entities that we experience in the world to point beyond themselves to that which is not another such entity but is rather the source of all entities, the condition that there can be anything whatsoever.

God in himself is an ineffable mystery, and if he were less than that, could we call him God at all? But if he has, as the community of faith confesses, touched and transformed human life, surely we can say something about him, and something that goes beyond a merely negative theology – though admittedly such a *via negationis* should not be undervalued, for it is a safeguard against over-familiarity and downright idolatry. Theologians claim that they can say something about him, and they do so by the use of images, symbols, analogues, models.[11] None of these can be taken literally. This means that they have to be both affirmed and denied, so that theological language has a paradoxical character. Nowadays, however, the use of non-picturing models is also familiar in physics.

The symbolic elements in theological language preserve the mystery and transcendence of God, and acknowledge that he is characterized by an 'otherness' that goes beyond the grasp of rational thought. Such symbols are evocative rather than straightforwardly descriptive. As examples, one may think of the symbolizing of the Holy Spirit as wind or fire or water, and of the meanings which these terms evoke.

But once again there is the danger of subjectivism, even perhaps of occultism, unless we can offer some rational interpretation of the symbols, while acknowledging that such an interpretation is never exhaustive. We speak of the Holy Spirit not only in the symbols mentioned above but in such concepts as creativity, procession, unification. Although no concepts can adequately express the being of God, we must deploy such concepts as are available for the interpretation and articulation of the symbols of faith. To acknowledge the mystery of God is not to renounce any effort to understand him as far as possible, and certainly the business of theology is elucidation, not mystification. So again we find theological language displaying a dialectical character, employing both images and concepts, and allowing them to interpret each other. A healthy tension has to be maintained at this point also. Theology has to develop intelligible concepts for the articulation of its subject-matter, but it has to do this without falling into sheer abstraction and without infringing the mystery of God.

We have been content for the present with showing some of the strands that enter into theological language and the dialectical tensions among them. The various possible ways of handling these tensions account for the many types of theology. Since we have had in mind Christian theology especially, and since this theology has its centre of reference in Jesus Christ, it will be obvious that some, though not all, of the tensions converge on Christ. According to Christian faith, he is human and divine, a concrete historical existent and yet the eternal Logos. Christ is himself that 'given' form of life which theology seeks to articulate in a language. How one discriminates among the variant types of theology and decides what language truly articulates the given, and whether one can probe into the credentials of the given itself are topics that must be left to other essays.[12]

Notes

1. Gilbert Ryle, *Dilemmas*, Cambridge University Press 1954, p. 1.

2. J. A. Martin, *The New Dialogue between Philosophy and Theology*, Seabury Press 1966, p. 110.

3. L. Wittgenstein, *Philosophical Investigations*, tr. G. E. M. Ascombe, Blackwell 1968, p. 8.

4. Op. cit., p. 11.

5. Op. cit., p. 226.

6. M. de Unamuno, *Diario Intimo*, Alianza Editorial 1970, p. 25.

7. D. Pears, *Wittgenstein*, Collins 1971, p. 168.

8. This was the subtitle of his book, *Religious Language*, SCM Press and Macmillan 1957.

9. D. Pears, op. cit., p. 57.

10. K. Barth, *The Humanity of God*, tr. J. N. Thomas and T. Weiser, Collins 1967, p. 9.

11. For a discussion of these terms, see J. Macquarrie, *God-Talk*, SCM Press and Harper & Row 1967, chapters 9 and 10.

12. This chapter is based on a paper prepared for the Lambeth Conference 1968, and published in A. M. Ramsey (ed.) *Lambeth Essays on Faith*, SPCK 1969.

2

Truth in Theology

Theology claims to be true, just as the faith which it explicates claims to be true. But if, as we have seen in the first essay in this book, theological language has a highly complex dialectical texture, then its truth and the assessment of its truth are no simple matters. The truth of a theological doctrine does not seem to be, for instance, like the truth of a mathematical proposition. The latter is true if it can be validly deduced from the fundamental axioms and definitions on which the mathematical system is based. But the 'given' of theology is not itself a set of propositions; it is a form of life, the life of a community of faith, and, in the case of Christian theology, a community centred on the person Jesus Christ. Now this living reality could never be transposed into words in anything other than a fragmentary way; and although the writings of the New Testament are, so to speak, the charter of the community and the witness to its origins, they are already themselves embarked on the theological task and are quite different from the givens of a deductive system. On the other hand, the truth of a theological doctrine seems to be different also from the truth of an empirical proposition. If theology is essentially God-talk, and if God is not a sensible phenomenon, then assertions about God are quite different from, let us say, assertions about the weather, and their truth must be differently evaluated.

Of course, I am not saying that deductive and empirical tests are never relevant to the question of theological truth. Theologies tend to be evaluated as wholes. Their several doctrines flow into each other and mutually support each other, and this is what one might expect if theology is the exploration of one primary datum. Within a theological system, one can usually distinguish some doctrines that are more central, others that are more peripheral, and very often the truth claim for the more peripheral doctrines will rest on the argument that they are deducible from the central doctrines. Again, since Christian theology appeals to events of history, it cannot help becoming involved in empirical truth claims. That Jesus Christ lived, and that he died on a cross, is an assertion implied by Christian theology, and it asserts a matter of fact that can be investigated empirically. If the existence of Jesus could be disproved or made to seem highly improbable, this would be a serious matter for many Christian theologies. But it should be noted that some would still say that this did not affect the truth of Christianity, and certainly that truth is not exclusively an empirical truth.

Is the truth of theology then something *sui generis*? The danger of saying this would be that theology might become shut up in itself as a kind of private language-game, and surely the whole point of laying claim to truth is to put forward a belief publicly as worthy of acceptance. On the other hand, perhaps every discipline has its own understanding of truth and its own tests for truth, though these would not be unrelated to other disciplines. Does this mean then that there is some overarching concept of truth? At least, we would have to say that neither in the past nor in the present have philosophers been able to agree what this is. They have advanced correspondence theories, coherence theories, pragmatic theories and so on.

Let me now set down three presuppositions which will serve to introduce the further discussion of truth in theology. These presuppositions can scarcely be demonstrated, but I believe that reflection upon them shows them to be reasonable assumptions to make.

The first presupposition is that *truth is multiform*. We have already taken note that the truth of a mathematical proposition is of a different order from the truth of an empirical proposition, and this would be generally accepted. But the multiformity goes further. We may quote a theologian, R. C. Moberly: 'Truth is manifold and multiform. There are truths of material fact; truths of abstract statement; truths of historical occurrence; truths of moral experience; truths of spiritual existence; and that truth is deepest and truest, which most includes and unifies them all.'[1] Moberly is acknowledging that truth is multiform, yet he is also claiming that somehow it is also one, or ought to be one. So even if one says that truth is multiform, one can hardly leave the matter there, and say that after all, the assertions of mathematics, of chemistry, of history, of theology are all true (or capable of being true), but the truth is in every case different. The nature of the differences has to be explored, and the criteria for truth made clear in each case. Can the theologian, for instance, point to criteria in his discipline that have anything like the clarity and definiteness that belong to the criteria of the scientist (or are commonly supposed to belong to them)? Unless the theologian can make plain what he means when he claims to be dealing in a different form of truth, his truth claims may well be disregarded. As well as claiming that truth is multiform we must, like Moberly, acknowledge that there is something unifying in truth. It is not just that we use the word 'truth' in every case. The point is rather that there is in every case a claim to be true. This claim may constitute what, in Wittgenstein's useful expression, we could call a 'family resemblance' among the many forms of truth. Moberly presumably had much more in mind when he visualized an inclusive, unifying truth. Let me tentatively suggest that what is common to the several forms of truth is that they all claim to let us see, as it is, without concealment or distortion, that which is talked about.

The second presupposition is that *truth has a personal dimension*. Truths do not float around the universe like clouds of cosmic dust. Truths are truths for someone. They are not so much properties as events – the truth takes place when it is appropriated by an intelligent agent. Truths, again, can be relied on; truth is trustworthy. Admittedly, the personal dimension varies in importance from one form of truth to another. Mathematical formulae can be circulated in textbooks, factual data can be fed into computers. In these cases, the personal dimension seems quite unimportant, though perhaps it is never totally absent. On the other hand, when one is dealing with religious or theological truth, the personal appropriation of such truth is of the highest importance. The point is well made by Kierkegaard. Truth 'is not the duplication of being in terms of thought ... the truth consists not in knowing the truth but in being the truth'. This truth of being is inseparable from the way that leads to it, and significantly Christ claims to be 'the way and the truth and the life' (John 14.7). Kirkegaard contrasts two kinds of truth – the kind that can be written down on a piece of paper and instantly appropriated, and the kind which calls for a long and perhaps painful process of inward appropriation. He gives as an example the case of a man who spends twenty years in discovering the formula for gunpowder. Once discovered, the formula is immediately available and the twenty years have become irrelevant. But 'when the truth itself is the way, the way cannot be shortened or drop out without the truth being corrupted or dropping out'.[2] One may compare his famous definition of truth as 'an objective uncertainty held fast in an appropriation-process of the most passionate inwardness'. This, he claims, 'is the truth, the highest truth attainable for an existing individual'.[3] In this definition, of course, he is explicitly thinking of Christianity, and contrasting the uncertainty of every historical assertion (such an assertion never goes beyond approximation) with the truth of faith, which inevitably involves risk. But we shall come back to these matters later.

Meanwhile, we pass to our third presupposition, that *truth is always culturally and historically conditioned*. At least, whenever a truth is formulated in words (as theology is), it must participate in the language and conceptuality of a given epoch. The New Testament witness to Jesus Christ is unquestionably conditioned by the world view of the first century and therefore by ideas like demon possession and apocalyptic expectation which form no part of our modern conceptuality. To be sure, there may be a truth which endures through its many historical formulations, but we never encounter this truth unformulated, in a supposedly pure form that is uncontaminated by a cultural outlook. A quite extreme statement of the relativity of truth is given by J. L. Austin, and it is interesting to note how at this point this analytic philosopher comes close to some existentialists in his denial that there are objective, timeless truths. 'True and false', he writes, 'do not stand for anything simple, but only for a general dimension of being a right and proper thing as opposed to a wrong thing, in these circumstances, to this audience, for these purposes and with these intentions.'[4] This view of truth certainly rules out the possibility that there could be a final theology or an immutable formulation of dogma. But on the other hand, there is no denial that the distinction of true and false is a real one. It is indeed a sociologist, Peter Berger, who has made much of the sociology of knowledge but who feels compelled to remind us that 'once we know that all human affirmations are subject to scientifically graspable socio-historical procedures, (we have still to ask) *which affirmations are true and which false?*'[5]

However different truth may be for the practitioners of different intellectual disciplines, in each case its locus is held to lie in the propositions or statements of the discipline. But now we must take cognizance of a still deeper difference in our talking about truth, for sometimes it is claimed that the locus of truth does not lie in propositions but in concrete realities of one kind or another. We can talk of 'true coin' (a thing), of 'a true meeting of minds' (a situation), or, most importantly, Christians, following the lead of the fourth gospel, are prepared to affirm that Jesus Christ is the truth (a person). Indeed, many theologians, especially at the present time, would probably say that the truth in which they are chiefly interested and which they are trying to bring to expression is the living personal truth of Christ; and that theological statements are true only to the extent that they are 'true to' the reality of Christ, pointing us to it and illuminating it. But theologians differ among themselves about how far they are willing to stress this point. Some would want to make more, others less, of the truth of the statements and propositions themselves. As Hans Küng has pointed out, Roman Catholic theology in the nineteenth century was very much concerned 'for clear and unequivocal propositions, for the maximum possible definition of the teaching of the Church'.[6] Thus there was the promulgation of such dogmas as immaculate conception and papal infallibility, each spelled out in detail. In the twentieth century, first among Protestants and more recently among Roman Catholics as well, there has been a swing away from propositional theology, even to the point of devaluing it quite drastically. But it seems clear that one cannot wholly escape the question about the truth of doctrines or the whole body of doctrine by appealing to a personal truth of Christ that is prior to all doctrines, for some spelling out of that fundamental truth in the verbal formulations of theological doctrines seems to be inevitable. One has then to ask how truly these doctrines communicate or reflect the fundamental truth from which they are derived. Certainly, the appeal to 'the truth of Christ' cannot be made the excuse for theological indifferentism or for maintaining that finally one theological formulation is as good as another.

But it is necessary for us to examine much more carefully what can be meant by saying that Christ is himself the truth. We do find this assertion in the fourth gospel and in some modern theologians of a personalist or existentialist bent. What is meant by the truth of a person or of a human reality, as distinct from the truth of propositions? The personal or existential understanding of truth is perhaps best expounded in the writings of Kierkegaard and Heidegger.

Kierkegaard directly raises the question: 'What is truth, and in what sense was Christ the truth?' He answers: 'Christ is the truth in such a sense that to *be* the truth is the only explanation of what truth is.'[7] Admittedly, there is an obscurity here. The claim is to be understood in the light of Kierkegaard's criticism of the ideal of objective truth, understood as the agreement of thought (or language) and being. 'The way of objective reflection makes the subject accidental.' Objective truth could be obtained only if two conditions were fulfilled: first, that being were finished and complete, and second, that the thinker had a vantage point outside of being from which he could pronounce on the agreement (or disagreement) between thought and being. But only God can view things *sub specie aeternitatis*. Thus the existing thinker, who is inserted into the midst of being, must choose a different way toward truth, a way that swings off from the objective way. 'A subjective reflection makes its way inwardly in inwardness.' Again, he writes: 'The truth consists in nothing else than the self-activity of personal appropriation.'[8]

Does this stress on inwardness and subjectivity contradict the point we have made that truth claims seem by their very nature to be public? It might be replied that if the truth with which we are concerned is not the truth of propositions but the truth of personal being, then the only way to the truth is precisely this inward way. It may be noted too that Kierkegaard cites Socrates as the supreme example of an 'existing thinker', for he was the philosopher who sought to follow the command, 'Know thyself!' and who believed that truth is to be recalled from the depth of the self.

But it will be interesting to set alongside Kierkegaard's teaching the more sober remarks of Heidegger. He too sees the locus of truth (or, at any rate, of the most important kind of truth) in existence rather than in propositions. He does indeed mention the example of someone standing with his back to the wall and saying, 'The picture behind me is hanging squint.' He acknowledges that the truth of this statement can be tested by the obvious procedure of turning round and seeing whether one's words are in agreement with the observed state of affairs.[9] But he maintains that what makes an assertion true is not the fact of agreement, but the fact that the assertion 'uncovers the entity as it is in itself'. Repeatedly in his writings, Heidegger reminds us that the Greek word for truth is *aletheia*, literally 'unhiddenness'. When concealments and distortions have been removed, and that which is can be seen for what it is, the event of truth takes place. While

Heidegger does not use Kierkegaard's language about the 'subjectivity' of truth, it is clear that for him too truth is always *for* a person, who can be in the truth and appropriate the truth. Man in his self-consciousness is the locus in the universe (so far as we know) where the opacity of things has come into the light. He is like a clearing in the forest. He participates in overtness. That is to say, he stands in the possibility of being the locus of truth or unconcealment, though there is likewise the possibility of untruth when concealment and distortion prevail.

Applying these understandings of truth to Jesus Christ as 'the truth', can we now see more clearly what it means to make this claim for Christ? What does he bring into the light and make unhidden? This at once raises the question of christology. This is not surprising. If, for the Christian community, Christ is the truth, then the study of who Christ is and what Christ means will converge with the investigation into the question of truth. Bonhoeffer grasped a somewhat similar point when he noted that if Christ is the Logos, then christology is logology. It is, he claimed, the highest science because it is *logos* concerning *logos* itself.[10] So it is neither an accident nor a digression if our discussion of truth in theology leads us into christology.

We come back then to the question: 'What does Christ bring into the light and make unhidden?' Following the trend of current christology, we may say that Christ brings to light a true humanity, he makes unhidden what man has it in him to become. If by turning within himself man discovers an image of a true humanity to which he is obscurely called, does he see this image fulfilled and made unhidden in Christ? The Christian community does indeed claim that this is the case. Of course, there is a reciprocity in this act of recognition. The project of a true humanity within points to Christ as its fulfilment; Christ in turn delivers the project from concealment and distortion. There is also a risk in this act. One could never step outside the human situation to obtain an objective confirmation of the agreement between Christ and a true humanity. Kierkegaard is therefore correct in saying that it is in the face of objective uncertainty that one must inwardly appropriate this truth. Yet it is not just a matter of subjective preference, as if one might equally have decided that the truth of humanity is best uncovered in Hitler or Casanova. There is a givenness of self-understanding in man (we could call it 'conscience', in one sense of that word) which points him in some ways rather than in others.

Furthermore, man does not exist in isolation. He is part of that intricate and interdependent system that we call Nature, and indeed (so far as we know) he stands at the head of that hierarchy of beings which Nature has brought forth. So the Christian is bold to claim that Christ is also the truth of the cosmos. He makes unhidden the meaning of the process of Nature. Christian faith goes further still and believes that Christ is the truth of the ultimate reality we call God. Hence, to recall Moberly's expression, Christ is 'that deepest and truest truth, which most includes and unifies all truths'. And Bonhoeffer moves in the same direction, because for him, as Heinrich Ott has shown,[11] Christ is reality, in the full ontological sense of the word.

At this point it should be added that the Christ-reality or the Christ-event must not be narrowly identified with the career of the individual person, Jesus of Nazareth. He is indeed the centre of it and the clue to its character, but it spreads out beyond him both in space and time. The community which he gathered around him and eventually the whole church or people of God are incorporated into the Christ-event. Again, that event did not begin with the birth of Jesus nor did it end with, let us say, his ascension. It has been preparing from the beginning and is still going on. Nevertheless, it is important to maintain some balance between the concrete identifiable figure of Jesus as the centre or focus of the event, giving the whole its character, and the more peripheral areas. If it would be a mistaken narrowing to concentrate entirely on the 'historical Jesus', there is also the danger of a diffuseness and loss of content if he is simply dissolved into a somewhat vague totality. Perhaps a useful analogy at this point would be that of the living cell. Jesus Christ may be likened to the nucleus of the cell, the centre which has a controlling role but which is inseparable from the surrounding area and which along its boundaries is in constant interaction with that surrounding area. The further importance of these remarks will become clearer later on.

But now we must return to language, and inquire about the truth that may belong to doctrinal statements or propositions. We have held that the primary truth is the truth of Jesus Christ himself. Christians believe that in his life and in the total event of which he is the creative centre, he makes unhidden the destiny of man and even the reality of God himself, so far as this can be grasped by human minds. This living concrete truth comes before all statements about it, and it cannot be fully transcribed into words.

It is more than a 'word-event', to use the expression favoured by Gerhard Ebeling. Yet in saying that the Christ-event comes before propositions about it, I do not mean that it can be appropriated apart from language. Ebeling is correct in drawing attention to the fundamental role of language in the constitution of man. We may say that the living personal truth of Christ is prior to any doctrinal language about him, in the sense that it is the personal reality which founds such language. On the other hand, it is the language that permits us to participate in the truth and articulate the truth of the personal reality. Part of the Christ-event is language – Jesus' teaching, his conversations with his disciples, his disputes with his enemies and so on – just as part of any human and personal event is language. Let us agree that the personal truth of Jesus Christ is more than words, yet we still have to say that it cannot be appropriated apart from words. The first words uttered about Christ by the disciples were exclamatory and confessional rather than descriptive, but they gave way to ever more subtle statements about Jesus Christ as the complexity of the living truth came to be more and more explored and articulated in the emerging discipline of Christian theology. But it has also to be said that with every elaboration of language and with the development of doctrinal formulation, there appeared the possibility of error, for language can obscure as well as illuminate.

What is it then that distinguishes true language from false language, true doctrine from false doctrine? We have already seen that the so-called correspondence theory of truth appears to have a very limited applicability. That theory rests on another – the picture theory of language, according to which a proposition exhibits a structure representing the structure of some fact. But this theory of language, though it was once widely held, is deficient at many points. It has little relevance in theology and even in the empirical sciences it has only a very limited degree of plausibility.[12] The business of language is not to provide us with a verbal or mental picture of the reality talked about, but rather to light up that reality itself so that we see it for what it is. When this happens, the language is true.

St Thomas' famous definition of truth as *adaequatio intellectus et rei* has usually been understood in terms of the popular conception of truth by understanding *adaequatio* as the 'agreement' or 'correspondence' of thought and thing, language and reality. But instead, let us take *adaequatio* simply as 'adequacy'. Then what we say is true to the extent that it is adequate to what we are talking about, that is to say, to the extent to which it is able to light up what is talked about, so that we see it for what it is. A myth, for instance, is true to the extent that it makes unhidden the reality it talks about; false to the extent that it obscures that reality. But its adequacy – or inadequacy – does not depend on its picturing the reality in the way of a direct representation. In fact, few people nowadays would claim that literal kind of truth for, let us say, the great central Christian myth of the Son who comes down from heaven, makes atonement through his blood for the sins of men, then rises from the dead and ascends into that heaven whence he had come. To attend to the literal sense of the myth might indeed amount to an obscuring of the reality to which it directs us, and would be to that extent a lapse into falsehood.

Attempts to isolate the 'historical' Jesus or to disengage the 'facts' of his life from their mythological and then theological interpretation have some academic interest but do not seem to me to contribute much to our understanding of the truth of Christ. Indeed, the interest in discovering the 'facts' can easily become a kind of fundamentalism in reverse, a preoccupation with literal and factual truth that misses the distinctively religious and theological truth. It is sometimes said, no doubt correctly, that the earliest Christians did not distinguish so sharply as we do between literal statements of fact and mythological interpretations. For instance, in the series 'born of the Virgin Mary, suffered under Pontius Pilate, was crucified, dead and buried; he descended into hell; the third day he rose again from the dead, he ascended into heaven ...' it seems to be clearly the case that being born and being crucified, descending into hell and ascending into heaven are treated as if they were all events of the same order. To our analytic mentality, this may seem intolerably naïve. Yet in the holistic mentality that expresses itself in the Apostles' Creed, the statements follow each other quite naturally as elements that all have their place in the attempt to express adequately the truth of Christ, to make unhidden the reality that came to light in him. This is no doubt clearer in the Nicene Creed, where the various moments of the Christ-event are preceded by the words 'for us men and for our salvation' and are thereby all bracketed within the theological context. The historical element is not unimportant, for it links the story to our existence in space and time. But it cannot be isolated or sharply separated from the rest of the story. It has been incorporated into a whole which, as a whole, seeks adequately to bring into the light the event of Christ. We have already seen that this event is not restricted to the individual life of Jesus of Nazareth but stretches out into the whole historical and human complex of which he is the centre and originator. What precisely belongs to him and what to the community's interpretative work cannot be always determined, but this is not of primary importance from the theological point of view.

Let me now try to set out a few criteria by which to judge the truth of doctrinal statements in Christian theology.

The first will be simply the internal coherence of the whole body of doctrinal statements. We have seen that the several theological doctrines are not separate, but belong together in a whole.[13] This coherence is not only logical consistency but is constituted also by the way in which the various symbols and analogues of a theology mutually support and illuminate each other. It is significant that we speak of 'catholic truth' for the mainstream of Christian doctrine in its wholeness. Deviations from this occur when parts of the whole are either denied or isolated.

A second criterion is to judge the coherence of the theological assertions with our non-theological beliefs. Sometimes it may be difficult to compare these, for different kinds of statements and different forms of truth are in question. But if Christian theology does make some empirical assertions, whether about history or other matters, then there are some points at which it is amenable to verification or falsification and where it may be either in agreement or disagreement with our secular beliefs.

A third criterion bids us ask about the possibility of development. Theological language is a dialectical language, and, whatever else this may mean, it means that the last word has never been said. Whatever has been said, something more remains to be said. Theological statements are true in the sense that they are on the way to truth, that is to say, they do not freeze the question but open up the possibility of new insights. This would hold for some of the classic Christian pronouncements on doctrine, such as the Chalcedonian definition.

The fourth criterion is to ask whether the theological statements light up, as adequately as words can, that form of life, the Christ-event in the broad sense, which it is the business of theology to explicate. And here we strike the ultimate 'given' of Christian theology, though I have suggested that even this given is not just arbitrarily accepted. Christians have assented to this given because of an inward testimony arising out of that self-knowledge which is part of our personal existence and which sees Christ as the fulfilment of man's inner tendency.

If one is working with a commonsense theory of truth as correspondence between language and facts, then propositions are either true or false, and it would make no sense to talk, as Moberly did in the words we quoted from him, of 'the truest'. But as soon as one substitutes adequacy for correspondence, as soon as one acknowledges the dialectical character of theological language, and as soon as one admits that all such language is socially conditioned, then one is inevitably driven in the direction of a doctrine of 'degrees of truth', perhaps not so very different from F. H. Bradley's teaching on this subject. No theological statement or system of statements is wholly adequate, and so never fully attains to truth; while possibly no theological statement is entirely devoid of some truth. But it has been made abundantly clear in all that has been said above that this does not imply a sheer relativism in which one theological position is as good (or bad) as another or that one can sit lightly to the theological task. On the contrary, the task of formulating doctrine as clearly as possible becomes more urgent if we are to gain a more adequate understanding of the form of life itself. Always one formulation will be more adequate than another, or more adequate in some respects, and this means that it will be truer and that it will have a stronger claim on our assent.

Notes

1. R. C. Moberly, *Atonement and Personality*, John Murray 1901, p. 234.
2. S. Kierkegaard, *Training in Christianity*, tr. W. Lowrie, Princeton University Press 1944, pp. 198ff.
3. S. Kierkegaard, *Concluding Unscientific Postscript*, tr. D. F. Swenson, Oxford University Press 1945, p. 182.
4. J. L. Austin, *How to Do Things with Words*, Oxford University Press 1962, p. 144.
5. P. Berger, *A Rumour of Angels*, Allen Lane: The Penguin Press 1970, p. 57.
6. H. Küng, *Infallible?*, Collins 1971, p. 138.
7. *Training in Christianity*, p. 199.
8. *Concluding Unscientific Postscript*, pp. 173ff., 217.
9. M. Heidegger, *Being and Time*, tr. J. Macquarrie and E. S. Robinson, SCM Press and Harper & Row 1962, p. 260.

10. D. Bonhoeffer, *Christology* or *Christ the Center*, tr. J. Bowden, Collins and Harper & Row 1966, p. 28.

11. H. Ott, *Reality and Faith*, tr. A. A. Morrison, Lutterworth Press 1971, p. 426.

12. Cf. J. Macquarrie, *God-Talk*, SCM Press and Harper & Row 1967, chapter 3.

13. See above, p. 15.

3

Mystery and Truth

To write on mystery and, still more, to suggest that mystery has indispensable value and can even provide an avenue to truth, is to invite the charge of being hopelessly out of touch with modern thought. For the history of science and philosophy since the Renaissance could be interpreted as the steady elimination of mystery. Clarity and intelligibility have been the goals of that history, and there has been a truly remarkable measure of success in attaining these goals.

The emphasis on clarity comes through strongly in the father of modern philosophy, René Descartes. 'Clear and distinct ideas' constitute the foundation of his philosophy. They are more fundamental than even the *cogito, ergo sum*. For when he asks what is the ground of his confidence in the validity of this argument, he replies: 'There is nothing at all which gives me assurance of the truth of these words beyond this, that I see *very clearly* that in order to think, it is necessary to exist.' He goes on to assert 'as a general rule, the principle, that all the things which we *very clearly and distinctly* conceive are true'.[1] From this principle he later deduces the negative rule that one forms no judgment 'except regarding objects which are *clearly and distinctly* represented ... by the understanding'.[2] Descartes does indeed acknowledge that there may be difficulty in determining just what, in particular cases, constitutes a clear and distinct idea. But the difficulty would seem to be due to our imperfect ability to give 'attentive consideration' to a complex subject, and, in principle, it might be overcome through a mental discipline in which the mind becomes 'gradually habituated to *clearer and more distinct* conceptions of its objects'.[3]

The drive for clarity has continued from Descartes for three centuries and is still powerful today. The author of the *Tractatus Logico-Philosophicus*, Ludwig Wittgenstein, said about that influential book: 'Its whole meaning could be summed up somewhat as follows: what can be said at all can be said clearly; and whereof one cannot speak, thereon one must be silent.'[4] Indeed, with Wittgenstein and others like him, philosophy, understood as logical analysis, may be said to have made clarity its only goal. For philosophy of this type leaves the pursuit of knowledge to the sciences and regards its own function as that of clarifying the procedures of thought. Thus the modern drive for clarity has become a two-pronged operation; quantitatively, the sciences reduce the area of mystery by bringing more and more phenomena within the sphere of intelligibility, while qualitatively philosophy eliminates mystery by removing confusions and sharpening investigatory procedures. The situation was well described by Michael Foster: 'Mystery will be conceived as arising from two sources: (i) lack of knowledge – it is the business of science to cure this; (ii) unclear thinking – it is the business of philosophy to cure this. The goal toward which both scientist and philosopher are working is a state in which there will be no more mystery.'[5]

Sometimes it has seemed that the theologian himself is working toward the same end as the scientist and the philosopher. In recent years there has been a strong tendency to deemphasize or even to eliminate both in theology and in liturgy whatever savours of mystery, transcendence, ultimacy. The extreme manifestations of this have been 'religionless' Christianity and 'death of God' theology. It has been assumed that the contemporary human being has lost any sense of the holy. Thus, if Christianity is still to be relevant to him, it must be reduced to 'clear and distinct ideas', that is to say, to the practical and the historical, shedding its traditional 'numinous' or 'supernatural' dimension. The noted secular theologian, Ronald Gregor Smith, wrote: 'It is doubtful whether the sense of what Rudolf Otto has called the "numinous" is able to play any dominant part in the life of modern man.'[6] Other theologians have gone even further in decrying the sense of wonder in man – and is it not inevitable that wonder must decline, in an age of striking scientific and technological advance?

Let me make it clear that I am entirely in sympathy with the drive toward clarity and intelligibility, even in theology. I have always believed that the theologian must aim at the maximum of lucidity and that he must not seek refuge in mystification. The advance in intelligibility and clarity that has taken place over such a wide field in the past few centuries has dispelled a great many pseudo-mysteries which never deserved the name of 'mysteries' in the first place. The theologian must welcome as much as anyone else the overcoming of ignorance and confusion, and I think that by now it is very well understood that faith in God cannot be based either on the gaps in our knowledge – many of which will soon be filled in any case – or on arguments of dubious logical validity. But my hope would be that the dissolving of pseudo-mysteries might lead to a clearer recognition of genuine mysteries and to a better appreciation of what they are and of their role in theology.

It must be admitted, however, that for the most part this has not been the case. Advances in understanding and clarity have tended to foster the belief that there are no genuine mysteries at all. What appear to be mysteries will be removed, either by further investigation or by a more careful use of language so that we do not stumble into the error of asking unanswerable questions. Even if it were acknowledged that there are some genuine mysteries, it might be said that we can only be silent about them – we must not even ask. This would seem to have been the position of Wittgenstein at the end of the *Tractatus Logico-Philosophicus*, though there is some ambiguity in what he says. He speaks on the one hand of the 'inexpressible' which is said to 'show itself', but he can speak also in terms that seem closer to positivism of 'the vanishing of the problem'.[7] One is reminded of the positivist trend in Ritschl's theology, expressed in his remark, 'I recognize mysteries in the religious life, but when anything is and remains a mystery, I say nothing about it.'[8]

When the pseudo-mysteries arising from ignorance and confusion have been cleared away, are there any genuine mysteries left? If so, what are these mysteries? Do they have any cognitive significance? Do such mysteries provide any openings on to truth? Can we inquire into them or say anything about them, or can we only remain silent before them?

In order to try to answer these questions, let us look again at what philosophers and theologians have had to say on these matters. Although the mainstream of Western philosophy has been directed toward clear and distinct ideas and has tended to equate mystery with a defective state of understanding that can, in principle, be remedied, there has been a minority point of view. This too deserves attention, and recently it seems to have been increasing in strength.

Undoubtedly the best-known defence of mystery in recent years has been that offered by Gabriel Marcel. No treatment of the subject can afford to ignore his analysis, but since his point of view is well-known, I shall content myself with a bare summary. In Marcel, the concept of mystery is contrasted with the concept of problem. We objectify our world and break it up into manageable areas. Such an area constitutes a problem for human thought. We can apply to it our techniques of investigation and wrest from it its secrets. A mystery, on the other hand, resists objectification. We are ourselves already involved in it. 'A mystery is something in which I am myself involved, and it can therefore only be thought of as a sphere where the distinction between what is in me and what is before me loses its meaning and its initial validity.'[9] There is no way of getting outside of the mystery so as to submit it to an objective scrutiny. The fact that one is oneself involved in it implies that there are unclear areas that cannot be brought within the scope of clear and distinct ideas. This does not mean, of course, that the mystery remains totally opaque. Our very involvement or participation in it, so it is claimed, is an important way of being open to it and constitutes a kind of knowing.

Marcel's account of mystery has as its background an existentialist type of philosophy and relies especially on the irreducibility of the existential experience to an objectifiable phenomenon. But we may set alongside it a quite different account of mystery, one which comes from the background of analytic philosophy and in some ways contrasts rather sharply with Marcel's. I refer to the account given by Milton Munitz, especially in his book *The Mystery of Existence.*

Munitz offers two main criticisms of Marcel. One is that 'Marcel's account of mystery nowhere raises a question about the existence of the world'.[10] Marcel is concerned with the personal and the interpersonal, with value and concern, rather than with what we might call the brute fact of the existence of the universe. The other main criticism is related to this. Because for Marcel mystery arises in the sphere of the personal, it tends not to be a question or an enigma at all, but is transformed into a revelation.

For Munitz, on the other hand, the mystery is cosmological and it is an enigma. He is concerned with the question, 'Why does the world exist?' Much of the book consists of a careful analysis and defence of this question. The traditional form of the question, 'Why is there something rather than nothing?', is rejected as too vague, especially in its use of 'something'. Furthermore, this word 'something' refers to some particular existent, and so does not evoke mystery. The very difficult terms, 'world' and 'exist', are scrutinized. When we say that the world 'exists', we are using 'exists' in a unique way. 'It designates what the world does.'[11] Munitz finally reformulates the question as follows: 'Is there a reason-for-the-existence-of-the-world?'

Munitz is by no means unaware of the emotional overtones of this question, but it is very important that the question should be subjected to the painstaking analysis which he provides and not be submerged in an aura of religious feeling. It is, of course, apparent that in taking seriously this question about a reason-for-the-existence-of-the-world, Munitz rejects the positivist veto which would forbid the asking of the question on the ground that it is meaningless. It seems to me that his analysis does amply establish that the question is a meaningful one. But what is interesting is not just his break with positivism – for this break is a common one in contemporary analytic philosophy – but his rejection of the belief that where there cannot be a meaningful answer, there cannot be a meaningful question. Wittgenstein had claimed: 'If a question can be put at all, then it can also be answered', and 'A question can exist only where there is an answer.'[12] Munitz, on the contrary, believes that in the case of the question about a reason-for-the-existence-of-the-world, we have a meaningful question to which there is no answer. The question, he claims, is neither spurious nor removable, but it must be accepted as unanswerable. The question is *sui generis*. To recognize its peculiar status as an unanswerable question is to become aware of the 'very meaning and irremovable character of the mystery'.[13]

How is Munitz' treatment of mystery to be judged? It seems clear that, in spite of his differences from Marcel, there is for both of them one basic mystery – the mystery of being. Where they differ is that Marcel looks to personal existence (and eventually to God) for the illumination of the mystery of being, while Munitz remains agnostic. Munitz intellectual treatment of mystery is surely of the highest significance, and he seems to be right in saying that there is no *rational* answer to the question he propounds. But it may be asked whether he does not draw too soon and too sharply the boundary between the rational and the non-rational, the cognitive and the non-cognitive. This is certainly a difficult matter, but I think that the border between cognition and affection is a very elusive one, and that feelings of awe and wonder may have some cognitive content. Again, are we to rule out in advance any possibility of revelation, of the self-communication of mystery?

A further point is this. Is the question about a reason-for-the-existence-of-the-world *totally* unanswerable? If the question could be fully answered, then we would not talk about a mystery at all. On the other hand, if the question were totally unanswerable, I do not think we would talk about a mystery either, and I would be inclined to agree with those who hold that a question of this character cannot even be significantly asked. For can we ask a meaningful question without having some idea of what a possible answer might be, or how we might recognize such an answer, or at least in what direction we ought to look for it? A mystery would not be a blank enigma, a completely unanswerable question, but a question in which we only glimpsed the shape or direction of an answer, and found that the more we penetrated into the answer, the more its horizons expanded so that we could never fully grasp it.

At this point I shall mention two contemporary theologians who give an affirmative account of mystery, and whose contributions to the subject may lead us eventually toward a reconciliation of the conflicting views of Marcel and Munitz in a more comprehensive concept. One is Bernard Lonergan. I doubt if any theologian has been more insistent on the drive toward intelligibility in all things, even in the profoundest questions of theology, but he does not hesitate to say that 'an orientation to transcendental mystery is basic to systematic theology'.[14] The other theologian is Eric Mascall. He too has a confidence in reason, but it is the very ability of reason to penetrate that leads to the acknowledgment of mystery. He writes: 'On being confronted with a mystery, we are conscious that the small central area of which we have a relatively clear vision shades off into a vast background which is obscure and as yet unpenetrated. We find, as we attempt to penetrate this background ... that the range and clarity of our vision progressively increase, but at the same time the background which is obscure and unpenetrated is seen to be far greater than we had recognized before. It is in fact rather as if we were walking into a fog with the aid of a lamp which was steadily getting brighter; the area which we could see with some distinctness would get larger and larger but so also would the opaque and undifferentiated background in which no detail was yet visible. Thus, in the contemplation of a mystery, there go together in a remarkable way an increase both of knowledge and of what we might call conscious ignorance.'[15]

Let us now for a time leave the philosophers and theologians and turn to the biblical material on mystery. The word 'mystery' is, of course, of Greek derivation, and it has sometimes been supposed that its occurrences in the New Testament are due to Hellenistic influences, and especially to the influence of the mystery cults. The word is derived from the verb *muein*, which meant 'to close the eyes' or 'to close the mouth' – both of them acts appropriate to the mysteries. Cognate words are 'myth' and 'mysticism' and it may be worth our while to ask later about the relation of mystery to myth and mysticism. But these again seem to be more closely associated with Greek religion than with the Bible.

Nevertheless, it has been claimed as a result of recent biblical studies that even if the Greek mystery religions were known to the New Testament writers and had some influence on them, the notion of mystery which these writers use can be adequately accounted for in terms of the Old Testament and Semitic background. Raymond Brown ends an interesting study of the question by saying: 'We believe it is no exaggeration to say that, considering the variety and currency of the concept of divine mysteries in Jewish thought, St Paul and the New Testament writers could have written everything they did about *musterion* whether or not they ever encountered the pagan mystery religions. "Mystery" was a part of the native theological equipment of the Jews who came to Jesus Christ.'[16] Somewhat more cautiously, Henry Chadwick leaves open the possibility of influence from the Greek mysteries, and says they 'are not to be set aside as wholly irrelevant'; but he too is inclined to find the major influence in the Old Testament and Semitic background.[17]

Both of these writers mention the ancient Hebrew idea of a heavenly assembly of God and his angels, deriving probably from a still older idea in the pagan Semitic religions of a council of the gods, wherein was deliberated the governance of the universe. The prophets were those who were admitted into the heavenly assembly and permitted to learn something of the mysteries or secret plans decided upon there. This is indeed a thoroughly mythological idea, and implies the belief that there are two worlds, the ordinary world of sense and the upper world, hid from view, where dwell God and his host of angels. This upper world is inaccessible from below, but what is decided there determines what will happen on earth. If one does not know what has been decided in the heavenly assembly, then the sequence of events on earth may be very puzzling. A good illustration of this is the story of Job. The reader is permitted to know what was decided in the assembly on the 'day when the sons of God came to present themselves before the Lord' (Job 1.6). But Job and the other actors in the terrestrial drama do not know what has been decided above. Events begin to happen which contradict their expectations and their theories about life. The mystery would be solved if they knew what had gone on in the heavenly assembly, but this could never be known from the earthly and human side, unless God chose by some means to reveal it.

This pictorial mythological background to the idea of mystery can be to some extent demythologized. The notion of the two worlds, which we would nowadays find unacceptable, can be expressed in a different way. The notion expresses the conviction that there is, so to speak, both an outside and an inside to events. We see the outside, in the sequence of phenomena observable by the senses; but it is supposed that there is also an inner logic of meaning that may not be evident to us at all. To put the matter in another way, we see the proximate causes and effects of actions and events; but their ultimate causation and their ultimate tendency, goal and meaning, remain hidden. To put the matter thus may be to get away from the more obviously mythological character of the picture of the two worlds, but clearly one is not getting away from some metaphysical understanding of mystery. One is making the assumption that there is some ultimate *rationale* in the happenings of the world, and clearly this is a large part of what it means to believe in God. No doubt one has to acknowledge that the idea of mystery is inevitably a metaphysical idea. If one asks about ultimate causes and goals rather than proximate ones, then one is asking 'why' questions rather than 'how' questions. Munitz' sophisticated argument that it makes sense to ask an unanswerable question indicates that the mythological quest for a causation and meaning that lie behind what is apparent to the senses, however crudely this quest may have expressed itself, is not to be dismissed as primitive confusion or sheer superstition. One could say that Munitz' account of mystery as unanswerable question is descended in a recognizable genealogy from such myth as that of the heavenly assembly. One has moved from mythology to the refinements of analysis, but the essential problem remains the same.

However, the Bible parts company with Munitz at a decisive point, in its belief that even if there is no way from the outside to the inside, the mystery nevertheless opens itself and communicates itself, without thereby ceasing to be mystery. In mythological terms, the prophet is admitted to the assembly and hears a snatch of what goes on there. In more sophisticated theological language, we may speak of 'revelation'. One cannot help noticing a curious paradox in most of the New Testament instances of the use of the word 'mystery'. Mystery and revelation seem to go together (Cf. Mark 13.11; I Cor. 2.7; 13.2; Rom. 16.25; etc.). In the New Testament we are not confronted with blank unanswerable questions, but with a reality in which we are allowed to participate in such a way that we are offered a glimpse of its character. In this respect, Marcel's view of mystery is closer to the New Testament than Munitz' view. The paradoxical character of mystery in the New Testament has been well expressed by Gabriel Moran who calls it a 'superluminous intelligibility'.[18] In his use of this expression, he is implying both that there is a mode in which mystery can be known and that when mystery is known, it remains mystery and is never reduced to a 'clear and distinct idea', in the sense of something manipulable and at one's disposal.

I have drawn attention in passing to the etymological relation connecting the words 'mystery', 'myth', 'mysticism'. We may now ask whether and how far the productions of mythology and the experiences of mysticism can be regarded as ways of penetrating into mystery.

Let us begin with mythology, the telling of imaginative stories. The ancient biblical idea which connected mystery with the heavenly assembly was also a typically mythological idea. Such a mythological idea presupposes some analogy between human experience and that hidden reality (the supposed ultimate causality, the inner or under side of events, the final meaning, God) which constitutes the mystery and about which the myth seeks to speak. This analogy supposes in turn that there are areas of mystery in the personal experience of the human being, areas where the horizons recede indefinitely. Among these areas, one would mention that of the creative imagination, the very area which produces myth. The ideas of a myth are not clear and distinct. They cannot be precisely defined. They are evocative, as we say, and this means that they burst out beyond the limits of any strict definition and make us aware of horizons that recede with every step that we take toward them. On the other hand, these ideas are not utterly vague or devoid of content. They belong to the growing edge of our experience as persons, and they have a directedness that points beyond that edge. I am inclined to say about mythological ideas what Ian Ramsey has said about non-picturing models, which seem to fulfil much the same function; namely, that in using them 'we are most characteristically persons, rather than mere organisms or social units; in this sense, we realize our transcendence, and the universe which discloses itself to us is similarly mysterious and likewise transcendent'.[19]

In stressing the importance of the underlying personal analogy, I am asserting that the kind of myth which would best disclose mystery would be a myth centred on a person or a community of persons, rather than on phenomena of nature. If it is permissible to call the central Christian story a myth, it is the myth of the God-man and (if we include the community which he brings into existence) the myth of God-manhood. The mystery and transcendence of manhood coalesce with the mystery and transcendence of Godhood.

When we turn from myth to mysticism, we meet with a corrective to any possible over-exercise of the creative imagination in the exploration of mystery. Myth invents ideas and language, but mysticism contemplates in silence. Though there are exceptions, the mystic is usually content with the negative mode of speech, 'not this, not that'. Yet the experience of the mystic is essentially like the experience that expresses itself in mythology – the experience of going beyond that realm which is reducible to clear and distinct ideas to a new level of reality. Could we say that these are two modes of *muein*? The mythopoeic mind closes the eyes to soar into the imagination; the mystical mind closes the mouth to contemplate in silence. For the mystic too brings together the transcendence that belongs to humanity and the transcendence of God. If he begins by turning into himself, he does not rest there but discovers that the very depth of his being leads him beyond himself. It is only a pseudo-mysticism that is individualistic and introverted. The true mystic is the ecstatic, the person who has gone out from himself. 'Mysticism', writes Berdyaev, 'is in profound contrast to every kind of closed-in individualism, isolated from cosmic life; it is in contrast to all psychologism. Mystical submersion in oneself always means going out of oneself, a breaking through beyond the boundaries. All mysticism teaches that the depths of man are more than human, that in them lurks a mysterious contact with God and with the world.'[20]

Thus mysticism and mythology are both concerned with mystery.

But whereas mythology speaks through its symbols, mysticism for the most part remains silent or speaks in the negative mode. Any adequate discourse about mystery employs both the symbols derived from mythology and, as a reminder of their shortcomings, the silence and negations of mysticism. Only so can the paradox of mystery be preserved. A striking illustration of this is provided by the Chalcedonian definition. The great symbol of the God-man is developed with almost metaphysical precision. But breaking into the talk about *ousia, phusis* and *hupostasis*, there appear the four negative adverbs: *asugchutos, atreptos, adiairetos, achoristos*. These negatives make it clear that this is no exhaustive description that is being offered. They hold open the mystery, and they make the Chalcedonian definition itself a signpost to fuller truth, rather than just a settling of earlier disputes or, still less, the end of the road in christological reflection.

We have now discussed the views of some philosophers and theologians on mystery, seen something of the biblical material, and noted the relations of mystery to myth and mysticism. It may be helpful if we now try to identify more clearly than we have done some concrete examples of mystery. If there are any genuine mysteries, can we name some of them and give reasons for regarding them as mysteries?

We may approach this question by asking about the range of our clear and distinct ideas. What things do we understand clearly, distinctly and (at least, in principle) exhaustively? If we can indicate these things, then we may inquire about what is left over.

I should think that mathematical entities are those which can be most clearly, distinctly and fully understood. I do not think there is any mystery in a triangle. To be sure, a schoolboy will not, upon immediate inspection, grasp all the properties of a triangle, and some of them he may never grasp at all. But this is due not to any mystery in the triangle but to the schoolboy's limited intellectual powers. Mathematics is commonly held nowadays to be an *a priori* science, so that its propositions are already all contained in the initial definitions and axioms. The fact that people can make discoveries in mathematics is due only to the slowness of our own wits, not to any inherent mystery in the subject-matter. There may be difficulty, but scarcely mystery. A. J. Ayer has remarked: 'A being whose intellect was infinitely powerful would take no interest in logic and mathematics. For he would be able to see at a glance everything which his definitions contained, and, accordingly, could never learn anything from logical inference of which he was not fully conscious already. But our intellects are not of this order. It is only a minute proportion of the consequences of our definitions that we are able to detect at a glance.'[21]

It was the mystery-free character of mathematics that made it appear the paradigm of knowledge to Descartes. In mathematics, everything is in principle able to be grasped in clear and distinct ideas. Thus Descartes and the modern Western intellectual tradition have tried to extend the mathematical method to all fields of knowledge. And it cannot be denied that the extension of the mathematical method to other areas of investigation has been extraordinarily successful. The key to unlocking the secrets of the physical world has been the application of a mathematical hermeneutic. We may think that less success attended the efforts of Spinoza to use the method of geometry in ethics. But some people would argue that this was due only to the vastly greater complexity of his subject-matter. There are still many people today who believe that the social sciences are in principle no different from the natural sciences, even if there is also a significant reaction against this view.

It would be hard to say at exactly what point the language of mathematics begins to be inadequate as we apply it to the range of phenomena, but this does begin to happen as we meet with more and more individuation and concretization, for these cannot be fully grasped in abstract concepts. Obviously, the language of mathematics is most adequate at the level of physics. When applied to human phenomena, it still has important uses, but the richness of the human reality escapes it, and especially what is most distinctive in that reality. Man, as Kierkegaard and also Hegel saw, has an untidiness that does not conform to clear and distinct ideas. Our understanding of man always has rough edges and unclear corners. The case of biology lies somewhere between that of physics and that of the human sciences. Mathematical concepts are more adequate in biology than in the human sciences, yet even here there are phenomena that escape the pattern.

Whether an element of mystery begins to enter as soon as we leave the pure abstractions of mathematics, I shall not presume to say. The presence of unclear corners in our ideas is not of itself an evidence of mystery. I suspect that even a philosophy of Nature will not be able wholly to dispense with the concept of mystery, but I do not have to commit myself to this point of

view. Perhaps this is only the pseudo-mystery of the gaps, and
the recent astonishing success of biologists in elucidating the
mechanism of genetics would certainly make one cautious about
asserting any mystery on the natural level. Yet in some ways,
Nature today seems more mysterious than it did in the nineteenth
century. We meet that paradox which Mascall associated with
mystery – the increase of knowledge together with the increase
of conscious ignorance. Physicist Harold K. Schilling writes: 'The
stubborn fact that it can never be sure that there is nothing beyond
its horizon at any time, constitutes for science a basic *unknown*
and *unknowable*, and is therefore an aspect of Nature's genuine
mystery.'[22]

But at the level of the human phenomenon, I think one can
confidently speak of mystery. There are areas of human life that
elude every attempt to bring them within the scope of clear and
distinct ideas and that break out beyond the categories of our
thought. And this does not seem to be a temporary state of affairs
that might one day be remedied. It belongs to the very nature
of these phenomena themselves. Freedom, creativity, the capacity
to bring forth the new and the unique, interpersonal relations –
these are the kind of phenomena which, though not utterly
unintelligible (for we know them from the inside, as it were)
nevertheless escape any method that seeks to exhibit them as
objective manipulable facts. These areas of man which recede
beyond the grasp of empirical science it has become customary
to call his 'transcendence'.

If the concept of mystery can be rehabilitated for our time (and
I do not believe that man can attain the full stature of his humanity
unless he nourishes himself on mystery), then I think that the
rehabilitation will take place along the lines I have described,
namely, through the exploration of the mystery that belongs to our
humanity. This is not to deny that there are other mysteries –
the mystery of the cosmos (Munitz), the mystery that seems to
deepen after every scientific penetration into Nature (Schilling).
But many mysteries that provoked awe in the past have been
dissolved or, rather, they have been shown not to be mysteries at
all. However, I do not think that this will happen in the case of
the mysteries we encounter in personal experience, both individual
and corporate, for these appear to be in principle unobjectifiable.

There is today a revival of the interest in mystery and of the
sense of wonder in our secular society, especially among young
people. This may mark the beginning of a revulsion against the

long established hostility to mystery in Western philosophy. Now, if it is true that the most natural (though not the only) way into mystery is through the exploration of man himself, then the Christian faith is singularly well situated to give a lead in the quest for mystery. By its doctrine of the incarnation, Christianity holds that it is precisely in a human person, Jesus Christ, that the final mystery of being has been opened up. According to Paul, Christ is 'the revelation of the mystery which was kept secret for long ages' (Rom. 16.25-6). This is commonly taken to mean that Christ has revealed or opened up the mystery of God. But would it not be correct to say that he has done this by opening up the mystery of man? Is there not a deep affinity between the mystery of God and the mystery of humanity? By becoming man in the fullest sense, that is to say, in a measure of fulness that transcends all our ordinary levels of manhood, Christ manifests God in the flesh. He pushes back the horizons of the human mystery so that they open on to the divine mystery, but he does this without ceasing to be man.

Let me now sum up some of the main points about mystery as these have emerged in our discussions.

1. Mystery arises in various ways. It arises in those situations in which the knower is himself involved so that he can never achieve the objectification of the situation; it arises in connection with the world as a whole, for the world provides the context for every explanation but has no context of its own. In both cases, we lack an external point of vantage from which the mystery may be objectified and grasped in its entirety. Thus understanding of mystery and language about mystery can never be more than partial.

2. But more than this, mystery is inexhaustible. Even that which can be brought within the focus of thought always stretches beyond the reach of our grasp. The more we penetrate into it, the more the horizons recede. This inexhaustibility is not something that in principle might be overcome through prolonged and detailed exploration of the mystery. The inexhaustibility belongs to mystery as such.

3. Mystery does not contradict logic, but it transcends logic. The inexhaustibility is not quantitative but qualitative. If it were merely quantitative, it might in time be abolished. It is qualitative because in mystery we encounter that which our categories of thought cannot contain. Among the many kinds of transcendence,

we ought to recognize logical transcendence. Medieval philosophers did in fact recognize it when they designated a few basic indefinable ideas ('being', 'unity', 'truth', etc.) the *transcendentia*. Perhaps not all of these medieval notions would rank as 'mysteries', but in our range of concepts they stand at the opposite end from those which are entirely intelligible and, *ipso facto*, least interesting.

4. Though transcending logic in the sense of going beyond it, mystery is neither absurd nor opaque. It has its own translucency. We stretch our concepts by using them analogously, we extrapolate the images of poetry and myth, we throw our symbols into the logical beyond. And we claim that in this way we obtain glimpses of the mystery, though the claim is restrained and the mystery is preserved by the simultaneous use of the negative language of the mystics.

5. The claim to have a glimpse of mystery is based finally on the nature of man himself. For man's nature is to transcend himself, to exist, to keep going out beyond the boundaries of his being in such experiences as freedom, creativity and love. For one whose very nature is to cast himself into the existentially transcendent, it is surely not impossible to cast his thoughts into the logically transcendent. This would be especially the case if there is any validity to the idea of revelation, the idea that the mystery beyond man opens itself to him and draws him beyond himself, because there is an affinity between this mystery and the spirit of man. 'The Whither of transcendental experience', writes Rahner, 'is always there as the nameless, the undefinable, the unattainable', and he claims that man's basic knowledge of God arises from his orientation to the Whither.[23]

Finally, what of truth? Does mystery have any claim to truth or any connection with truth?

We have seen that mystery, although it touches on the whole human experience, has its intellectual dimensions and is certainly not merely emotional. It may fairly be claimed that there is a truth of total experience, alongside which the truth of propositions is abstract. This truth of total experience is a progressive one and is never completed as man transcends toward the mystery of his Whither. It is the truth which arises in the unfolding of the mystery. From one point of view we may call it the truth of self-discovery, from another the truth of the discovery of God.[24]

Notes

1. R. Descartes, *A Discourse on Method, Etc.*, tr. J. Veitch, J. M. Dent 1912, p. 27.

2. Op. cit., p. 119.

3. Op. cit., p. 18.

4. L. Wittgenstein, *Tractatus Logico-Philosophicus*, tr. C. K. Ogden, Kegan Paul 1922, p. 27.

5. M. B. Foster, *Mystery and Philosophy*, SCM Press 1957, p. 20.

6. R. G. Smith, *Secular Christianity*, Collins 1966, p. 111.

7. Wittgenstein, op. cit., p. 187.

8. A. Ritschl, *The Christian Doctrine of Justification and Reconciliation*, tr. H. R. Mackintosh and A. B. Macaulay, T. & T. Clark 1900, p. 607 n.

9. G. Marcel, *Being and Having*, tr. K. Farrer, Dacre Press and Harper & Row 1949, p. 117.

10. M. K. Munitz, *The Mystery of Existence*, Appleton-Century-Crofts 1965, p. 31.

11. Op. cit., p. 93.

12. Wittgenstein, op. cit., p. 187.

13. Munitz, op. cit., p. 11.

14. B. Lonergan, S.J., *Method in Theology*, Darton, Longman & Todd 1972, p. 341.

15. E. L. Mascall, *Words and Images*, Longmans, Green 1957, p. 79.

16. R. E. Brown, *The Semitic Background of the Term 'Mystery' in the New Testament*, Fortress Press 1968, p. 69.

17. H. Chadwick, 'Mystery', *Hastings' Dictionary of the Bible*, ed. F. C. Grant and H. H. Rowley, T. & T. Clark 1963, p. 683.

18. G. Moran, *Theology of Revelation*, Herder & Herder 1966, p. 133.

19. I. T. Ramsey, *Models and Mystery*, Oxford University Press 1964, pp. 68-9.

20. N. Berdyaev, *The Meaning of the Creative Act*, tr. D. Lowrie, Harper & Row 1955, p. 296.

21. A. J. Ayer, *Language, Truth and Logic*, Gollancz ^{2}1946, pp. 85-6.

22. H. K. Schilling, *The New Consciousness in Science and Religion*, SCM Press and United Church Press 1973, p. 107.

23. K. Rahner, 'The Concept of Mystery in Catholic Theology', in *Theological Investigations*, Darton, Longman & Todd 1961-8, vol. IV, pp. 49-50.

24. This was the Père Marquette Lecture for 1970, published as a pamphlet by Marquette University, Milwaukee 1973.

4

Some Thoughts on Heresy

From time to time, when a theologian, priest or minister has strayed too far in his writings or utterances from the accepted norms of belief, we still hear the cry: 'Heresy!' The purpose of this essay is to show that the concept of heresy has become a very elusive one, that heresy trials are definitely an anachronism in the twentieth century, and the Christian community must find a more adult way of dealing with threats to the integrity of its faith.

Perhaps the identification and rejection of heresies were necessary and useful activities during the first five centuries of the church's existence. In confrontation with the culture of that age, the Christian faith was assuming its classic shape. There was always the danger of distortion or of the merging of Christianity into the welter of pagan cults, and a constant vigilance had to be maintained.

Looking back, we may well believe that the church made the right choices. But we must also acknowledge that the great heretics were, for the most part, sincere and able men. Sometimes the church took a long time to make up her mind between the competing views. The more important heresies were suppressed only after high theological debate. Admittedly, plenty of pettiness and animosity appeared in these early controversies, but in the main I think we can agree with John Courtney Murray when he writes that this was no 'trivial logomachy', but 'great religious argument'. He adds: 'Certainly in no subsequent arguments have the issues been wrought out so clearly and argued with such amplitude for stakes that were incalculably high.'[1]

But who could make such claims for debates over heresies (or alleged heresies) in modern times? It is certainly not obvious that the ecclesiastical authorities have been always, or even on most occasions, in the right. Frequently, these authorities have been poorly qualified to judge the issues. Usually the appeal has been to some dogmatic standard. There has been little attempt to arouse theological debate – indeed, one suspects that it has been avoided. Not surprisingly, the heretic or supposed heretic has often ended up with all the glamour of a martyr, and sometimes he has deserved it.

Let me recall one case that is typical of many during the emergence of the church into modern times. In 1856, John McLeod Campbell published *The Nature of the Atonement*, one of the classics of Scottish theology. Twenty-five years earlier, he had been solemnly deposed from the ministry of the Church of Scotland. His 'error' was that he taught that God's reconciling grace is offered to all men and not just to a predestined few.

Some members of his congregation in the village of Rhu had taken notes of his sermons, and complained about this teaching to the presbytery, which recorded its 'detestation and abhorrence' of his views, as being contrary to the Calvinist doctrine of election. The case went to the General Assembly of the Church of Scotland, and there was an overwhelming majority of votes against Campbell. He was held to have taught doctrines 'at variance with the Word of God and the standards of the Church of Scotland', and received the extreme sentence – deposition from the sacred ministry. Writing more than a century later, J. G. Riddell could say: 'It is almost ironical to read, across the intervening years, that after prayer the Moderator pronounced sentence of deposition in name and by authority of the Lord Jesus Christ, the King and Head of the Church.'[2]

Today in the theological hall of Glasgow University there is a little shrine with some souvenirs of Campbell, preserved almost like the relics of a saint. People are now free to believe what he taught, but it is a shameful page in the church's history that tells how this freedom was bought. Campbell himself died before the rigid Calvinist standards were relaxed.

Let me now set out five propositions on the subject of heresy today. These are not systematic theses, but even if they are somewhat disjointed, most of them are theological in nature.

1. *All theological formulations are approximate.*

This follows both from the nature of faith and from the nature of revelation. Faith is the response of the whole man to God, and this cannot be completely transcribed into words. Likewise, the

Christian revelation has been given in the person of Jesus Christ, not in words.

To say such things is in no way to minimize the importance of theology or to deny the need to seek the clarification of Christian faith through its expression in the best language available. Neither is it to deny that great bewilderment and harm can be caused by distorted teaching. But, even so, one must acknowledge that all formulations fall short of the reality they try to express and are therefore subject to revision and reinterpretation.

Some Christian communions have wisely refrained from attempting a too precise formulation of dogmas. I believe that the present tendency in all branches of the Christian church is to recognize the provisional and historically conditioned elements in all theological statements. The whole question about the meaning and logic of theological and dogmatic language is extremely complex and is much discussed at the present time. Almost all scholars would agree that theological language is not a simple direct kind of language. Its reference is indirect and symbolic, and so it resists efforts that would force it into the mould of final and exact statements.

As soon as one departs from the notion that the Christian faith can be precisely and fully expressed in verbal formulations, the notion of heresy becomes very blurred, and attempts to demonstrate that any particular opinions were heretical would be extremely difficult. Such attempts could not succeed simply by showing that the allegedly heretical opinion contradicted some particular dogmatic formulation. It would be necessary also to show that there was a conflict with the reality of faith that this dogmatic formulation sought to express, and that the allegedly heretical opinion was excluded as a possible reinterpretation or re-expression of the faith.

2. Genuine heresy is extremely rare.

By 'genuine' heresy, I mean really culpable heresy that offers a serious threat to the integrity of the Christian faith. It must be remembered that heresy has to be distinguished not only from attacks on the Christian faith made by persons outside of the church, but also from apostasy, the denial of the faith by persons who have severed themselves from the church. The point about the heretic is that he continues to count himself a member of the Christian community, and this matter of the relation to the community must be borne in mind. A heresy consists in the denial or distortion of some particular aspect of the faith, but the heretic believes that it is possible to hold his point of view and remain within the church, and he continues to give a general allegiance to the Christian faith.

Now almost every member of the church and every theologian has probably at some time entertained erroneous opinions about the faith, even opinions that have been judged heretical. Of course, he may have entertained such opinions only through ignorance. But if his allegiance to the Christian faith as a whole is sufficiently strong, this outweighs the heretical tendency, for Christian doctrine constitutes an interlocking whole. As we have noted, all theological formulations are provisional and are historically conditioned. There is no final and complete theology, and no doubt every theology has had its imbalances as it has responded to particular situations.

A genuinely culpable heresy would be found only where the denial or distortion of a particular doctrine turned out to be stronger than the person's allegiance to the faith as a whole, so that the denial or distortion threatened to undermine and destroy the entire structure of faith. Schleiermacher believed that there are in fact only a very few basic heresies, and what makes any one of these a heresy is that when the implications of the position are followed out, the whole Christian faith collapses.[3] I think one would add that the true heretic is also one whose conduct departs from the Christian norms, especially in the matter of charity. Heresy of a really culpable and dangerous kind has therefore a systematic and deliberate quality.

It follows that such heresy cannot be demonstrated from isolated and possibly ill-considered statements, or even from popular unsystematic theological writings. One would have to consider these matters in the context of the entire understanding of the Christian faith held by the supposed heretic, and in the light of his intention of remaining within the Christian community and of his actual relation to that community. Even if it were shown that some of his opinions were destructive of the fabric of faith, I doubt if such a person could properly be considered a heretic unless he persisted in these opinions in opposition to the expressed common mind of the church. Such a situation would be of the rarest occurrence.

3. *Theological freedom carries an element of risk that must be tolerated.*

While theologians have a responsibility to their communities of faith, they must also have reasonable freedom to pursue their work. This is especially the case in the twentieth century, when there are taking place in the world such rapid intellectual and social changes that even drastic reformulations of Christian truth may be called for, if the church and her message are to make their impact on the contemporary world. In the search for such reformulations, some mistakes are bound to be made. Truth is occasionally sacrificed in the interests of a supposed relevance, and sometimes novelty is prized for its own sake. Yet it is better that such risks should be taken than that the church should be left only with the formulations of earlier times, often couched in antiquated terminology and conceptuality. Even the mistakes can be helpful as exercises in experimental thinking, for it may only be after a position has been explored that one becomes aware that it leads to a dead end or is subversive of some vital Christian truth.

In general, the church is able to contain such aberrations, and may even be stimulated by them to find new and more adequate formulations of doctrine. Today almost all branches of the Christian church are coming to recognize the principle of theological freedom and, in varying degrees, to accept its risks. Some of them, notably the Anglican communion, have had an outstandingly enlightened record on these matters. Others, including the Roman Catholic Church, find it more difficult to be flexible. But wherever the threat of heresy charges lurks in the background, not only is the concept of theological freedom placed in doubt but there may well be an inhibiting effect on the work of theologians who are seeking as responsibly as they can to find ways of relating Christian faith to the contemporary world.

4. *The theological objections to the use of the concept of heresy in the modern church, stated above, are supported by many practical considerations.*

The latter are too well-known to need more than a cursory mention – division in the church, the projecting of a repressive image, the impression given that theological truth is ready made, and so on. These practical issues would not of themselves carry decisive weight if some grave theological issue were at stake, as was sometimes the case in the early church. The understandable desire of ecclesiastics not to rock the sacred boat could not count against a real threat to the integrity of the Christian faith. But I have tried to show that such threats would be very rare and, in modern times, very hard to identify with certainty. When the theological and practical objections to heresy proceedings are taken together, the case for regarding such proceedings as quite anachronistic in the twentieth century is surely overwhelming.

These remarks, of course, should not be taken to imply that the church must remain silent in the face of teachings that may be one-sided, ill-considered or irresponsible. I have simply been saying that the church ought not to proceed to accusations of heresy. If there is freedom in theology, there ought also to be responsibility in the use of this freedom. Theologians who are aware of their responsibility to the church will always welcome expressions of the common mind of the church, such as may help them in their task. Likewise, persons in the church who may be bewildered or distressed by the teaching of some individual theologian or minister have a right to expect some guidance from the church. What then is the church to do in such situations? This question leads me to the final proposition.

5. *Heresy, or suspected heresy, is best combated by a clear affirmative statement of the church's position.*

In other words, the only real corrective for bad theology is better theology. Indeed, heresy and other forms of distortion usually arise when the church's teaching on some matter has been unclear and inadequate. Karl Rahner makes the essential point when he writes: 'The temptation arises to combat heresy to a certain extent only by administrative means, by putting books on the Index, dismissing suspect professors, and so on, instead of by means of the *teaching office*, that is, by such positive formulation of the true doctrine that the error really is supplanted.'[4]

Thus, when some important doctrine of the Christian faith has been challenged, with resultant doubt and confusion in the church, the first move of the ecclesiastical authorities should not be a negative act of condemnation or dissociation, but the positive step of reaffirming their allegiance to the realities of the Christian faith. At the same time, recognizing that the challenge has probably arisen because the doctrine in question has been unclearly or imperfectly formulated, the church should encourage constructive theological efforts to reformulate and reinterpret the doctrine in language intelligible to our time and in ways that will show the place of this doctrine within the whole body of Christian truth.

In stressing an affirmative response by the church when there is a challenge to its beliefs, am I saying that not only should there be no heresy proceedings but that there should be no merely negative or repressive action against the exponents of 'far out' views? Perhaps this is what one must indeed say, in a world where it is recognized that the adult way of coming at the truth is through free and responsible discussion of the issues. Of course, this assumes that the supposed heretic is also ready for responsible discussion. In any case, his views can be really overcome only by showing that the truth lies elsewhere.

One must say that it is questionable whether an ecclesiastical authority, though refraining from a formal accusation of heresy (and thereby escaping the trouble and undesirable publicity attendant on a heresy trial), should nevertheless rebuke the person concerned.[5] Such a rebuke could hardly be for his opinions, if there had been no proper trial or investigation at which the person concerned had been heard; and if the rebuke was for something else, then these dubious opinions would have been left unchallenged and the confusion that they might have caused would not be allayed. In other words, nothing of importance would have been done to deal with the situation, though sympathy might well have been aroused for the person rebuked.

Still worse is the policy in some Roman Catholic dioceses where the troublesome teacher or cleric is dealt with by transferring him to a rural parish or a remote seminary, or even by assigning him to a missionary post in Patagonia. This is the opposite of what ought to happen. His opinions ought to be brought out into the open and seen for what they are worth. Instead, they are quietly suppressed, and we hear only the faint sounds of strangulation in the distance.

At least one can say that this has been, if the expression may be permitted, an evenhanded injustice. In the years following Vatican II, the chopper has fallen with admirable lack of discrimination alike on the ultraconservatives and on the ultraprogressives, on those who want to celebrate the mass in Latin as well as on those who want to organize clerical trade unions. But this should not happen to any of them. The Roman Catholic Church is big enough and strong enough to contain considerable diversity in theology and churchmanship. In spite of all its undoubted *aggiornamento* in some matters, it still has not sufficiently softened its authoritarian attitudes. And perhaps there is nothing more ridiculous than an autocratic prelate attempting to impose 'liberal' reforms by decree.

The repressive measures described above are, unfortunately, still to be found from time to time in various Christian communions. Obviously, such measures can only be stopgaps, and they may even lead to more explosive rebellions. In the long run, the only effective answer to heresy, near heresy and errors of other kinds is for the church to show that she has a better theology than the person suspected of error. In ninety-nine cases out of a hundred, it should not be difficult to do this. But the hundredth case may be that of the McLeod Campbell, the true saint and prophet possessing an insight and a sensitivity ahead of his contemporaries, and in such a case, like Gamaliel, we have to beware that we are not 'found opposing God' (Acts 5.39). Looking around the theological horizon today, I see many people who pride themselves on being 'far out' and *avant garde*, but I must frankly say that among them I do not see anyone even remotely approaching the stature of McLeod Campbell.[6]

Notes

1. J. C. Murray, *The Problem of God*, Yale University Press 1964, p. 32.

2. J. G. Riddell, *The Calling of God*, St Andrew Press 1961, p. 48.

3. F. Schleiermacher, *The Christian Faith*, tr. H. R. Mackintosh and J. S. Stewart, T. & T. Clark 1928, pp. 95-6.

4. K. Rahner, *Inquiries*, Herder & Herder 1964, p. 458.

5. This is what happened in the case of the late James Albert Pike, formerly Bishop of California. His own account of the affair, using thinly veiled pseudonyms, is found in his book, *You and the New Morality*, Harper & Row 1967, pp. 110-18.

6. This essay originated as a letter sent to the American House of Bishops at the time of the controversy over Bishop Pike.

5

What is the Gospel?

What is the gospel? This must sound like a strange question. After almost two thousand years of Christian preaching and reflection, are we still uncertain about what the gospel is? I think we must acknowledge that this is indeed the case, and that at the present time there is still an unresolved debate about the true nature of the Christian message. The gospel has been interpreted in many ways during the centuries of preaching. It is receiving new interpretations in our own time, and some of these are in startling contrast to the traditional forms. Two obvious examples from recent years of drastic reformulations of the gospel are *The Secular Meaning of the Gospel*, by Paul van Buren, and *The Gospel of Christian Atheism*, by Thomas J. J. Altizer. According to the former, the gospel is 'the good news of a free man who has set other men free'. This good news was first proclaimed by the immediate disciples of Jesus, but men have continued to be liberated 'by accepting the liberator, Jesus of Nazareth, as the man who defines for them what it means to be a man and as the point of orientation for their lives'.[1] For Altizer, on the other hand, the gospel is the good news that the death of God in Christ has freed us from the tyranny of a transcendent power: 'Only by accepting and even willing the death of God in our experience can we be liberated from a transcendent beyond, an alien beyond which has been emptied and darkened by God's self-annihilation in Christ.'[2] It is worth noting that however different these two versions may be, they are agreed – as are many other contemporary versions of the gospel – in putting liberation at the centre of the message, and this is certainly an authentic New Testament note.

To be sure, these drastic new versions of the gospel have won few converts. Christians have not been much attracted to them, for such presentations of the gospel are so one-sided and reduced that, when fully pondered, they can hardly qualify as 'good news' any more. Non-Christians have been even less attracted, for they see no good reason for introducing a residual Jesus-language into their own straight secularism or atheism – this could only lead to confusion. Yet if these contemporary versions of the gospel are judged to be inadequate, can we be sure that some of the traditional versions were really much better? To many people in the British Isles and the United States, the very word 'gospel' (and likewise the adjective 'evangelical') are associated with a style of preaching and a form of Christianity which, as we increasingly recognize, were too intensely individualistic, other-worldly and 'pious' in a bad sense of that abused word. That form of the gospel, so influential among the parents and grandparents of many of ourselves, had, in spite of its many strengths, its serious inadequacies and blind-spots. Some of the defects were intellectual, others were ethical and social. These defects have been, in large measure, responsible for calling forth the new secular versions of the gospel, though, in the event, the violence of the reaction has made some of these secular versions even less adequate than the old ones.

But how do we determine the adequacy or inadequacy of a particular version of the gospel? What norms do we have for passing the kind of judgments made in the preceding paragraph? Is there a pure, original, unchanging gospel that can serve as a yard-stick for measuring the authenticity of all pretended versions? Sometimes people have supposed that there is such an original gospel, and they have even claimed to know what it is. But always their own interpretations have entered into their accounts. No doubt there is an inalienable core of Christian truth which persists through many different formulations. It is there in the Bible, but cannot be simply read off, for the Bible itself is susceptible to varying interpretations. The subsequent teaching of the church has ruled out some interpretations as erroneous, but even so, there is still plenty of scope for widely differing presentations of the gospel.

And surely this is a testimony to the continuing vitality of the gospel. Even if there is a constant core of Christian verity, the gospel is something dynamic rather than static. In the course of history, the gospel is addressed to changing situations and assumes different formulations. Now one aspect of the good news, now another, is specially emphasized in response to some special situa-tion; and in the course of this history, we may hope that a genuine unfolding and development of truth takes place.

To say that there is no pure unchanging formulation of the gospel available as a norm is not to deny that there may be some norms. We must look for other ways of judging the adequacy or inadequacy of any particular formulation of the gospel. We have seen that the vitality of the gospel demands that there shall be a situational element in its presentation. But the danger is that we understand our situations too narrowly, that is to say, too much in terms of our own immediate feelings. Then the situational element can become a merely parochial element, and thus something that distorts and impoverishes the version of the gospel which it influences. Let us remember too that there are parochialisms of time as well as of place, and that, for instance, a 'gospel for the seventies' might turn out to be very poor and meagre news if it allowed its understanding to be dominated entirely by the current mood. Every cultural mood sharpens our perception of some matters, but it seems to do so only at the expense of dulling our awareness of some other matters. We can see this easily enough when we look back at some former time, say the Middle Ages or the Enlightenment. But we cannot become aware of the limits imposed on us by our own cultural mood, for we are still in that mood and cannot look back on it from a situation in which men will have been set free from it. For that very reason, however, we tend to absolutize the current mood. As sociologist Peter Berger points out, we frequently use a double standard on these matters: 'The *past* is relativized, in terms of this or that socio-historical analysis. The *present*, however, remains strangely immune from relativization.' He chooses a theological example to illustrate his point: 'The New Testament writers are seen as afflicted with a false consciousness rooted in *their* time, but the analyst takes the consciousness of *his* time as an unmixed intellectual blessing.'[3]

This absolutizing of a position which is itself relative and even parochial can be well seen in those secular versions of the gospel mentioned above. It is not surprising that van Buren and Altizer have found irrelevant a version of the gospel thought up by Victorian evangelicals, but what they fail to see is that their own versions were far too narrowly tied to a particular phase of affluent, technological, middle-class, white America. Thus we should not be surprised in turn when we find that black theologian James H. Cone brands the 'death of God' theology as irrelevant to the experience of black America. He identifies this theology with 'a cultural structure which enslaves', the structure, namely, of 'an advancing secular technological society which ignores the reality of God and the humanity of man'. And he asks: 'Do whites really have the right to affirm God's death when they have actually enslaved men in God's name?'[4]

What then is the gospel? Our reflections so far would indicate that the gospel is not a timeless formula laid up in the heavens, but must assume different forms as it is addressed to different situations, for only if it reaches men where they actually are is it a gospel. Yet we have also seen the danger of a legitimate situational concern being turned into a mere parochialism which deprives the gospel of its universality. How can the gospel have the freedom and the dynamic that are needed if it is to meet people where they are and yet to be protected from the stifling idiosyncrasies that arise from our tendency to absolutize or at least to inflate out of all proportions our passing cultural moods? Let me suggest two criteria in answer to this question.

The first criterion is a *material* one. It has to do with the content of the gospel. Let us agree that the New Testament itself already contains a plurality of theological interpretations. Nevertheless, if we employ good critical methods and careful exegesis, it is impossible to derive *just any* interpretation from the New Testament. There is richness and diversity to it, but there are also limits as to what one can legitimately read out of it. When we are faced with any particular formulation of the gospel, we have to ask whether it adequately expresses the many-sided, perhaps inexhaustible, good news of the Christian proclamation as set forth in the New Testament, or whether it is in conflict with it.

As soon as we begin to ask about the content of the gospel in the New Testament, we strike, as is well-known, on an ambiguity. The expression, 'the gospel of Jesus Christ', can be taken in either of two ways. We may understand it as a subjective genitive, so that it means 'the gospel proclaimed *by* Jesus Christ'. In this sense, the content of the gospel is the kingdom of God and its advent upon earth. 'Jesus came into Galilee, preaching the gospel of God, and saying, "The time is fulfilled, and the kingdom of God is at hand; repent, and believe the gospel"' (Mark 1.14-15). We may also understand the expression, 'the gospel of Jesus Christ', as an objective genitive, and then it means 'the gospel proclaimed *about* Jesus Christ'. Its content is now Christ himself. There has been discussion about the precise content of the apostolic kerygma, but certainly the core of it was Jesus, the crucified and risen Lord. St Paul writes: 'Now I would remind you, brethren, in what terms I preached to you the gospel', and he goes on to speak of Christ dying for our sins and being raised from the dead (I Cor. 15.1ff.).

These two possible ways of understanding 'the gospel of Jesus Christ' have occasionally been in some tension with each other. Harnack believed that the essence of the gospel lay in Jesus' proclamation of the kingdom of God, understood in ethical terms, and that the replacing of this content by a christological one had been an unfortunate development. Liberal theology on the whole agreed with him in stressing the kingdom rather than the cross. With the rise of neo-orthodoxy, the pendulum swung the other way and the gospel was proclaimed in fully christocentric terms. I think, however, that the most recent theology is seeking to overcome the disjunction. The fulness of the gospel is neither an ethico-political exhortation separated from the truth that God was in Christ, nor is it a message of personal justification and salvation through the cross without regard to the practical social implications of such a message. Although I find myself critical of some aspects of the 'theology of hope' associated with Moltmann and others, I believe that one of the merits of this type of theology is the determined attempt to overcome the dichotomy between an undogmatic liberal version of the gospel in ethical and social terms, and an unsocial, unethical version in terms of inward personal piety. Carl E. Braaten, one of the most articulate American advocates of the theology of hope, writes thus: 'The Pauline Christ who is the righteousness of God, and the Synoptic Jesus who announces the coming kingdom, are one and the same. For righteousness is the content of the kingdom. The message of the New Testament is the message of both the *basileia tou theou* and the *dikaiosune tou theou*. We should declare an end to the competition and seek a correlation between the kingdom and the cross *motifs* in the Christian tradition.'[5]

If our concept of the gospel must be comprehensive enough to embrace both kingdom and cross, it must likewise be broad enough to let Christ be seen in his multidimensional significance. The mystery of Christ is inexhaustible, and today we are still exploring it. Already in the New Testament the many facets of Christ were being recognized in the many titles and images used to speak of him – Messiah, Son of Man, Lord, the Word, Son of God, the True Vine and so on. Each title or image draws attention to a definite aspect of the impact Christ made on the early Christian community, and each one contains in itself the seeds of a definite christology and so of a version of the gospel. The title 'Messiah', for instance, did have political connotations, even if these are played down. As John Knox remarks: 'The gospel tradition does not permit us to miss the political bearings of Jesus' career, but they are certainly obscured.'[6] The use of this title 'Messiah' allows for the development of Christ's claims upon our common life and for the so-called 'social Gospel'. It belongs as an essential constituent to the mystery of Christ, and it has a special relevance today to black Americans and others. Yet neither this title nor any of the others is exhaustive of the mystery of Christ. To present him as only or even primarily a political revolutionary is utterly inadequate, and at this point New Testament criticism and exegesis are needed to correct subjective tendencies in theological interpretation.

While at any given time, one aspect or another of the reality of Christ may need to be emphasized in relation to a particular human need, that aspect cannot be cut off from all the others or it becomes sterile and ineffective. Some of the other ways of preaching and understanding Christ may not appear to be so relevant to the immediate situation as Christ the liberator, but they must not be denied or completely ignored, or else the whole gospel of Christ is distorted and loses its force. Christ as the God-man or the divine Word are not speculative luxuries but foundational affirmations, without which we cannot make other affirmations. For Christ is not just the sum of the roles attributed to him in the various titles by which he has been known. He is the reality who comes before all these titles, and makes them possible. Thus any one of them by itself is an abstraction, and cannot finally be severed from its context without distortion; and any proclamation of the gospel, whatever its particular emphases, cannot be adequate unless these emphases are related to the whole mystery of Christ.

Let us now turn to the second criterion, which is a *formal* one. That is to say, it has to do with the concept of anything that could properly be called gospel. What characteristics must belong to a message or proclamation that would lead us to acknowledge its claim as gospel? I suggest that we must be able to discern at least two characteristics before we can properly speak of the 'gospel'. The first is that such a message must bring good news for the *whole* man, not just for some department of his being or activities. The second point is that such a message brings *ultimate* good news; the message is not merely temporary or provisional or liable to be set aside by changing circumstances, even if all that is true of its particular formulations, but is the final Word behind all partial words or, in theological terms, the Word of God.

The first point has to do with the wholeness of man. Today man's understanding of himself has left behind the old-fashioned quarrels between spiritualistic and materialistic theories of man. The human person is not just a soul dwelling in (or even encumbered by) a body; yet his soul is no mere epiphenomenon of a material body, but a depth and transcendence of being, inexplicable in terms of a reductive naturalism. A pietistic gospel addressed only to man's soul and a secular gospel addressed only to his worldly needs are both pseudo-gospels. Nothing that does not touch the whole man is fully gospel. Furthermore, the contemporary phenomenology of man stresses the inescapably social dimensions of his being. The practical consideration of our increasing interdependence increases the importance of the phenomenological finding. This surely calls in question that idea of individual salvation that was so prominent in some ways of presenting the gospel, and makes us look rather for a universal salvation.

The New Testament seems to apply this criterion of a wholeness of outreach as the test of an adequate gospel. The story of Christ's temptations may be read as his quest for an adequate gospel. Various pseudo-gospels are considered and rejected. The words he uses in turning away from the temptation to turn stones into bread are surely significant: 'Man shall not live by bread alone' (Luke 4.4). Man is more than a body and needs more than a secular gospel. But it is abundantly clear that Jesus was not indifferent to the needs of the body. He does not say that man can live without bread – perhaps he thought that was such an absurd idea as to be scarcely worth mentioning, though in fact later 'spiritual' versions of the gospel have come near to such an absurdity.

I turn to the other point, that gospel, properly so-called, is an ultimate word, the Word of God. As such, it comes before all particular, relative, verbal formulations. Jesus Christ is himself the Word incarnate. One might say that he is the 'performative' Word of God – the Word in which doing, saying and being are together in concreteness before getting transcribed into words and sentences. Christ is the living communication of God's Word, and the words in which we try to seize and express the meaning of the communication can at best be fragmentary and abstract.

The ultimate Word transcends all grammatical forms. Yet we cannot be excused from the task of transcribing it into words and sentences, and we have to be on our guard that we do not rob it of anything belonging to its essence. Our grammatical forms are many – assertions, questions, commands, acclamations and so on. Perhaps the primal Word which founds the gospel is all of these. To be sure, it is above all *assertion*, the assertion that the final mystery whom we call God is to be understood in terms of the love of Christ. It is also *question*; there can be no authentic version of the gospel that does not put in question our human institutions, customs, standards of conduct. The gospel is also *command* – not command in isolation, which would be merely disheartening, but command in the context of assertion, the command to join with God and Christ and the Spirit in their already ongoing work of raising the creation to the level of the kingdom. I mentioned also *acclamation*, and the gospel is this too, for, as ultimate good news, it is a declaring of the glory of God.

How then, finally, do we answer the question about the gospel? It cannot be answered by any brief, simple formula. I have stressed the many dimensions of the gospel, and its inexhaustibility. I have acknowledged too that in any historical situation, some aspects of the gospel will come into focus, as specially related to the needs of that situation. Every generation has to discover and rediscover the gospel.

For our own time, the gospel should be presented differently than it was in the time of our grandfathers. Their excessively individualistic approach needs to be replaced with an emphasis on the social and even global implications of the gospel; in this age of affluence alongside starvation, their pietism and otherworldliness needs to be supplemented with concern for the whole man; their emphasis on believing needs to be countered by a call to action and participation in the world's affairs; where they felt summoned to passive obedience, we are more likely to understand the calling of God as one to responsible stewardship.

Short of the *eschaton*, I do not suppose that any generation will hear and receive the gospel in its fulness. And I cannot imagine any greater arrogance than that of supposing that for the first time in two thousand years one's own generation is really beginning to understand what the Christian gospel is all about! If we hear some things more clearly than an earlier generation, we may be thankful; but we can also be sure that we are failing to hear some things and that our understanding will be defective in ways we cannot see. We can best minimize the bad effects of our parochialisms and insensitivities by keeping ourselves open, as far as possible, to all the dimensions of the gospel. Above all, we must remain open to its transcendent, creative origin in God, for without that we could not speak meaningfully of a gospel at all.

Notes

1. P. van Buren, *The Secular Meaning of the Gospel*, Macmillan and SCM Press 1963, p. 138.

2. T. J. J. Altizer, *The Gospel of Christian Atheism*, Westminster Press 1966, p. 136.

3. P. Berger, *A Rumour of Angels*, Allen Lane: The Penguin Press 1970, p. 58.

4. J. H. Cone, *Black Power and Black Theology*, Seabury Press 1969, p. 99.

5. C. E. Braaten, *The Future of God*, Harper & Row 1969, p. 93.

6. J. Knox, *The Death of Christ*, Collins 1959, p. 29.

6

Liberal and Radical Theologies Compared

The number of theological labels is very great – 'liberal', 'radical', 'progressive', 'modernist', 'fundamentalist', 'evangelical', 'catholic', 'orthodox', 'neo-orthodox', 'conservative', and so on – but they all tend to be somewhat vague and they overlap at various points. Some refer to the spirit in which theology is done, while others have come to indicate some more or less definite body of opinions. The wisest theologians avoid getting themselves labelled too precisely. Yet when anyone sets out to understand the welter of conflicting movements that have had a place in the history of Christian theology, some attempt at typology and therefore inevitably some labelling is demanded.

Our present concern is to consider two of the types mentioned, liberal theology and radical theology. Our task will be to trace in outline the historical genesis of these two types, and so to illuminate the relation between them. But to begin with, I shall indicate in a general way the meanings which I attach to the words 'liberal' and 'radical' when used in a theological context, though the content of these words can be filled in only at the end of the inquiry.

In much of the writing of the present century, 'liberal theology' has been understood in the restricted sense of that movement (much diversified in itself) within Protestant theology which had its roots in Schleiermacher, continued through Ritschl and reached its culmination in the work of Harnack around the end of the nineteenth century. But in a broader sense, the name of liberal theology has been applied to much theology falling outside the narrower definition, yet related to it in so far as it is done in the spirit of 'liberality', to use a term popularized by Karl Jaspers on the continent and by Alec Vidler in England. In this broader sense, liberal theology is characterized above all by an openness to secular culture. It looks for continuity between Christian faith and the beliefs and attitudes of intelligent responsible persons outside of the church. In modern times, liberal theology has been especially open to the insights of the natural sciences, and likewise of psychology and sociology. It has encouraged exchanges with philosophy. It has welcomed and responded to the historical criticism of the Bible and the sources of Christian faith. Liberal theology has tended to be optimistic in outlook, and has found it easy to ally itself with doctrines of evolution and progress, while playing down the seriousness of sin. In many cases, liberal theologians have been very willing to recognize the value of non-Christian religions, and have tried to relate to them in affirmative ways. Though liberal theology has always been much concerned about intellectual integrity, it has been very much aware too of the ethical and social implications of faith. It has been critical of speculative types of theology if these have seemed to have little relevance to practical questions, but it has not denied the need of a theological basis for action. The openness toward culture on the part of liberal theology has led to a corresponding tentativeness in the formulation of dogma (often considered a bad word among liberals!) and to the scaling down of the authority to be attached to scripture and churchly traditions.

According to *The Oxford English Dictionary*, the use of the word 'liberal' to designate a style of theology originated around the middle of the nineteenth century. In 1846 Oliver Wendell Holmes mentioned 'a cheerful Christian from the liberal fold'. In 1886 W. P. Roberts published a book entitled *Liberalism in Religion*, in which he strongly maintained that liberal Christianity is not anti-theological.

'Radical theology' is also an expression with several usages, some broader and some narrower. It has been used recently in a quite narrow sense for those forms of theology which have accepted as their point of departure the 'death of God' – and in this sense William Hamilton and Thomas Altizer have been able to describe radical theology as 'a contemporary development within Protestantism'.[1] But there is a broader sense in which radical theology is a much older phenomenon. Historians have long talked of the 'radical' Reformation, meaning those extreme revolutionary movements which gathered around such prophetic figures as Thomas Münzer. One might say that the fundamental character of radical

Christianity and of the theology which grows out of it is its attempt to accomplish what Nietzsche called a 'transvaluation of all values'. Münzer has been called by the philosopher Ernst Bloch the theologian of revolution. Radical theology is a theology of revolution, and in this respect contrasts rather sharply with liberal theology, which is much more a theology of evolution. If we take the transvaluation of all values as a central characteristic of radical theology, then there have been many Christian theologies far more radical than 'death of God' theology, in spite of the appeals of the latter to Nietzsche. Just as liberal theology has its ethico-social implications, so has radical theology. It seeks the overthrow and transformation not only of traditional religious values but of the values of the prevailing culture as well. In its opposition to the culture (a fact which usually means that the theological radical is a political radical as well) radical theology again differs markedly from liberal theology, which attempts a *rapprochement* with the culture. In this respect, it becomes clear that 'death of God' theology belongs to an extreme liberal type rather than to the radical type. Some further points about radical theology may be noted. As revolutionary, it is strongly future-orientated and therefore interested in apocalyptic. Since it criticizes all 'religion', understood in the Barthian sense of the word, it is not concerned in the same degree as liberal theology to establish good relations between Christianity and other faiths. Some radical Christians would go so far as to claim that their allies are to be found not in other religions but in such secular movements as Marxism. Radical theology is more concerned with the ethico-political implications of Christian faith than with attaining a 'high' intellectually viable theology, and to the extent that it does construct a theological framework, its images and concepts are more likely to be drawn from politics than from metaphysics or natural science. But this also means that a radical theology may well be more definitely biblical than liberal theology often is, even if the biblical emphases of the radical are selective.

Even these preliminary generalizations have made it clear that liberal theology and radical theology are very different from one another. It is quite wrong to suppose that radical theology is just liberal theology pushed to the limits. Radical theology has different presuppositions from liberal theology. It is not an extreme form of liberal theology, but in many respects stands just as much opposed to liberalism as both the liberal and radical viewpoints stand opposed to conventional orthodoxy. It is equally wrong to suppose, as Altizer and Hamilton seem to do, that radical theology is something new and a more recent phenomenon than liberal theology. On the contrary, radical theology has been around much longer and, of the two, it is liberal theology that must be accounted the *parvenu*. In fact, it arrived with the *nouveaux riches* of modern bourgeois society.

But the generalizations I have made must now be substantiated by an examination in more detail of the evidence. Only the briefest of historical surveys will be possible, and, since I have claimed that radical theology is the older of the two types we have been considering, it seems appropriate to begin with it. What then are the origins and development of radical theology?

An interesting story is told about Martin Buber. After the Nazis came to power, Buber, who was still teaching in Germany, gave a lecture which brought the secret police to his home to question him. One of the officers asked: 'Do you have any radical literature here?' 'Yes', Buber answered, and handed him a copy of the Jewish scriptures.[2]

I tell the story because the origins of radical theology are so obviously right there in the Bible. The Old Testament, with its continual cry for justice and social renewal, is a radical document. The prophetic spirit is the spirit of radicalism. And this is continued in the New Testament, which is even more radical. The Sermon on the Mount challenges the whole existing value-system: 'You have heard that it was said to the men of old ... but I say to you ...' Jesus himself was the centre of the challenge to the established order in religion and society. He was certainly not a violent revolutionary, as some have tried to make him out to be. His radicalism went much further than that, for it undercut not only the values of the established culture but equally those of the conventional revolutionary who, in spite of his opposition to the prevailing order, has in large measure taken over its values and methods. But although Jesus is at the centre of this radical movement, it is evident in New Testament Christianity as a whole – in Paul, with his insistence that the time is short, and even in Luke who sets out the Christian programme in the *Magnificat*.

Can we push the matter further, and ask what it is that gives to the Bible, and especially the New Testament, its radical character? The answer to this question seems fairly clear. It is eschatology, or even apocalyptic. The prophets of the Old Testament, Jesus himself, and the earliest Christians all looked forward to the coming of a new order. To be sure, this was visualized in different ways at different times. But it was never regarded as evolving naturally out of the existing order. The more intense the eschatological expectation, the sharper the looked for break between the old order and the new, then the more radical was the teaching. For if the old order stands already condemned, none of its institutions, whether religious or political, has a permanent claim upon men. These institutions are already perishing, the time is short, and what is needed is to prepare oneself for the new order with its new values, new life styles, new forms of association and community. All the essential categories of radical theology – the new, the future, the transvaluation of values, the rejection of the existing order (including 'religion', in so far as this has become a part of that order), the new society of the kingdom of God – all these are grounded in the eschatological expectation. I think it may also be said that in the subsequent history of the church, whenever the eschatological element in Christianity has been stressed, theology has taken a radical turn; and at times when eschatology has been discretely soft-pedalled, Christian theology has been lacking any radical character.

Christianity in what might be termed its raw form has in fact been too frightening for most people, so that its radical and eschatological aspects have been more often than not suppressed. There is some evidence that the evangelists themselves were already toning down some of the more radical teaching of Jesus, so that New Testament scholars are inclined to the opinion that the more radical any teaching of Jesus is, the more authentic it is likely to be. I mentioned already the antitheses of the Sermon on the Mount, and these (or, at least, most of them) seem to be beyond question genuine utterances of Jesus.[3] As the *parousia* was more and more delayed, and as Christian theology coalesced more and more with Hellenistic philosophy, the eschatological and consequently the radical elements in the Christian faith were increasingly muted.

Yet, what might be called the radical-apocalyptic strain in Christian faith is so deeply rooted that it could never be quite suppressed, and it has kept bursting forth from time to time, though often in sects and 'far out' groups rather than in the mainstream of the church's life and thought. I have time to mention only a few of the more striking manifestations.

For our first example, we go to the time of the revival of the church through the rise of monasticism in the early Middle Ages. There were many radical features in the movements of that time, and perhaps this radical tendency received its best expression at the hands of Joachim of Fiore, who in 1202 issued his *Treatise on the Four Gospels*. This could be described as an eschatological interpretation of history. According to Joachim, world-history is divided into three ages – the age of the Father, the age of the Son and the age of the Holy Spirit. The age of the Father was announced by Adam and Abraham, and brought in by Moses. This was the age of the law and of the Old Testament dispensation. The second age was announced by John the Baptist and inaugurated by Christ. This was the age of the institutional church, the age of clerics and sacraments. But this age, Joachim believed, was fast approaching its end. By a calculation based on the genealogy of Jesus given in Matthew's gospel, he claimed that the year 1260 would see the beginning of the new age of the Spirit. Its forerunners had already appeared to announce it – Antony, Benedict and Bernard. The new age would bring about a radical transformation and would be a truly pentecostal time. The temporary institutional forms of the church would disappear and be superseded by a free spontaneous form of Christian life in the Spirit, to which monasticism was already pointing the way. On the political side, feudalism would likewise be abolished and social inequalities be done away.

Joachim, in turn, had an influence on Thomas Münzer, the best-known representative of radical Christianity in the Reformation period. Around 1520, Münzer believed himself to be receiving the direct inspiration of the Holy Spirit, and sought to found a spiritual community, rather on the model of the third age in Joachim's scheme. On the political side, Münzer preached revolt and allied himself with the rebels in the Peasants' Revolt, while mainline Protestantism, led by Luther, supported the princes.

Of the various radical Christian groups in England in the seventeenth century, probably the Fifth Monarchy Men stand closest to the tradition I have been describing. The fifth monarchy, supposed to have been prophesied by Daniel, was to succeed the empires of Assyria, Persia, Greece and Rome. During it, Christ would reign with his saints for a thousand years.

The coming of the Enlightenment led once more to the neutralization of the eschatological and apocalyptic elements in Christianity. One of the tragedies of the eighteenth and nineteenth centuries, the formative period in which the industrial and technological society was taking shape, was that with the suppression of eschatology in the interests of intellectual respectability, the radical aspects of Christian teaching were likewise suppressed, and then reappeared outside of the Christian church altogether. Certainly, at a time when chiliasm and eschatology were being played down by Christian theologians as intellectual embarrassments, they were receiving a powerful and, as it has turned out, a most influential treatment at the hands of Karl Marx. Sometimes Marxism has been called a Judeo-Christian heresy, and the description is justified to the extent that Marxism has isolated the radical–apocalyptic strand in biblical teaching and, separating it from its theistic context, has sought to provide it with a new context in a materialistic interpretation of history. The question must arise how the responsibility for this lies at the door of those eighteenth and nineteenth century theologians (would we have to call them liberals?) who extruded eschatology from Christian faith on the ground that it was a primitive survival and who thereby forced it to seek new soil in which to grow.

At the end of the nineteenth century, the interest in eschatology was revived, chiefly through the work of Weiss and Schweitzer. These men also made clear the bond between eschatology and the radical ethical teaching of the New Testament. Schweitzer called it an *interim* ethic, and so it is, whether the *interim* period is short or long. The renewed interest in eschatology led in turn to a renewal of radical theology. The great radical theologian in the early part of the present century was undoubtedly Karl Barth. For him, at that time, theology was identified with eschatology. Bitterly he blamed the theologians who had turned God into the guardian of our Western culture and our Christian religion. God, he taught, is rather the judge who accuses both culture and religion and demands their radical transformation in the face of the end. But after the first fine careless rapture, Barth, for better or worse, lapsed into church dogmatics.

Schweitzer and Bultmann, though they made much of the place of eschatology in the New Testament, sought in their several ways to demythologize it in their contemporary presentations of Christian theology. They took away the eschatological sting or offence, and both ended up as liberal rather than radical theologians. But the story did not end there. Moltmann and his associates have hit back at the demythologizers with a full-blooded reassertion of eschatology. The old themes are heard again – the godlessness of the present age, the earnest expectation of a future of hope, the resurrection of the dead as the renewal of society. This is the most radical theology of the day and, like many radical theologies of the past, it is highly biblical in its orientation. Whether or not Moltmann is successful in his aim, the aim itself is highly laudable.

That aim is to reintegrate into Christian theology the radical–apocalyptic strand which the Enlightenment threw out and which has found a home in Marxism. Moltmann's influence is discernible in some of the other forms of radical theology that have recently developed, especially black theology in the United States and some of the theological work being done in the third world. Also in the Roman Catholic Church there is a movement of radical theology, in which the eschatological *motifs* are present.

But it is time for us now to turn to the history of liberal theology. Since this is more recent in origin, we can deal with it more briefly. There would be general agreement with H. P. Van Dusen's judgment that 'liberal theology was, in its origin and formulation, something *genuinely new* in the pilgrimage of Christian faith'.[4] That origin is to be placed around the period of the Enlightenment, and what was new was the conscious and systematic attempt to reconcile Christian faith with modern thought, or to construct a Christian theology which would be fully compatible with our modern understandings of man and Nature. The question inspiring liberal theology is this: 'How can I be both a Christian believer and a child of the modern world of the intellect, receiving its well-established findings and remaining open to its constantly new discoveries?' Although this is an intellectual question, it is not a narrowly academic one. It is the question of intellectual honesty, and therefore a profoundly existential and even agonizing question.

Admittedly, while liberal theology as a conscious systematic endeavour is a phenomenon of modern times, its practitioners have felt an affinity with earlier theologians who displayed a spirit of 'liberality'. Such were some of the early Fathers, who tried to reconcile Christian teaching and Greek philosophy. Origen was voicing a liberal sentiment when he wrote: 'We are careful not to raise objections to any good teachings, even if their authors are outside the faith.'[5] Again, Renaissance scholars such as Nicholas of Cusa have been claimed as forerunners of liberal theology. But the movement proper belongs to the last two or three centuries.

The volume of what may be broadly called 'liberal theology' produced in this period is so vast that even the barest historical sketch is not possible, and would be of little use in any case. But what can be done is to point to a number of areas in which liberal theologians have tried fairly to meet the challenges of modern culture, and the successes and dangers that have attended them.

Perhaps the fundamental encounter has been with the modern historical spirit. It is often thought that Christianity has been weakened through the historical criticism of its sources in the past two or three centuries, but it seems to me to have been one of the great triumphs of Christian theology that at least its more liberal exponents have been able fully to accept the historical method and to submit theology to the self-criticism which this method implies. If it has meant abandonment of the old belief in the infallibility of the Bible, it has led to far better insights into the meaning of the Bible and of Christian faith generally. Furthermore, the claim of theology to be a serious intellectual discipline has been greatly strengthened by the determination of liberal theologians to be in earnest about historical criticism and to follow the evidence wherever it may lead. The liberal theologian, whatever else he may be, is one who thinks historically, and this is a great strength.

It has become clear in the modern period that to think historically is to admit a measure of relativism, and this too is a nettle that the liberal theologians have firmly grasped. The liberal was quick to recognize that doctrine develops and that no dogmatic formulation has finality. Where it is a question of greater or lesser adequacy rather than a question of all or nothing, the liberal theologian was also able to be appreciative of positions other than his own and of the truth to be found in non-Christian religions and philosophies. In this matter, he has often had recourse to the Logos doctrine of Justin and other early Fathers.

As the authority of the Bible and tradition was relativized, a new source of religious truth came to be stressed – human experience. Schleiermacher, often called the father of liberal Protestantism, made human experience and particularly the religious consciousness the keystone of his theology. Most liberal theologians have followed him in emphasizing the place of experience. Again, this has meant a strengthening of theology in a world where the empirical has come to be highly valued. Yet we must notice that one of the principal dangers to which liberal theology is liable has arisen from this stress on experience. Schleiermacher himself was careful to appeal to *corporate* experience, but many later liberal theologians have moved in the direction of individualism and subjectivism, and have been accused of retreating into an inner world of feeling because they had no objective supports for faith left. This is a criticism which many liberals would find difficult to answer.

To the credit of liberal theology is to be reckoned also its steady endeavours to come to terms with the sciences – not only the natural sciences, but also psychology and sociology. To some extent, theology was helped in this endeavour by the acceptance of the historical method. For instance, when one recognizes the historical provenance of the creation stories in the Bible, they have been relativized in such a way that there is no longer a head-on crash when one is confronted with modern scientific theories of evolution. But liberal theologians have gone far beyond this in constructive theology, and have shown how such traditional notions as creation, miracle and the like can be reconceived in a modern context and can have continuing value. Demythologizing is only one example of the methods used to make the traditional teaching intelligible and credible to modern minds.

One might mention too the dialogue between liberal theology and the various types of philosophy that have come and gone since the Enlightenment. No doubt there has sometimes been the danger that liberal theologians would lean so far that they might subordinate Christian faith to whatever happened to be the philosophical fashion of the moment. More generally, liberal theologians have been tempted to accommodate Christianity to the cultural moods expressed in these philosophies. Yet such risks must be taken if Christianity is to be communicated in new and changing intellectual climates. Even to be aware of the danger is already to be on guard against its worst consequences.

According to Karl Barth, liberal theology failed both the church and the world very badly at the time of World War I. It may well be conceded that too many accommodations to secular culture had been made. Yet there were abiding insights in liberal theology that could not be suppressed, and although it was in eclipse for a time, it is still with us today in many forms. Process theology, common in the United States, is one form of liberal theology, specially dedicated to the task of expressing Christian doctrine in terms compatible with the modern dynamic understanding of nature. Bultmann's demythologizing, I have already hinted, may be counted a form of liberal theology, even if its author would disown the label and was at pains to distinguish his position from that of the older generation of liberals in Germany. Tillich's theology of culture is one of the most elaborate attempts to reconcile Christian faith and modern thought. As I have suggested above, the 'death of God' theologies are not so much radical theologies as extreme forms of liberal theology, carrying accommodation to the cultural mood to the furthest lengths; and this diagnosis is confirmed by the criticism which has been directed at 'death of God' theology by the genuinely radical black theologians of America. The theology of

Teilhard de Chardin may be regarded as a kind of liberal Catholicism, and shows many of the features which we have seen to be characteristic of liberal Protestantism.

Now that we have before us the outlines of the historical genesis of liberal and radical theologies, and the main characteristics of each, let us try to draw the comparison. The conflicts are more obvious than the similarities, and this confirms my original claim that liberal and radical theologies are quite different and not merely two stages of a single movement. Liberal theology is orientated to the present, radical theology (as eschatological) to the future. Liberal theology seeks to relate affirmatively to the prevailing culture, radical theology is negative to the culture, as the present age which must perish so that the new can be born. Liberal theology is tolerant to the point of indifference, it is ecumenical and well-disposed even to the non-Christian religions, while radical theology has the intolerance (not necessarily a persecuting intolerance) of an urgent conviction, and tends to operate through the self-conscious sect or pressure group. Liberal theology sets itself above all the goal of intellectual honesty and employs categories drawn from science and philosophy, while radical theology is in the main practical and draws inspiration from biblical images, especially those with a political slant. But the fundamental point is that liberal theology is embarrassed by apocalyptic, which must therefore be either eliminated or demythologized, while for radical theology such ideas as the end of the age and the resurrection of the dead belong to the very essence of the Christian faith.

I do not think that I have drawn the contrasts too sharply, though, of course, there are intermediate positions, and there are different ways in which the various characteristics described may be combined. For my own part, I find attractive features in both liberal and radical theology, though I would not want to identify myself wholly with either position. We have to remember that these are only two of many types of theology – I listed about ten at the beginning of this essay, and that list was not meant to be exhaustive.

Furthermore, there is no easy way of combining the liberal and radical positions. The tensions between them are probably healthy for the state of theology and for its future development. I am suspicious of 'consensus' theologies of the kind that issues from committees and commissions and is usually so dull as to destroy any further interest in the subject. In the foreseeable future, Christian theology is likely to be pluralistic. New truths will be won out of the constructive confrontations of the different points of view. The conflicts will sometimes be sharp, but they need not be bitter, and in subjects like theology, the truth is never found entirely in one position. I believe that both liberal and radical theology have important contributions to make to the theological dialogue of the future.

Notes

1. T. J. J. Altizer and W. Hamilton, *Radical Theology and the Death of God*, Bobbs-Merrill 1966, p. ix.

2. A. Hodes, *Martin Buber: An Intimate Portrait*, Viking Press 1971, p. 130.

3. Cf. E. Käsemann, *Essays on New Testament Themes*, SCM Press 1964, pp. 37-40.

4. H. P. Van Dusen, *The Vindication of Liberal Theology*, Scribner 1963, p. 17.

5. Origen, *Contra Celsum*, tr. H. Chadwick, Cambridge University Press 1965, vii, 46.

7

Word and Idea

The word is *logos* or discourse, that which is uttered, heard and understood, that which pertains to *legein*, the activity of saying. The idea is *eidos* or form, the image, percept or concept which arises in the mind and pertains first to *idein*, the activity of seeing. When the two expressions, 'word' and 'idea' (we could equally well say, 'the two words' or 'the two ideas') are set down side by side, we are first aware of some opposition between them. Yet, as soon as we try to analyse this opposition, we find that it becomes elusive and that the two terms constituting it tend to run together. Word and idea stand together in a tension that comprises elements both of opposition and affinity.

The oppositions are obvious. For instance, there is the contrast between seeing and hearing. These are two of the senses by which man is open to the world and to his fellows. These are, furthermore, the senses by which we are able to extend our awareness into the distance. Through seeing and hearing, we become aware of a vastly extended environment. But we perceive this environment very differently through each of these senses. The word belongs primarily to hearing, the idea to seeing, and so in their origins these two come from quite different media.

There is the further contrast between particularity and universality. A word embodies itself in the physical world as an event in that world. It possesses a certain uniqueness, as it is spoken by a particular person in a particular situation. It becomes publicly accessible, as something that happens in the world. Even if one tries to preserve it by writing it down, it still retains its concrete innerworldly character – it is ink on paper, though never merely that. The idea, on the other hand, seems to float above the world. It cannot be pinned down as an event that has happened at a particular time. It does not have any physical embodiment. The value of an idea is precisely that it can be universalized, so that it transcends the particularity and mutability of an event, of becoming; and this, of course, was the virtue that Plato saw in ideas. And if it is characteristic of the word to be publicly accessible, it is equally characteristic of the idea to be private to the mind which entertains it – until, indeed, that mind expresses the idea by transforming it into the word.

Likewise, one could mention the opposition between the dynamic character of the word and the static character of the idea. This follows from, and simply develops a little further, the point I have just been making. The word is an event, a happening in time, whereas the idea has a peculiar timelessness. Thus the word is often performative; it commands, it incites, it encourages, it gets things done. But the idea seems rather to belong to the sphere of contemplation. The word goes out from man and initiates activity. The idea, however, is received and entertained, and we experience a measure of passivity before it. One is tempted to see the word as masculine, the idea as feminine, always remembering that every human being, whether man or woman, has masculine and feminine aspects of personality.

There is a related contrast between intellect and sense. The word is appropriated by understanding. 'Do you hear me?' is equivalent to 'Do you understand me?' *Logos* gives rise to logic. But *eidos* gives rise to eidetic and esthetic. It is concerned with shape and form.

One could go on enumerating the contrasts that can be set up between word and idea. Yet we soon come to recognize that all these contrasts stand in need of qualification, and that it would be a one-sided procedure that would be content to place word and idea in opposition to each other. If the word goes forth with dynamic effect, it can also be passively received by the hearer; if the idea is received or conceived in passivity, it may nevertheless eventually emerge as a dynamic force. We find that word and idea often converge and overlap, and even that they sometimes seem to exchange the roles that we conventionally assign to them, so that now the word is operating as idea, and now the idea has become word. The Word of Philo, for instance, has so many of the characteristics of an idea that we could recognize it as having much in common with the Idea of Hegel. Each expression points to the principle of rationality and order that bodies itself forth in the world. And perhaps both are embraced in a wider concept of meaning.

The possibility of moving from word to idea and then perhaps to a more comprehensive concept is present from the moment that we begin to use such complex notions as word and idea. It will be recalled how Goethe tells of Faust's dissatisfaction with the traditional rendering of the prologue to St John's gospel: 'In the beginning was the Word'. He tried instead: 'In the beginning was the Idea (Thought)'. But this too was unsatisfactory. 'In the beginning was the Deed.' Now we reach something more comprehensive. A word is a deed, and no deed, properly so-called, is lacking thought.

The relation between word and idea, then, is fluid and ambiguous. We could easily proceed to turn around some of the contrasts set up at the beginning of this essay. If, in one sense, the word has particularity, especially the word of living speech, in another sense the word makes possible abstraction and universal ideas. If it is the idea or *eidos* that primarily signifies form, nevertheless it is language that first allows men to give form to the world. When man names the phenomena of the world he brings to them a manageable order. There is no longer just an infinite and bewildering profusion of unique existents, for the word has permitted man to categorize, to classify, to distinguish, to join together. Indeed, philologists tell us that the root meaning of *legein* was 'to gather'. To use words is to gather, to set up connections, to articulate, to grasp common characteristics. In other words, it is to universalize, in the sense of building a universe, an ordered whole as distinct from a chaotic flux of unrelated particulars. But to gather and connect together is at the same time to separate and distinguish. Every affirmation is also an implicit negation. Every *logos,* as Aristotle expressed it, is at once *synthesis* and *diairesis,* putting together and taking apart. The use of language, that is to say, makes possible conceptualization, and concepts are simply universal ideas.

I have drawn attention in another writing[1] to the interesting connections that are to be found in a wide variety of languages between verbs of saying and verbs of seeing. Such verbs frequently come from a common root, in which the notion of seeing is usually primary, that of saying derivative. The connection is very evident in the English language, where 'to say' originated as a causative form of 'to see'. To say is to cause to see, though it is also, and possibly more obviously, to cause to hear. To say the word or *logos* is to exhibit the form or *eidos* of what is seen. The philosophical understanding of the word or *logos* in Greek thought, perhaps from as early as the time of Heraclitus right down to the times of the Stoics and the Christian fathers, is that of the universal form or *eidos* of the world, and one might say that this philosophical interpretation of *logos* is the furthest remove from the word of living speech in the direction of pure idea, the fullest development of the innate tendency of word to pass over into idea.

On the other hand, one could point to the convergence of the idea upon the word. Ideas are not just images, even if the word 'idea' originally did point to the visual appearance of anything. For as soon as images enter into experience, they become subject to the process of putting together and taking apart, and it is hard to suppose that this could happen to any extent apart from the use of words, the activity of *legein*. Is it possible to think without words? Perhaps, in some rather special ways, it is. To name one example, musicologists have claimed that music is a thinking without concepts, and Beethoven's late string quartets have been called (surely for good reason) 'metaphysical'. But our familiar kinds of thinking are different. In all the usual forms of thinking, ideas must clothe themselves (or incarnate themselves) in words, if they are to be articulated within the structure of thought itself.

The notion of 'meaning' is important for understanding the relation and convergence of word and idea. Of course, 'meaning' is itself a very difficult word to define, and there are different kinds and levels of meaning. In the present context, I would say that something has meaning when it can be seen as part of a larger whole, and in such a way that it constitutes in some measure the unity of the whole; but the whole too has meaning as a unity with order and structure, and not just a collection of parts. Thus, a word has meaning in a sentence, while the sentence in turn has a meaning of a different level in an argument or a story. A puzzling object in the distance has meaning when we discern that it is part of a building. A tool or piece of equipment has meaning when we see it getting used in the context of a manufacturing process. But the process itself has meaning, in the wider context of human life, as well as in the fact that it has order and structure within itself. Evidently a stage must be reached when no further context can be supplied. The words 'world' and 'God' are difficult to define, because they themselves supply contexts but appear to have no contexts of their own. Such words point to realities in which intelligibility is qualified by mystery, that is to say, by inexhaustibility.[2] And at this point too the locus of meaning tends to shift from words to the realities of which we speak in our words.

Words are not just sounds. They are formed sounds that have become bearers of meaning and possible constituents of wider meanings. Ideas, likewise, are not just images or bare sense-data. They are percepts and even concepts and, as such, participate in meaning.

We have taken note that Goethe's Faust set alongside the traditional verse, 'In the beginning was the Word', the alternative, 'In the beginning was the Idea'; and then gathered both of these in the more comprehensive, 'In the beginning was the Deed'. My own inclination, however, would be to use the notion of meaning as the comprehensive term here. It is perhaps hardly necessary to say that I would understand 'meaning' not in too narrowly intellectual a sense or as confined to words and sentences, but in a broad existential way that includes elements of intellection and sense, of conation and feeling, of intention and appreciation.

Then, if I might be bold enough to join those who have tried to translate or paraphrase the prologue to St John's gospel, I would render it somewhat as follows:

Fundamental to everything is meaning. Meaning is closely connected with what men call 'God', and indeed, meaning and God are the same. To say that God was in the beginning is to say that meaning was in the beginning. All things were made meaningful, and there was nothing made that was meaningless. Life is the drive toward meaning, and life has emerged into the light of humanity, the bearer of meaning. And meaning shines out through the threat of absurdity, for absurdity has not destroyed it.

Every man has a share of the true meaning of things. This follows from the fact that this meaning has been embodying itself in the world from the beginning and has given the world its shape. Yet the world has not recognized the meaning, and even man, the bearer of meaning, has rejected it. But those who have received it and believed in it have been enabled to become the children of God. And this has happened not in the natural course of evolution or through human striving, but through an act of God. For the meaning has been incarnated in a human existent, in whom was grace and truth; and we have seen in him the final meaning or glory toward which everything moves – the glory of man and the glory of God' (John 1.1-5 and 9-14).

In our earlier discussion, I have several times linked the word to hearing and the idea to seeing. It is meaning that unites what comes to us through these very different channels of sense. One of the most amazing things about our human experience is the way in which the several senses are co-ordinated, so that although hearing and sight are quite different media, they belong together in the unitary world that we know through them. When one sits and talks with a friend, the words that the friend utters and the facial expressions that accompany them are experienced as a unity. A handclasp too may become part of the experience, and then still another sense, that of touch, has been incorporated into the total meaningful situation. We may talk, if we wish, of a common sense or a coenesthetic awareness, building the deliverances of the several senses into a unified awareness. But from the philosophical point of view, one must point again to the role of meaning. The raw data of the senses, whether sight or hearing or touch or something else, are always immediately subjected to interpretation, that is to say, they are transformed into meanings. It is very difficult ever to be aware of a mere sense-datum. We do not see just a coloured patch, for already it is seen as a cloud, as a house, or whatever it may be. We do not hear just some noise or other, we hear an automobile or an aeroplane. We are puzzled, even startled out of our everyday awareness, if we cannot interpret a sight or a sound or if it is ambiguous, that is to say, if we cannot assign to it the appropriate meaning or (alternatively expressed) assign it to the appropriate context of meaning. Once the meaning has been assigned, the experience is articulated into our world of meaning, which is also our world of words and ideas.

Of course, the way in which a human being experiences the world is already determined for him by the particular senses which he possesses and their range. Our eyes, for instance, are sensitive to light-waves, but one could at least imagine a creature that had receptors sensitive to electro-magnetic waves of a different frequency, such as radio waves. To such a creature, the appearance or *eidos* of the sky would be very different from the way we see it. Similarly, our ears pick up sounds within a certain range of frequencies, but there are other creatures which are, so to speak, 'tuned in' to quite different frequencies and their experience of the world of sounds must be quite different. The phenomena of the world we know through the senses are far from exhausting all reality. It is true that by means of instruments we can extend the range of the human senses and fill in some gaps. The radio telescope yields a new map of the skies, and there are instruments which can detect and then 'translate' into audible sounds 'noises' that are beyond the range of our normal hearing.

Out of this vast fund of sensuous and trans-sensuous material is built up an ever expanding and ever more complex world of intelligible meanings. The whole process is a dynamic one of enormous complexity. Word and idea are alike basic ingredients in this process, and their dynamic character has already become apparent to us in the tendency of every word and idea to pass beyond itself – the word into idea, the idea into word, and both into larger wholes of meaning.

One classic description of this dynamic, expanding process is the one given by Hegel in *The Phenomenology of Mind*. Sense-certainty passes over into perception, perception into understanding, understanding into reason and so on in an unrelenting dialectical drive. The dialectic, according to Hegel, inheres both in the mind or spirit which unfolds itself in the process, and in the notions which that mind develops in itself. On the contemporary scene, a philosopher who has devoted himself in a signal way to exploring the mental act in all its complexity is Bernard Lonergan in his book, *Insight*. Understanding and imagination, definition and judgment, sense and intellect – these and many other notions which both refine and gather up some of the oppositions and affinities that we have noted in our own discussion of word and idea are used to delineate the mental act in its diversity and unity. But once more it is all seen in dynamic terms. Lonergan speaks of 'transcendence', and this supplies the dynamic element, just as 'dialectic' did in Hegel. Lonergan tells us that 'despite its imposing name, "transcendence" is the elementary matter of raising further questions'. He describes it in the following terms: 'Transcendence means "going beyond". So inquiry, insight and formulation do not merely reproduce the content of sensible experience, but go beyond it. So reflection, grasp of the unconditioned and judgment are not content with mere objects of supposing, defining, considering, but go beyond them to the universe of facts, of being, of what truly is affirmed and really is. Moreover, one can rest content with knowing things as related to us, or one can go beyond that to join the scientists in searching for the knowledge of things as related to one another. One can go beyond both common sense and present science to grasp the dynamic structure of our rational knowing and doing, and then formulate a metaphysic and an ethic. Finally, one can ask whether human knowledge is confined to the universe of proportionate beings or goes beyond it to the realm of transcendent being; and this transcendent realm may be conceived either relatively or absolutely, either as beyond man or as the ultimate in the whole process of going beyond.'[3]

One may have many reservations about aspects of the philosophies of both Hegel and Lonergan, but they both excel in their descriptions of the intellectual drive in man. It is clear too from the treatment in their writings of ethical and other matters that although their preoccupation is primarily with the intellectual, the concepts of dialectic and transcendence apply to the whole man. I would say myself that no entirely rigid lines can be drawn between aspects of our being that are strictly cognitive and others that might be called conative and affective. It was in this sense that I wrote above of the quest for meaning as an existential quest rather than a purely intellectual one, though I would certainly want to stress – as Hegel and Lonergan do – the intellectual dimension, especially in the face of some contemporary tendencies toward anti-intellectualism.

Word and idea, *logos* and *eidos*, belong together in human experience in a relation of both tension and affinity, and so do the various distinctions that are elusively associated with them – intellect and sense, hearing and seeing, concreteness and abstraction. Word cannot be exalted over idea, or the other way around. It is true that in a given historical and cultural situation, one or the other may predominate, but they are not finally separable, and both are needed if the richness and dynamism of experience is to be maintained and enhanced. These remarks have relevance to some contemporary problems in theology and the philosophy of religion, as I shall now seek to show.

A good starting-point for this part of the discussion would be a brief consideration of the sharp contrast sometimes set up between Hebrew and Greek modes of experience and thought. The Hebrew mode is said to be concrete and oriented to the *logos*; the Greek mode is said to be abstract and oriented to the *eidos*. This view has been very influential in much recent biblical theology, though I think its force has been much weakened by the impact of such books as James Barr's *Semantics of Biblical Language*. However, the alleged Greek–Hebrew contrast keeps reappearing, even in systematic theology (Moltmann) and philosophy of religion (Dewart). To be sure, the contrasts are really there, but they become grossly exaggerated. If, as we have seen, *logos* and *eidos* are both necessary to a rich and dynamic experience, so, I believe, Hebrew and Greek contributions come together to form a richer and more dynamic Christianity than would be possible if we tried to extrude one or other of these contributions.

As an illustration, we may consider a contrast between seeing and hearing. Rudolf Bultmann writes: 'The Greek tends to think of the world as an objective closed system, susceptible of mathematical measurement. Thus, for him, sight tends to be the most important of the senses. For the Old Testament, however, hearing is the most important.' Bultmann then explains the point by arguing that to see God would be to make an object of him and so 'to be able to stand upright in his presence'. (Contemporary liturgical reformers please take note!) On the other hand, 'hearing is the sense of being encountered, of the distance being bridged, the acknowledgement of a speaker's claim on us'.[4]

I doubt very much whether seeing a person and hearing a person can be contrasted in this way. The richest experience of encounter would be one in which we both saw and heard the other – and touched him as well, if that were possible. To hear a word in isolation from the other senses would be a somewhat ghostly encounter. Undoubtedly it is true that in the Hebrew experience of God, hearing the word was normative. The notion that God might be seen or depicted was for the most part abhorrent to the Hebrew mind, as redolent of idolatry, though in a very few ancient passages of scripture, God is in fact seen (Cf. Gen. 32.30; Ex. 24.10). Sometimes, however, vision is joined to audition, most notably in the noble vision of Isaiah (Isa. 6.1ff.). And if, in the beginning, creation took place through the *word* of God, the highest moment in the work of creation was the imparting of the divine *image* (*eikon*) to man (Gen. 1.26-7).

In the New Testament, Christ is certainly the incarnate Word, but in St John's gospel there is talk also of seeing his glory, and it is claimed that those who have seen him have seen the Father (John 1.14 and 14.9). Franz Mussner has written on the importance of verbs of seeing in this gospel, and claims that although seeing is not understood by the evangelist as inward mystical vision but has its beginning in ordinary acts of seeing, it nevertheless 'transcends what is on the surface, the temporal and the historical, and penetrates to the mystery', which is 'the epiphany of the eternal divine Logos'.[5] We may further note concerning the New Testament that while the fourth gospel speaks of Jesus as the eternal Word, the Epistle to the Hebrews calls him the 'express image' (*charakter*) of the Father; the potentiality of 'reflecting the glory of God' – a potentiality which belongs to every man in virtue of his being a bearer of the divine image (*eikon*) – is in Christ actualized on a transcendent level (Heb. 1.3).

Here we have dwelt on the contrast between seeing and hearing, and we must conclude that finally these two are not opposed but complementary. The same is true of the other contrasts which arise from the relation of word and idea. Let me now conclude by pointing briefly to the necessity for both word and idea in three vital areas of Christian concern – theology, worship and practical service in the world. In all three, strains and tensions between word and idea are experienced, and different emphases are appropriate at different times, yet each area would be much impoverished if either word or idea were too severely reduced for the sake of the other.

In theology, we need both logic and imagination (including poetry, myth, symbolism). Theology may be deemed a science, in the sense that it participates in the *logos* of rational discourse and contributes to the sum of human knowledge. As such a *logos*, theology must have its standards of intellectual integrity and it must seek coherence both in its own structure and in relation to other intellectual disciplines. Theology does not simply tell a story or present us with poetic symbols. It interprets and criticizes the story. It has its propositional and conceptual elements, and there must be some recognized logic of God-talk if theology is to be taken seriously. Yet just because the subject-matter of theology is finally God, the ineffable mystery, it can never be contained in propositions or finite categories but is always bursting out of them. This it does by developing its eidetic side, the images and symbols which are not strict concepts but imaginative leaps out into the mystery that is never fully grasped. The mystery always stretches beyond the furthest reaches of thought, and an adequate theology requires both a logical structure and the open texture of an imaginative outreach.

In worship, we need both word and sacraments – and the latter cannot be reduced simply to *verbum visibile*. The word is needed if worship is to be an intelligent activity, and safeguarded from lapsing into superstition, fanaticism and sentimentalism. The sensuousness of the sacraments is needed if the full range of faith is to be experienced as something much more than intellectual conviction. Separation of word and sacraments has always been disastrous, leading either to an intellectualized and individualistic faith based on the word alone, or to an uninstructed quasi-magic when the sacraments are divorced from an effective ministry of the word. It is interesting to note that Christian sacramentalism effects a peculiar synthesis of *logos* and *eidos*. In the eucharist, for instance, the use of bread and wine contrasts on the one hand with the Greek representation of the gods by means of statues and direct visual portrayal; it contrasts on the other hand with the Hebrew enshrining of the written word. Admittedly, this has led to a tension that has been experienced in Christian history with special acuteness in the rise of various iconoclastic movements, notably in the seventh and eight centuries, and again at the Reformation. But the visible eucharistic species of bread and wine have provided an eidetic focus which transcends both image and word, and which leads into a context of meaning to which both word and image contribute. It would seem that at the present time both Catholics and Protestants are striving to overcome the false disjunction of word and idea, such as occurs when word and sacraments are separated. For a long time, many Protestants have become increasingly aware of the onesidedness and eventual sterility of an exclusively word-centred worship, while Catholics on their side have been developing an increasing respect for the ministry of the word.

In the Christian life, there is need for both action and contemplation. We have already noted the dynamic character of the word. The Hebrew *dabar* could mean either 'word' or 'deed', and the prophetic word was closely connected with action. But ideas, images, stories, pictures have a certain dynamism too, and can be creative. They may lie hidden and germinating for a long time, but during this time they are silently at work in forming the lives of those who entertain them. This kind of formation may prove to be far more effective than verbal instruction or exhortation. A time comes when the ideas break forth into deeds. Activism has in recent years been greatly prized in the Christian church, and no doubt this has been a necessary corrective to past inaction. But activism is short-lived and self-defeating if it is not founded and nourished in the kind of thought and contemplation that are scarcely to be distinguished from prayer. Christian discipleship demands not only obedience to the word but an inward dwelling on the images and symbols of faith with their formative power.

Although I have argued that *logos* and *eidos* must always have their place in any adequate presentation of a faith, theology, liturgy or even philosophy of religion, I have also acknowledged that, in different historical and cultural circumstances, now one and now the other may come to dominance in the never-ending dialectic between them. How do we read the situation today? I think we may be

coming into a time when *eidos* is reasserting itself. There are
symptoms of a revolt against the long domination of the West by
logos and logic, against the Gutenberg man of the printed page,
against the Apollinian man who appropriates everything in inward
intelligibility. Perhaps the culmination of the word-centred type
of Christianity was the secular theology which reduced Christianity
to ethics, proclaimed the death of God and abolished mystery. But
there are stirrings of a reaction, which seeks to recover the sensuous,
the visual, the sacramental. Sam Keen well expressed the new spirit
when he pleaded for a revival of what he called 'Dionysian religion',
and he rightly noted that Dionysian theology is oriented more
to the eye than the ear.[6] This new direction is to be welcomed,
as an attempt to recapture the dimensions of wonder and celebration. But even as this happens, the word will renew its
claims, the tension between *logos* and *eidos* will be felt again,
and each will force the other to yield new contributions. Without the word and its logic, the eye alone, wonder alone, celebration alone, can lead to a merely uncritical sentimentalism –
what I call 'celebration without cerebration'. That would be no
help. *Logos* and *eidos* will continue to belong together within the
immense complexity of man's mental life and, even if they struggle,
they can never finally do without each other.[7]

Notes

1. J. Macquarrie, *God-Talk*, SCM Press and Harper & Row 1967,
pp. 63-4.

2. See above Chapter 3, pp. 28ff.

3. B. Lonergan, *Insight*, The Philosophical Library 1957, p. 635.

4. R. Bultmann, *Primitive Christianity*, Thames & Hudson 1956,
p. 23.

5. F. Mussner, *The Historical Jesus in the Gospel of St John*, tr.
W. J. O'Hara, Herder & Herder 1966, p. 22.

6. 'A Dionysian Manifesto', *Transcendence*, ed. H. W. Richardson
and D. R. Cutler, Beacon Press 1969, p. 50.

7. A lecture given at Loyola College, Montreal in 1969.

PART TWO

Reconstructing Theism

8

The Problem of God Today

Though the problem of God is not so loudly debated in theological circles as it was a few years ago, this problem remains at the top of the theological agenda. It cannot be swept under the carpet by the emergence of new theological fashions – theologies of hope or theologies of celebration or anything else of the sort. For unless reality is trustworthy at the deepest level (and this, I take it, is the fundamental meaning of belief in God) there is little ground for hope, and celebration becomes irrelevant, if not downright insensitive. Langdon Gilkey is correct in asserting that 'questions of the reality of God and the possibility of language about him are still our most pressing theological problems, prior to all other theological issues.'[1]

The problem of God, as it presents itself today, is not a problem that has suddenly emerged. To trace the roots of the problem and to show why it takes the particular form that it does, would be a colossal task, amounting to nothing less than an exploration of the entire intellectual history of the West. On the philosophical side, one would first have to reach back to the atheistic thinkers of the nineteenth century, to the work of men like Feuerbach, Marx and Nietzsche; but these men, in turn, could be understood only in the light of their own predecessors, thinkers such as Hume and Kant and Hegel. Once one is embarked on this process of delving back into the past, it is doubtful if there could be any stopping-place short of the very origins of Western philosophical reflection in ancient Greece, for it can be argued with some plausibility that already in the form which the philosophical quest assumed among the pre-Socratics, the future direction of Western thought was being determined, for better or for worse. There would be an equally formidable task on the theological side. The great figures of the nineteenth century,

men such as Schleiermacher, Ritschl and Newman, have power-
fully shaped our contemporary problematic; and in their case also
we would have to push our search into the earlier periods and
eventually back to the sources of faith in the Bible itself. It is not
my purpose to offer even the barest sketch of this vast historical
background.[2] But it is important to remember that the crisis of
theism has arisen out of a long and very complex process of development. Powerful intellectual pressures have been at work and
these cannot be ignored. It has become increasingly recognized in
theology that Christian doctrine is not static but subject to development. The traditional doctrine of God cannot be simply maintained
as if nothing had changed. It must be brought into confrontation
with the critical pressures that have built up. If there can be a
doctrine of God that is valid in our time, then it must have taken
full account of the developments, both philosophical and theological, that seem to have militated so strongly against traditional
theism. Philosophically, the contemporary radical empiricism and
radical existentialism have between them brought to expression the
thought of the secular age, and seem quite hostile to any belief
in God; or, if not actually hostile, they seem to make belief in
God a peripheral matter. Theologically, the decline of natural
theology, the rise of demythologizing, the distrust of supernaturalism are among the symptoms of a deep bewilderment concerning
the significance of God and his acts. Thus, even in the church, the
idea of God has become elusive, and it would seem that many of
those who profess to believe in God would find it very hard to state
clearly what they mean by professing such a belief or just how they
differ from those who take up an atheistic stance.

It cannot be denied that the atheist today seems to come forward
with a strong case. Furthermore, contemporary atheism has a
different and more attractive character than had much of the
atheism of the past. That traditional atheism was usually associated
with pessimistic world views. It was motivated by the recognition of
the evil and absurdity of so much that happens in the world, and
by the difficulty of reconciling this with belief in a God of love.
To be sure, this pessimistic type of atheism is still to be found.
Some of the French existentialists have stressed the senselessness of
the world and the vanity of human existence. Sartre and Camus
have in some of their writings represented this point of view. A
somewhat different type of atheism finds expression in the writings
of Richard Rubenstein. After Auschwitz, he believes, it is impossible any longer to have faith in the God of Judaism and the Old

Testament, the God who was supposed to have guided history.[3] Perhaps it is good that we should have these realistic reminders that there is much in the contemporary world that is absurd, and even nightmarish and demonic. There is an honesty and sensitivity about the pessimistic versions of atheism, and these qualities are not always obvious either in the more optimistic versions of atheism or in some forms of theistic belief.

But most contemporary atheism has a different mood from the one we find in Sartre, Camus and Rubenstein. The mood is one of liberation and even of exhilaration. This is a humanistic atheism, inspired by man's discovery of his apparently unlimited powers to shape his world and his future. It is humanistic in the further sense that, in its best forms, it aims at realizing to the highest degree human dignity and responsibility, and it believes that such an aim is incompatible with man's subordination to or reliance on any superhuman reality. This contemporary atheism is often no more than a practical atheism. But when it is expressly formulated, it is no weary pessimistic resignation in the face of an intractably evil world, but a summons to the human race to become adult and to take its destiny fully into its own hands. By their own science and technology, it is believed, men and women can build for themselves a better life than the gods have ever provided in response to faith and prayer.

It cannot be denied either that much in the atheistic critique of belief in God has been justified. Feuerbach, Marx, Nietzsche, Freud and their successors have all had their point. Images of God have often been the all-too-human projections of our own imperfect aspirations, and they have then distorted human life by casting a glamour of sanctity over our all-too-human ambitions. Preoccupation with God in his transcendence has often turned away men's eyes from the immediate tasks of this world and made them complacent in the face of social ills. Differences concerning belief about God have led and still sometimes lead to bitter and bloody disputes. Superstitious ideas of God have held back the advance of knowledge. Infantile reliance upon him has produced neurosis and prevented adult responsibility. If belief in God can survive these criticisms, then it can only be by taking cognizance of them and responding to whatever is true in each of them.

Yet, in acknowledging the force of the atheistic critique, I am not conceding the case of the atheist. In spite of the persuasiveness of some of its arguments and the justice of many of its criticisms of theistic belief, atheism is neither so attractive as it may seem at first sight nor is it able to establish its case as clearly as some of its advocates would seem to suggest. There is an atheistic dogmatism just as there is a religious dogmatism, and we hear a good deal of this atheistic dogmatism today, as if atheism were the only belief an intelligent up-to-date person could hold. This is an utterly ridiculous claim. I think there is much more truth in the claim of James Richmond that 'theism is not only possible but also an illuminating and compelling theory which integrates all of our experience into a rational unity'.[4] Today, as in the past, it seems to me that a world that has brought forth personal beings is much more reasonably accounted for on some theistic theory than on an atheistic one. Furthermore, I think that human life itself is only fulfilled when man communes with a reality that utterly transcends his own. While we have acknowledged that human life has been stunted and perverted in many ways through inadequate or distorted images of God, it has also been the case that belief in God has again and again stretched man beyond himself and has led him into new understandings of what it means to be a person in a community of persons.

The truth is, however, that we live in an ambiguous world where no final proof, one way or the other, is available, and where we either believe or disbelieve on the strength of such evidence as we can find; though it must be added that whatever stance one may take up is not an arbitrary one, for it will be based initially on what seems at the time to have the best claim to truth, and then this claim will be subject to all kinds of testings as one tries to live in accordance with the belief.

But just what does belief in God (or disbelief) mean, and what is the difference between theism and atheism? Modern theology itself has abandoned the God of mythology, a God who might sensibly manifest himself, as he is reported to have done in some parts of the Old Testament. Likewise this modern theology has grown doubtful about the God of supernaturalistic theism, a God conceived in subtle metaphysical categories rather than in the crude imagery of mythology, but nonetheless a God 'up there' or 'out there', separate from and independent of the world. If these ways of understanding God have been abandoned or put in question by theologians themselves, what remains, or how can one still talk of a difference between theism and atheism?

My own way of expressing the meaning of belief in God is to say that this belief is equivalent to 'faith in being',[5] and by this I understand an attitude of acceptance and commitment in the face not only of my own being or even that of the society in which I find myself, but ultimately of that wider being within which human society and history have themselves their setting. The notion of faith in being could also be defined in words that I used at the beginning of this chapter – it would mean that 'reality is trustworthy at the deepest level'. In a somewhat different theological and philosophical tradition, Schubert Ogden, it seems to me, is defining belief in God in a very similar way when he declares that 'the primary use or function of the word "God" is to refer to the objective ground in reality itself of our ineradicable confidence in the final worth of our existence'.[6]

Understood in the way indicated, the question of God is not a question about the existence or non-existence of some being additional to the world, a being who may, or may not, be out there on the periphery of things. It is not a question belonging to the edges or still unclosed gaps in human knowledge. Rather, one may say that this is the most central question of all, and the question that underlies all others. For any question that we ask leads to further questions, and if we push our questioning far enough, we come to the question of God, even if God-language is not explicitly used. It is this centrality of the God question that invests it with such serious existential concern. If God were simply a piece of metaphysical furniture, so to speak, if we understood him in the perhaps unconsciously deistic manner that has been prevalent even among Christians in the past few centuries, then his existence or non-existence would be a speculative matter, not touching us too closely. But if God is the central reality underlying all others and giving the whole its fundamental character, then the way the question of God is answered can hardly fail to have profound practical consequences for the way in which people understand themselves and order their lives.

Let us now consider some of the questions which, as we probe them and tease them out, lead us into the question of God.

We can begin with the question of ourselves. For man certainly constitutes a question, and in more ways than one. It can hardly fail to arouse some wonder in us when we reflect on ourselves as free, personal, rational agents who find themselves in an existence which they did not choose for themselves or create for themselves. This might be called the 'shock of being', as distinct from Tillich's 'shock of non-being'. As Austin Farrer once expressed it: 'It seems terribly improbable that we should exist.'[7] Our very existence as thinking and therefore questioning beings carries with it the question about the whence of this existence. But equally our human existence constitutes a question when we consider what it will become. For man is unfinished, always on his way to becoming something that still lies ahead. As Nietzsche put it, man is a bridge. But a bridge to what? Man's whither is as much a question as his whence. It is true that we answer the question about ourselves in many partial and relative ways. We can answer it in terms of our place in the animal kingdom, or our place and function in human society. Yet all these partial answers and the sum of them still leave unsatisfied the human quest for self-understanding. 'The given datum', wrote Abraham Heschel, 'is man's bewilderment about himself, the fact of his being a problem to himself ... It is not enough for me to ask questions; I want to know how to answer the one question that seems to encompass everything I face: "What am I here for?" ' The same writer went on to point out: 'Human existence cannot derive its ultimate meaning from society, because society itself is in need of meaning. It is as legitimate to ask, "Is mankind needed?" as to ask, "Am I needed?" '[8] Thus we may say that the question of God is concealed in man himself. For to use the word 'God' is one possible way of answering the question of man. To say 'God' in this context is to assert that man is no anomaly or accident in the universe, and that his life is sustained by a creative source not less than spiritual and personal.

Or again, let us suppose – *per impossibile* – that the time had come when the sciences had answered all possible questions within their competence, and all the gaps had been closed so that there was no place left for the so-called 'God of the gaps'. There would still be a question which no science can answer and which, indeed, no science claims competence to entertain: 'Why a world at all, rather than just nothing?' The question might be framed more specifically: 'Why an ordered world, capable of being rendered intelligible to the intelligences that it has itself brought forth, rather than an unknowing and unknown chaos?' These are questions which, as I have said, no science either entertains or answers, but they are questions which man cannot renounce unless he is prepared to renounce what is most distinctively human in him. But such questions may lead again to God-language. One might say that there is a world rather than nothing because there is God. This answer could be interpreted in various ways and might be developed into a doctrine of creation, but in the first instance it is the assertion that rationality and righteousness are better clues to the riddle of the universe than are chance and necessity.

Let me turn to a third approach to the God question. We are moral beings – that is to say, we have a moral consciousness, even if we do not live up to its demands. This means that every day of our lives we have to ask ourselves what we ought to do in the situations that confront us, and what goals we ought to be pursuing. But all such questions presuppose a deeper one. Why *ought* we to do anything at all, and what is the meaning of oughtness or moral obligation? This question can always be given a partial, relative answer in terms of a social and cultural situation. Yet beyond and embracing every actual relative obligation, there is the absolute demand of morality as such, a demand which cannot be refused without a renunciation of one's humanity and personal being. As Fritz Buri has expressed it, 'The voice that calls us to responsibility speaks to us from out of our surroundings; and yet, it is not merely the voice of my heart, my neighbour, my situation ... "God" is the mythological expression for the unconditionedness of personal responsibility.'[9] So here again we find a lead into God-language.

Still another approach starts from the quest for meaning. We live all the time in various contexts of meaning. These give direction and purpose to whatever we are doing. These contexts are of very many kinds, and they intersect and overlap at many points, but each of them is relative and limited. Sometimes we find ourselves asking whether there is an ultimate context of meaning, embracing all the others, gathering up the many different activities, giving sense and worth to history and to human striving as a whole. This quest for meaning is one that has been particularly insistent in recent and contemporary literature and the arts, perhaps in reaction against another phase which stressed the meaningless and the absurd. One observer of this scene, Nathan Scott, writes: 'Nothing is more intolerable for man than being unable to descry opposite himself anything other than necessity, inert objectivity, faceless mechanism ... Almost everywhere, the new *avant-garde* – in literature, in painting, in theatre, in music – is searching for ways of reconceiving the universe as a world which offers the promise and possibility of life under the law of participation.'[10] Admittedly, this search does not appear in the form of the old question, 'Does God exist?' But it is essentially the question of God in a modern guise, the question of an ultimate context of meaning.

I have mentioned four approaches which converge on the question of God. I believe that we are driven to this question as soon as we begin to reflect in any depth, and also that we can scaicely help giving some answers to the question by the very stances we take up and the policies we adopt. We are often told, however, that many persons today do not ask the kind of questions we have been discussing. They move simply from one limited task to the next, from one limited area of meaning to another. Perhaps this is a practical atheism, even if never explicitly formulated. Undoubtedly, the description is in some respect true of the lives of all of us. We live on the level of the everyday, as it may be called. But surely if one never allows oneself to be jolted out of the level of the everyday, one lives superficially; never to look beyond the demand of the immediate situation betokens a shallowness in existence. Positivism must be reckoned an escapism, to a much greater extent than religion has ever been. I doubt whether intelligent and thoughtful people can really be positivists for long. Certainly, in the strange and troubled world in which we live, we are now learning the price that has to be paid for the successes that have attended the excessively specialist and analytic style of Western thought. The ecological crisis is the most obvious example of the trouble that has overtaken us because of the refusal to think in sufficiently global terms, and it is doubtful if that crisis can be overcome until we once again have a philosophy of nature in addition to the specialized sciences. More and more we are being driven to consider the ulterior, and possibly the ultimate, import of our activities, and therefore also of our existence. But I think too that if our humanity is to be fully stretched and its potentialities realized, then we must reach out to that which is ultimate. John Baillie wrote of 'certain painful restrictions of outlook, of interest, of understanding and of sympathy' which can so easily affect the predominantly specialist and analytic mind, and which, he claimed, leave those of us so affected as 'very incomplete human beings'.[11] If our contemporary technology makes a fuller life possible for some people – as undoubtedly it does – it is also having a diminishing effect on some of our most basically human qualities. What shall it profit us, if the human race becomes a people rich in having, but poor in being?

When the question of God is posed in the way we have tried to expound it, it seems clear that while the distinction between theism and atheism remains, it is less clear cut than when one thought of it in terms of the existence or non-existence of a being beyond the world, the God of much traditional theism. For if we are content to be somewhat less explicit, and to define belief in God as faith in being, then one has to recognize that there are many gradations between, let us say, the Christian conviction that the character of reality has been manifested in Jesus Christ, so that God is love, and the doctrine of those existentialists who seem to be at the other end of the scale and declare that the world is absurd and godless. One could not simply draw a line through humanity, and say that the theists are on one side of it and the atheists on the other. For instance, Marxism, although it is officially atheistic and materialistic, is far removed from a doctrine of the sheer absurdity (godlessness) of the world, or from a doctrine that man is the measure of all things. There are at least some elements in classical Marxism which lean more to theism than to atheism: its eschatological outlook, its 'matter' endowed with creativity, its insistence on an ontological reality over against man. Perhaps no one in his heart can really and permanently believe in the utter vanity or godlessness of things, for it is hard to see how one could live on such terms. And perhaps many who deny God nevertheless recognize, either explicitly or implicitly, something like a godward trend in the world.

Am I then suggesting that finally there are no atheists? No, I certainly do not wish to make such an assertion. It is true that several distinguished theologians have held some such belief. John Baillie claimed that the serious-minded atheist, though he denies God with 'the top of his mind', believes in him at the bottom of his heart'.[12] More recently, Karl Rahner has familiarized us with the idea of the 'anonymous Christian', the man who lives in a manner similar to the Christian way, but without any profession of faith. Perhaps if such language is very carefully qualified, it is not altogether indefensible. But it can easily be misleading, and ought to be avoided. In the first place, it infringes the integrity of the man who professes himself an atheist, and does not permit genuine dialogue with him; for it says in effect that if he only understood himself as well as the Christian understands him, he would see that after all he is really a believer! This is thoroughly offensive. Further, we must realize that this is a two-edged weapon which the atheist can, and sometimes does, turn against the Christian, claiming that he, though he professes to believe in God, is really an atheist at heart. This style of argument has been used against Paul Tillich and John Robinson. Arguments of this kind, on whatever side they are used, are futile and childish. The most serious objection to such methods of debate, whether practised by Christians or atheists, is the logical one that terms become eroded and distinctions blurred. If the words 'theist' or 'atheist' or 'Christian' can be used so broadly that they can apply to almost anybody, then they no longer signify anything at all. Donald MacKinnon is right in saying that 'faith cannot somehow swallow up atheism; the latter has to be acknowledged as something which has its own laws, even its own dignity'.[13] Likewise, of course, atheism cannot swallow up faith.

So far I have been talking about the form which the question of God might take in our time, the situations which impel us toward asking the question, and the difference between theism and atheism. But beyond asserting that theism continues to be more plausible than atheism, while at the same time admitting that there can be no conclusive proof on such matters, I have done little to show why one should opt for belief in God. Of course, even to have made clearer what belief in God implies is to have done something to commend it. But the case must now be strengthened by filling in some details.

I begin on the philosophical side. There is no one philosophical approach to theism dominant today – indeed, as I have mentioned, the most prevalent types of philosophy tend not to be theistic. We have noted too that the traditional natural theology has languished. Yet there are a number of approaches to theism, and even their variety is a strength, for we find them converging at various points and so lending support to each other. The convergence produces, as it were, a family likeness among these different forms of contemporary theistic philosophies. I may mention three features which they seem to have in common. The first is a move away from the thought of God as substance to a more dynamic conception; the second is a determination to take time and becoming more seriously than traditional theism usually did; the third is an effort to overcome dualism by stressing the intimate relation of God and the world, even to the point of panentheism, though not, of course, of pantheism. These common features can be traced in the forms of theism built on existentialist philosophies, notably those of Heidegger and Jaspers. They are likewise to be seen in process theology, which is very influential in the United States and which founds itself on the philosophies of Whitehead and Hartshorne. In Roman Catholic thought, both the transcendental Thomism of Marechal and his successors and the evolutionary theology of Teilhard de Chardin and his school lay the same stress on the dynamic character of reality, though it is only Teilhard who goes to great lengths in stressing God's immanence in the world. There are signs of convergence too in the neo-Barthianism of Jüngel and Torrance. Any one of these forms of theism would need a whole series of lectures for its proper exposition and evaluation, but it is sufficient for us to notice that there is today this varied yet converging intellectual grappling with the problem of God, and that the emerging thought of God is one that has overcome many of the older criticisms.

But how do these sophisticated concepts of contemporary philosophy stand in relation to the God of the Bible, the God of Abraham, Isaac and Jacob, and the Father of Jesus Christ? An equally important part of rehabilitating the idea of God is to return to the sources of the Christian tradition and to explore them anew. When we do so, it becomes clear that many of the atheistic criticisms, while indeed they have struck home at distortions of belief prevailing from time to time in the Christian church, usually miss that understanding of God that we find in the Bible and in the classic formulations of Christian dogma. The atheist may well criticize the God who is a meeter of needs and a solver of problems, the God who is a projection of wish fantasy or neurosis, but this has nothing to do with the biblical God, who is characterized under the great categories of truth, justice, mercy and holiness. Of this biblical God, Jean Cardinal Daniélou has said: 'His ways disconcert us. But it is just at this point that he imposes on us his objective reality. He compels our reason and our will to forsake their own ways and adjust themselves to his. He brings us into the mysterious sphere that is his.'[14] Likewise the triune God of classical Christian theology is, in so far as language can express this, a dynamic God who could never be a dead God. The doctrine of the one in three and three in one falteringly expresses something of the unimaginably complex and never-ceasing activity implied as the source of a universe such as ours.

Thus contemporary philosophical work in theism and the traditional biblical and dogmatic sources of the Christian doctrine of God mutually interpret each other and mutually strengthen each other. If the atheistic critique has disposed of some unworthy forms of belief in God, this is no matter for regret. Rather, it makes way for better understandings of God, more worthy of the biblical tradition and more worthy to receive our intellectual and moral allegiance.[15]

Notes

1. L. Gilkey, *Naming the Whirlwind*, Bobbs-Merrill 1969, p. 104.

2. Cf. C. Fabro, *God in Exile: Modern Atheism*, tr. A. Gibson, Paulist Press 1968.

3. R. Rubenstein, *After Auschwitz*, Bobbs-Merrill 1966.

4. J. Richmond, *Theology and Metaphysics*, SCM Press 1970, p. 87.

5. J. Macquarrie, *Principles of Christian Theology*, SCM Press and Scribners 1966, p. 70.

6. S. M. Ogden, *The Reality of God*, SCM Press and Harper & Row 1966, p. 37.

7. A. M. Farrer, *The Freedom of the Will*, Scribner 1960, p. 173.

8. A. J. Heschel, *Who is Man?*, Stanford University Press 1965, pp. 53, 59.

9. F. Buri, *How Can We Still Speak Responsibly of God?*, tr. C. D. Hardwick and H. H. Oliver, Fortress Press 1968, p. 27.

10. N. A. Scott, *The Wild Prayer of Longing*, Yale University Press 1971, pp. 26, 31.

11. J. Baillie, *The Sense of the Presence of God*, Oxford University Press 1962, p. 253.

12. J. Baillie, *Our Knowledge of God*, Oxford University Press 1939, pp. 47ff.

13. D. M. MacKinnon, *Borderlands of Theology*, Lutterworth Press 1968, p. 65.

14. J. Daniélou, *God and Us*, Mowbrays 1957, p. 105.

15. The Drawbridge Memorial Lecture for 1972, published as a pamphlet by The Christian Evidence Society, London.

9

How can we think of God?

How can we think of God? How can we talk of him? There was a time when questions like these would have seemed absurd, for most people did talk about God and believed they had a sufficiently clear conception of what they were meaning when they talked about him. The idea of God was part of the conceptual apparatus in terms of which people thought about themselves and about the world, and so the word 'God' communicated when it was uttered. God explained many things. But communication depends on the sharing of basic ideas and presuppositions which allow one person's discourse to be intelligible to another person. Let us suppose that some of these presuppositions are gradually eroded away, and that new modes of thinking about ourselves and the world take their place. The same words that once communicated may not communicate any more. They may become increasingly vague and indeterminate and may end up by having no assignable meaning at all. We find that we cannot place them within the framework of our thinking. Something like that has happened to the word 'God' in our own time, so that we are forced to ask the questions: 'How can we think of God? How can we talk of him?'

Such questions have been sharpened above all by the rise of analytic philosophy. This type of philosophy takes as its primary task the logical analysis of our language in its many forms. What do we mean by the assertions we make? What procedures are relevant for either verifying or falsifying these assertions? As soon as we begin to raise problems of this kind, we see how slippery and misleading our language can sometimes be. What look at first sight to be important and even sweeping assertions may turn out on investigation to be quite jejune and indeed to have very little ascertainable meaning at all. It has been alleged that this is especially the case with assertions about God. The background of contemporary analytical philosophy is empirical science, and this has developed fairly well established procedures of observation, experiment, measurement, verification and so on. But these procedures seem quite irrelevant to the kind of assertions the religious man may make, or perhaps I should say that his assertions seem irrelevant to the established procedures. Yet this religious man is probably also for at least six days of the week a man whose thinking is more or less informed by the attitudes of empirical science. Where does his thinking about God tie in with his other thinking? Does he have to confess that there is no relation between the two, that his thinking about God is something altogether free floating, vague and problematical? Thus, if he is asked the question, 'What do you mean when you talk about God?' he may seem to have no clear answer to give, and may have to acknowledge that such talk is only a survival that has come down to him from an earlier time but has no secure place any longer.

Of course, even in times when human thinking made much use of religious ideas, there were many ideas of God, and it was never possible to point to any single idea of God such as would have been acknowledged by everyone who talked of him. Some have thought in terms of one God, others in terms of a plurality of gods. Some have thought of God as having a nature we can understand – very often they have thought of him as a kind of magnified human being – while for others God has utterly transcended human understanding. Of course, in the case of the latter, we might ask why they use the word 'God' and address to them the question of David Hume: 'How do you mystics, who maintain the absolute incomprehensibility of the Deity, differ from sceptics or atheists who assert that the first cause of all is unknown and unintelligible?'[1] Some have thought of God primarily as transcendent of, external to, and even remote from the world, while others have stressed his immanence, even to the lengths of pantheism, where God and the world become scarcely distinguishable. It can hardly be claimed therefore that there ever has been a clearly defined and universally accepted signification for the word 'God', as there has been for the word 'cat' and a great many others that we commonly use; though it should be noted that even the concept of a cat has some unclear borders.

Furthermore, there has been development in the idea of God, and the development has followed roughly parallel lines in different religions. The oldest ideas of God were mythological. In mythology,

God is another being within the world and may be the object of sense perception. There are some surviving elements of this mythological thinking in the Bible, in both the Old and New Testaments. God might actually be seen on the earth, and when the belief that he could be directly seen became intolerable, it was still believed that he might be heard (voices from heaven), or that he might show himself in extraordinary perceptible events (signs, wonders, miracles). But gradually these mythological ideas were left behind. The gods were no longer located in the universe, not even on the mountain tops or in the sky, nor was it any more believed that they could be seen or perceived by any of the senses.

There followed more sophisticated ideas of God. The Old Testament prophets were already speaking of his transcendence and incomparability, and philosophical reflection further refined these ideas. God was no longer located in any particular place, though metaphorically he was said to be 'above' or 'beyond' the world. He was conceived as a being who is personal, but bodiless, invisible, intangible, inaccessible to any kind of sense perception. He was believed to have created the world in the beginning and to exercise a general government over it, perhaps intervening in its affairs from time to time to keep it on the right lines. But with the rise of modern science and its apparently unlimited capacity for accounting for events within the world in terms of other innerworldly events, the need for positing such a God has been gradually eliminated. There seems to be nothing left for him to do. At best, he might remain as a constitutional monarch, presiding as a figurehead with no real power over a world that regulates itself. So the God of metaphysical theism seems to have suffered the same fate as the God of mythology, and fades out of the picture.

Does this mean the end of God? Is God dead, as Nietzsche claimed? Are those of us who think it worthwhile to discuss how we can think of God as out of touch with reality as the old saint whom Nietzsche's Zarathustra met in some secluded spot and about whom he felt constrained to ask: 'Can it indeed be possible? This old saint in his forest has not yet heard that God is dead!'[2] Or does it mean that we have to think anew and more deeply on what this word 'God' signifies and that we have to be prepared for just as revolutionary a development in our conception of God as took place when the old mythological ideas of God were discredited and then superseded by subtler conceptions. Let us see whether it is possible for us to sharpen our thinking about God. Is it possible to find a meaning for this word 'God', and to assign it a place in the framework of contemporary thought?

One move in recent theology has been to take the word 'God' as a proper noun. This gives the word great concreteness. It designates a person, just as names like Peter and Paul do. Many modern theologians have revolted against the more abstract and metaphysical conceptions of God, and have claimed that the word 'God' has meaning only in an encounter or meeting, like a meeting of two persons. Such meetings belong to a different dimension of life from those experiences of things which it is the business of science to explicate. To use Buber's familiar terminology, encounters belong to the dimension of the I–thou, whereas scientific knowledge belongs to the dimension of the I–it. Those who speak in this way sometimes add that we cannot properly talk *about* God, for that would make him an object. We can only address him or name him in the moment of encounter. Thus they sharply distinguish their own understanding of God from the traditional metaphysical ways, which they regard as an illegitimate objectification of God. At the same time, they claim that their own approach is much closer to the Bible, which is a recital of a whole series of encounters between God and man.

Let us at once grant that the distinction of the I–thou and the I–it is an important one, and may help us to avoid some of the difficulties in which we find ourselves when we try to think of God in metaphysical terms. In this other way of taking the word 'God', it points not to some remote, invisible, intangible entity, some 'first cause' or 'prime mover', but to a person who meets us in an encounter and who has that kind of concreteness which belongs to God in the Bible.

But this way of thinking of God runs into its own difficulties. Perhaps these are just as serious as the ones from which it tries to escape. When I encounter another person, certainly I address him, rather than talk about him. But surely this does not preclude me from subsequently talking about him or thinking about him. Why should it do so in the case of God? But if we go on to talk of God or think of him or make any assertion concerning him, then how can we avoid metaphysics or something that covertly entails metaphysics?

There is a further difficulty. In the ordinary way, a meeting or encounter between persons always includes some physical relation. The meeting is mediated through their bodies. Typically, the physical relation takes the form of words spoken and heard. In a face-to-face meeting, as we call it, part of the encounter will consist in the visible expressions, gestures and the like of the inter-locutors. Granted that a personal encounter is something quite different from, let us say, the collision of two automobiles, never-theless the personal encounter has its physical component. This would seem to be necessary as the bearer of whatever communica-tion or communion takes place on the intellectual or spiritual level. Now, we do not think of any corresponding physical component in the encounter with God. Indeed, at this point the logic of God-language differs significantly from the logic of person-language. In the case of finite persons, we can and do predicate of them physical characteristics, but we never do so of God.[3]

At the most, therefore, to speak of a meeting or encounter with God is to use an analogy. It may be *like* a meeting between two persons, but it is not such a meeting *simpliciter*. The question then arises: 'How like is it? Can the analogy stand up?' Clearly there are the difficulties which we have already noted. Of course, it might be said that the encounter with God is always mediated through some physical reality which serves as the bearer of the relation. This may be true, but to establish its truth would call for an intricate metaphysical or ontological exposition, and this is pre-cisely what the encounter theologians were trying to avoid. We must say, however, that their appeal to a self-authenticating personal encounter is a far too simple-minded attempt to deal with the problem, and cannot be accepted.

When faced with these difficulties, some theologians have moved in the direction of a reductionist theology. If it is so difficult to think of God or talk of God, can we not find a surrogate or rep-resentative who can take the place of God and with whom we can have a personal relation? Christianity, after all, teaches a doctrine of incarnation. The Word has been made flesh, God has assumed a body. And so it is claimed that it really is possible to have a meeting with God 'in the flesh' or 'face to face', or at any rate, a meeting with God's representative, the person who has the status or value of God for the human race. Such a meeting was possible in the first place for those disciples who were contemporary with Jesus and who conversed with him precisely as you and I might converse with each other. It is still possible for later generations of Christians through the records of the New Testament or through the word of preaching or through the sacraments of the church. We can have a personal encounter with Christ and so with God in the same sense in which historians might allow that we can have something like a personal encounter with notable figures of the past, through such words or deeds or attitudes as have been transmitted to us.

A good illustration of the theological position I have in mind was provided by some of the Ritschlian theologians at the end of the nineteenth century, notably Wilhelm Herrmann, teacher of both Barth and Bultmann. Philosophically, Herrmann was a positivist and denied the possibility of metaphysics. To his philosophical positivism he added a theological positivism. 'God is Jesus' was his creed, and Jesus, or at any rate, what he called the 'inner life' of Jesus, is accessible to us as a verifiable historical phenomenon. This was an extreme development of the saying attributed to Christ, 'He who has seen me has seen the Father', though perhaps it was also an evasion of the words Christ is said to have used on the same occasion: 'I am in the Father and the Father in me' (John 14.9-10), words which point to a relationship a good deal more complex than simple identity. A very similar and much more up-to-date statement of a positivist theology, and one that is probably better known to English-speaking readers, was put forward by Paul van Buren in *The Secular Meaning of the Gospel*. He made the same attempt to assimilate theology to christology and to get rid of the embarrassment of God by identifying him completely with Christ.

But these attempts to solve the problem fail. In the first place, they represent much too easy a capitulation to positivism, and a premature despair of making sense of the word 'God' in its own right. In the second place, we have here an arbitrary narrowing of the word 'God', which is, after all not a private possession of Christianity but a word with a much wider currency used to designate one who has made himself known at many times and in many ways. What, for instance, do Jews or Muslims mean when they speak of 'God'? Not Jesus Christ. So the Christian who identifies God with Jesus cuts himself off from dialogue with Jews and others and implicitly denies any validity to their religion. In the third place, the identification of God with Jesus or Christ is a serious deviation from the traditional faith of the church – a deviation into what has been called 'unitarianism of the second person of the Trinity'. For while Christian faith has maintained that Christ is God, this has never been regarded as a convertible proposition, so that one could turn it around and say that God is Christ. God, in Christian teaching, is more complex in his being; he is Father, Son and Holy Spirit. The claim that Christ is God is not an assertion of identity but a predication of Godhood. Finally, if we push Herrmann and van Buren far enough, what they seem to be saying is that Jesus of Nazareth, idealized as the Christ, is the supreme standard of value to whom we ought to give allegiance. It is interesting that this claim is made, but can it be made without idolatry or fanaticism unless we are prepared to show what is *ultimate* in Jesus Christ, that is to say, in what sense he is God?

This last discussion brings us to another possible way of thinking about God. If it is not satisfactory to think of 'God' as a proper noun or to identify him *tout court* with Jesus, perhaps we should take the term 'God' as meaning something like 'supreme value', that to which we must pledge our utter allegiance. The word 'God' is often used in this way in ordinary speech. We are familiar with such expressions as 'he made a god of money' and 'the Nazis made the state their god'. The classic theological statement linking God and value is found in Martin Luther: 'A god is that to which we look for all good and in which we find refuge in every time of need. To have a god is nothing else than to trust and believe him with our whole heart. As I have often said, the trust and faith of the heart alone make both God and an idol. If your faith and trust are right, then your God is the true God. On the other hand, if your trust is false and wrong, then you have not the true God. For these two belong together, faith and God. That to which your heart clings and entrusts itself is, I say, really your God.'[4]

Now unquestionably this is at least part of what the word 'God' means. No religion teaches about the gods in a disinterested way, as though the purpose were just to give information about them. All religions urge their devotees to love God, to worship him, to serve him, to put their trust in him, to set their hearts on him. 'God' is not a neutrally descriptive word. It is a word that evokes commitment, and this aspect of meaning is well brought out in Paul Tillich's expression, 'ultimate concern'.

The humanist John Dewey, in his book *A Common Faith*, declared himself willing to reintroduce the word 'God' provided that it was stripped of all transcendent and existential reference and all metaphysical connotations, and made to stand only for those human ideals and values which command our ultimate devotion. I have sympathy with those humanist and secular followers of Dewey who were confused and dismayed by his proposal and felt that he had compromised their cause by reverting to God-language, even in a diluted form. For while one may indeed agree that 'God' is 'that to which your heart clings', this is only part of the meaning, and it is misleading to isolate it. The fact that Luther could distinguish between the true God and an idol, though subjectively both are the object of utter trust, shows that there is something more to the meaning of 'God'.

This 'something more' is another aspect of meaning, just as fundamental as the notion of supreme value or ultimate concern. God combines highest value with highest reality. The true God differs from the idol in being the real God, the genuinely ultimate concern is the concern with what is really ultimate. God is reality, or as I prefer to say in the classic language of theology, God is being. He is not indeed one being among others, or even one being above others or the supreme being – a title which, significantly, was much used among the deists. Even to call God *ens realissimum* is so to distinguish him from all finite being (*entia*) that we see that God is not finally an *ens* at all, for a qualitative leap has taken place and God is seen to be *esse*, the very act of being which is prior to all beings and emerges in, with and through every particular being.

We must bear in mind, however, that to say God is being is no more exhaustive of the meaning of 'God' than was the description of God as supreme value. Both meanings have to come together before we can properly use God-language. 'God', we have said, is not a neutral word, but a word evoking faith and commitment. Being can be called God if the *ens realissimum* is also *summum bonum*, and both can be conceived in the dynamic concept of *esse*.

To think of God as being would go far toward solving some of the most intractable problems of traditional theism and would also restore to God his place at the centre. But it needs something like a revolution in theology to move from the thought of God as supreme being (*ens*) to the act of being (*esse*). At least, it would need something like a revolution as against the kind of theism which has been dominant in recent centuries and which has surely been infected by deism. Perhaps in earlier times, among some of the Fathers and in St Thomas, God was understood as *esse*, but today we have to push this insight through in a more thoroughgoing way, and this is happening in much contemporary theology. Some people perhaps feel that in this process God is being quietly eliminated and that in spite of all the talk about reconstructing theism, we are in fact adopting a covert atheism. I do not think that this is so, but certainly some further explanations are needed.

The thought of God as being has a long history in Christian theology, from the Fathers to Tillich, but the objection is sometimes made that this is a philosophical idea of God having little relation to the God of the Bible, or to the God whom other Christian theologians set in the context of personal encounter. Is not God, conceived as being, an impersonal, abstract Deity, a mere shadow of the God of the Bible?

I think it can be argued that there is a much more adequate basis in the Bible for the doctrine of God as being than is often recognized. The whole point of our argument that God is both *esse* and *bonum* is neatly summarized in a sentence from the New Testament: 'Whoever would draw near to God must believe that he is, and that he rewards those who seek him' (Heb. 11.6). God is the supreme reality – he is; and God is the supreme good – the reward of those who seek him.

The classic passage is of course the one in which God makes known his name to Moses: 'I am who I am' or simply 'I am' (Ex. 3.14). There has been much discussion over the meaning of these words, and it may be conceded at once that the scriptural authors did not hold the subtle philosophical theories that were read into the words in later times. But one thing we can be sure about – the words would be understood in a dynamic way, for the Hebrew verb 'to be' includes the notion 'to become'. E. L. Mascall makes a perceptive comment: 'Whether or not *Qui Est* is an accurate translation of the Hebrew name of God revealed to Moses, there is little doubt that St. Thomas' radically existential interpretation of *Qui Est* as signifying not a static perfection but the absolutely unlimited Act and Energy is thoroughly in line with Hebrew thought; and it is this that underlies his assertion that God is pure act.'[5]

Some scholars have interpreted the words in Exodus as having a causative sense. In that case, we could translate, 'I let be what I let be'. This would certainly be appropriate. God not only is; he is in the most dynamic and creative sense. The way a finite being is provides only a remote analogy to the way God is. He is being that imparts existence to all the beings. He is better described as He Who Lets Be than as He Who Is. There is confirmation of this when we turn to the creation story at the beginning of the Bible: 'Let there be light' (Gen. 1.3). This is the beginning of God's letting be, his own dynamic creative mode of being. Likewise in the New Testament we read of God that he is the one 'who gives life to the dead and calls into being the things that were not' (Rom. 4.17).

In St John's gospel, this language of being is placed on the lips of Jesus Christ, the incarnate Logos who has been with God from

the beginning and who is God. The recurring words 'I am' in this
gospel are an unmistakable echo of the words of Exodus. 'I am the
bread of life ... I am the true vine ... I am the light of the world
... I am the resurrection and the life' (John 6.35; 15.1; 8.12; 11.25).
It is as if all that man needs for his existence – bread, wine, light,
the very life itself – all point beyond themselves to the I Am who
gives them being. Most profound and dramatic of all are the
words in which Christ replies to the Jews: 'Before Abraham was, I
am!' (John 8.58). Before anything was, there is the dynamic
creative letting be that we call God.

Enough has been said to show that the language of being as
applied to God is not a philosophical invention but is well founded
in the Bible. In any case, one can go too far in distinguishing the
God of philosophy from the God of Abraham, Isaac and Jacob.
Biblical faith cannot finally avoid the ontological questions raised
by philosophy.

Certainly the Bible and also subsequent Christian theology
has many other ways of talking about God. He is Spirit, Light,
Love; he is Father, Shepherd, King. The list of titles could be
vastly extended. A plurality of titles and images is needed to
give us even an inkling of the inexhaustible richness and complexity
of God. But a priority belongs to being, for it is the most fundamental of all the words we have considered. Even love is a kind
of being. It is precisely that letting be which describes the dynamic
being of God, for what is it to love someone if not to do whatever
is in one's power to deepen, liberate and enrich the being of that
person?

We need many concepts and many images in which to think of
God and to speak of him, and whatever we think or say will still
be inadequate. But a special place belongs to this language of
being. It is biblical, and it has had a secure place in Christian
theology from the beginning to our own time. It is concrete and
dynamic. It makes God meaningful to man, who knows at first
in his own existence what it means to be, in an active dynamic way.
It clarifies the relation of God to the world, seen not as the relation
of two beings, but of being to the beings, of *esse* to the *entia*. As a
consequence, it makes room for both the transcendence and the
immanence of God, and avoids the opposite errors of pantheism and
deism. It preserves the divine mystery, yet also makes possible
analogy. It opens the way to endless possibilities of prayer and
comunion – and this last point is all-important, for we could not
think of God apart from the possibility of prayer to him.

Presumably we are standing only at the beginning of the revolution in the idea of God. Its application to particular Christian doctrines is something that has still to be fully worked out. That it will be more mature and more satisfying than the way of thinking of God that has been dominant in the past few centuries, the way that regarded him as a 'Louis XIV of the heavens', I cannot doubt. It tries in our technological age to awaken again the kind of thinking that brings us into the dimension of the holy. So far is it from voiding the traditional ideas of God of content that it rather complains that these traditional ideas have fallen too short of the reality. It strives to open up for our time and culture new glimpses into that mystery, at once awesome and fascinating, which we designate by the word 'God'.[6]

Notes

1. David Hume, *Dialogues concerning Natural Religion*, Hafner 1948, p. 31.

2. F. W. Nietzsche, *Thus Spake Zarathustra*, tr. A Tille and M. M. Bozman, Dent 1933, p. 5.

3. See above, p. 6.

4. M. Luther, in *The Book of Concord*, tr. T. G. Tappert, Fortress Press 1959, p. 365.

5. E. L. Mascall, *Existence and Analogy*, Darton, Longman & Todd 1949, p. 52.

6. A lecture given before the Institute of Social and Religious Studies in the Jewish Theological Seminary of America, New York, in 1964.

10

God and the World:
Two Realities or One?

The question posed in the title of this chapter does not admit of any simple answer if we stay within the bounds of Christian theology. There are, of course, simple answers, but these would not seem to be Christian. One might be a thoroughgoing pantheist, and declare that God and the world are really identical; or one might be a Manichaean or dualist of some kind, and say that God and the world are quite independent and opposed realities. But there are many subtle gradations between these extremes, and presumably the Christian answer to the question has to be sought somewhere among the gradations.

Pantheism has its undoubted attractions. The word 'world' shows many of the logical peculiarities belonging to the word 'God'. Furthermore, the world arouses in many people feelings of mystery, awe and even reverence. Among recent philosophers, the early Wittgenstein seemed to hint at some form of pantheism. At least, this is the interpretation which David Pears has placed on the somewhat enigmatic statements toward the end of the *Tractatus Logico-Philosophicus*.[1] But in spite of its seeming attractions, pantheism finally breaks down. If the world is God, it must be not only awesome and mysterious but also adorable; and this, surely, our ambiguous universe is not. The world is not itself divine.

Dualistic beliefs have arisen from the recognition that the world is so little divine that – so the dualists believe– it must be adjudged to be infected with great evil. Yet the dualistic view has paid as little attention to the ambiguity of the world as has pantheism. If the world is not divine, it is not utterly bad or godless either, for whatever good we know has been encountered by us within the world.

Christian theism eschews both the pantheistic identification of God and the world, and their dualistic separation. As against pantheism, it asserts the distinction of God from the world and his priority to the world; as against dualism, it asserts that there is one ultimate reality, God, and that the world is dependent on him for its existence. Yet there are various models on which the complex God–world relation can be understood. In most Christian theology, the monarchical model (as I shall call it) has been dominant. On this view, God's transcendence over and priority to the world have been stressed. The relation between God and the world has therefore been understood as an asymmetrical relation. The world needs God, but God has no need of the world; God affects the world, but the world does not affect God; the world owes everything to God, but God is not increased by the world; and so on. In some Christian theology, however, there has been offered an alternative model, the organic model, as it may be called. On this view, the God–world relation is – not indeed in all respects, but in some respects – symmetrical. This model envisages therefore a much more intimate relation between God and the world than the monarchical model does. The organic model does not abolish the ideas of the transcendence and priority of God, yet it qualifies them, and it tends to see God and the world as distinguishable but not separable within an organic whole which embraces both of them. So on this view it might be held, for instance, that a God who is outgoing love cannot be conceived without a creation; or again, that a God of love must be in some sense vulnerable, so that he is affected by his creation as well as affecting it. Thus elements of symmetry are introduced. Sometimes views of this kind have been called 'panentheism', but the term itself is not important. I should prefer myself to regard such views as forms of theism, differing from classical theism in the stress which they lay on elements of intimacy and reciprocity in the God–world relation.

The name 'panentheism' draws attention to the fact that this way of conceiving the relation between God and the world has its origins in philosophical speculation rather than in biblical theology. This may be conceded, and it is true that contemporary versions of panentheism are to be found chiefly among those theologians who have been influenced by such philosophers as Alexander, Whitehead, Bergson, Heidegger, Hartshorne. Yet it would be wrong to suppose that the organic view generally is without support in the Bible. While in the Old Testament the monarchical model is the dominant one, there are others. For instance, the prophet Hosea pictures God as the faithful husband, and this model introduces notions of reciprocity and even of vulnerability on the part of God. In the New Testament, the monarchical model is further qualified. This happens above all through the doctrine of the incarnation. God enters his creation by taking a body, and in so doing he places himself at the disposal of his creatures. The incarnational principle is extended in the sacramental principle. In recent theology, Teilhard de Chardin has drawn a connecting line from the incarnation through the eucharist to the vision of the whole creation's becoming the body of Christ. Sometimes, admittedly, his language comes close to pantheism, and no doubt his emphasis is one-sided. But he is nevertheless drawing attention to elements in the Christian tradition that have been all too often neglected.

We have used the term 'organic' to name the model on which the relation between God and the world is understood among those philosophers and theologians who lean toward panentheism. The name at once suggests a relation in which there is reciprocity and in which the terms so related cannot be conceived as existing apart from one another. Yet it is not a model which excludes some elements of asymmetry in the relation, or the subordination of one term to another. To offer an illustration, St Paul uses the model of the head and the body to express the relation between Christ and his church (Eph. 1.22-3). This is an organic model. It implies an intimate relation, such that the church exists only through Christ, and yet Christ is completed only through the church and could not exist as the Christ apart from the church, any more than a head could exist without a body. Yet the model also implies a definite subordination of the body to the head. Christ is prior to the church, he transcends the church, he lets the church be. Returning to the God–world relation, let me say that it is wrong to think of the organic model as merely a rival to the monarchical model. Some writers do seem to set up a sharp opposition between the various forms of panentheism and classical theism, no doubt in reaction against the latter. But no single model is in itself adequate, and neither is any theory. The organic model of theism is better understood as a corrective to the monarchical model than as a rival which seeks simply to supplant it. The monarchical model has been one-sided through its exaggerated stress on transcendence, and on such allied conceptions as omnipotence, impassibility, and the like; and similarly in its tendency to put a low value on the created order. The organic model qualifies rather than abolishes the monarchical model. God is not reduced to sheer immanence, but his transcendence is qualified by taking his immanence more seriously than it has been taken in much Christian theology. God is not brought totally within time and history, but time, history and becoming are, so it is claimed, to be taken with a new seriousnes too and permitted to qualify traditional ideas of the immutability and eternity of God. Again, God is not turned into a finite, struggling God, striving not very successfully to master a recalcitrant world, but it is recognized that his omnipotence and impassibility are qualified by the creation which he has himself brought forth and that he is somehow involved in the travail of creation.

I do not wish to identify myself with the version of theism found in A. N. Whitehead, for my own approach to these questions is very different from his, and I would have many questions about points of detail in his system. But there is a valuable element in his conception of God to which I wish at this point to draw attention, namely, his doctrine of the dipolarity of God. This is a significant attempt to build a concept of God that will take account of both the monarchical and organic models. God is said to have both a primordial and a consequent nature, and these represent respectively the poles of transcendence and immanence, eternity and temporality (or historicity), impassibility and passibility, and so on.

Let us consider for a moment the difficult question of God in relation to time and history. It seems to me that the God of Christian faith as a God who acts, a God who has made himself known in history, a God who through the incarnation has entered the historical process, a God who has promised to bring all history to a glorious consummation – it seems that such a God is so deeply involved in time and history that we cannot consider these to be quite external to him. There is no doubt a sense in which God transcends history, yet history is also the region or the medium in which he realizes his purposes, and surely this is important to him and makes some difference to him. God is not simply above history, unaffected and unchanged by it, nor is he simply within history as a kind of evolving God in the way that some empiricists have visualized him. He is both above and within, however difficult it may be for us to conceive this. At the end of his life, the late Ronald Gregor Smith was struggling with the question of God. He was in violent reaction against classical theism, and especially against the notion of an eternal unchanging God, throned above the chances and changes of time. Though a secular theologian – and he understood that to mean an historicizing theologian – he did not run away from the God question, as many of the secularizers did. 'The real audacity', he wrote, 'does not consist in declaring that God is dead but in daring at all to take that name on our lips.' At times he seemed to want to bring God wholly into history, or even to identify God with history. But history, like the world, is ambiguous and is certainly not divine. In the last fragmentary chapter of his book, we find Smith declaring that God is not included in history, but rather history in God. Almost immediately, however, he adds that 'the notions of inclusion and exclusion do not yield an adequate model'.[2] Of course they do not, and there is no model that is entirely adequate. I would say myself that the best clue we can have is our own relation to time – we are in time and subject to its flux, yet fundamental to personal being is a capacity to transcend time as mere succession. Even the finite existing person is, as Kierkegaard put it, 'an atom of eternity' in time.[3] Our own experience of time therefore may afford us some glimpse of God's double relation to time.

Similar considerations apply if we turn to the questions of God's omnipotence and impassibility. If he is worthy to be called God, then there must be a sense in which 'the Lord sits enthroned over the flood; the Lord sits enthroned as king for ever' (Ps. 29.10). Yet it seems equally true to say that if he is worthy to be called God, he cannot be unaffected by the storms that rage through the world. That God risks participation in his own creation and makes himself in some sense vulnerable to it seems to be entailed by the belief that he is a God of love and the God who became incarnate in Jesus Christ. And this certainly does not make God less adorable or less truly God, but rather more so. The fulness of God seems to demand both poles – the pole of transcendence and the pole of immanent participation. This dipolarity is reflected in the two central *motifs* of the Christian faith – cross and resurrection. The cross speaks of God's placing himself at the disposal of his creation, suffering with it and for it; the resurrection speaks of his power to open up a new way forward, his indefectibility, as we might say, though this is a term that has usually been employed with respect to the church. But God is neither more nor less God in the cross than he is in the resurrection. It is as much his nature as God to suffer with his creatures as to reign in triumph.

The difference between the classical type of theism and the alternative types which we have been discussing may be illustrated by calling to mind John Wisdom's essay, 'Gods'.[4] In that essay he considered whether the existence of God can today be regarded as an experimental issue, and the issue is proposed in terms of a parable. 'Two people return to their long neglected garden and find among the weeds a few of the old plants surprisingly vigorous. One says to the other, "It must be that a gardener has been coming and doing something about these plants." Upon inquiry, they find that no neighbour has ever seen anyone at work in their garden. The first man says to the other, "He must have worked while people slept." The other says, "No, someone would have heard him, and, besides, anyone who cared about the plants would have kept down these weeds." '[5]

Many readers are familiar with this opening section of Wisdom's parable and it may be regarded as a useful illustration for illuminating the traditional argument between theist and atheist, the argument which took the form, 'Is there or is there not a being beyond the world who laid it out in the first place and who will still maintain it when necessary?' – just as a gardener might lay out a garden and then give it such attention as was needed to maintain it in good condition. But what has been less readily noted – and indeed, may not have been noted by Wisdom himself – is that the subsequent dispute between the two people takes two fairly distinct forms. They begin by returning to their neglected garden, and the question at issue is whether a gardener comes to tend it. This seems to represent the dispute between classical theism and the corresponding atheism. But not much further on, the grounds of the dispute have shifted and the argument takes a different form. Now one man says to the other, 'You still think the world's a garden and not a wilderness.'[6] Here the argument is no longer about the question of a gardener who may or may not come to tend the plot. It has become an argument about the character of the plot of ground itself – whether or not it is a garden. As the argument proceeds, it seems to assume increasingly the second form. It becomes less and less an argument as to whether there is a gardener, separate from the garden and coming and going at will, and it becomes more and more a question as to whether the plot displays such a character as would constitute it a garden, or whether it must be reckoned a wilderness. The checking procedures differ also. For there is less and less talk about the possibility of hearing, seeing or otherwise detecting a gardener at work, and more and more talk about the immanent characteristics of the plot of ground, and especially whether one can trace in it what might be called the pattern of gardenhood.

This shift within Wisdom's parable is not dissimilar to the kind of shift that takes place when one moves from the classical type of theism to one of the types which take more seriously the immanence of God in the world and his organic relation to it. Yet it is clear also that this shift does not mean the abandonment of all belief in transcendence, or the reduction of God to a predicate of the world. The world, like the garden in Wisdom's parable, remains ambiguous. The world is certainly not itself God, and God has not been collapsed into the world. Yet God is not separate from the world or even an inference from the world, but rather a reality that opens up in and through the world itself when we see it in a certain perspective or pattern it in a certain way.

Moreover, this is not just a question of how one *feels* about the world. To be sure, one's feeling toward the world is likely to be different, according as one sees it under the God-pattern or in some other way. But the feeling here is dependent on the way one sees the world, not *vice versa*. (Wisdom, incidentally, makes much the same point about the feelings of the two men in relation to the plot of ground.) Further, it does not seem to be the case that the believer sees something that the atheist does not see, such as a gardener furtively entering or leaving the plot, or some secret sign that the gardener had left behind. That would bring us back to the idea of God as a being separate from and external to the garden. Believer and atheist alike see the same garden or world, the same phenomena, but they pattern these phenomena in different ways and dispute with each other over the presence or absence of such patterns.

Not only is the difference more than one of feeling, it is more than a verbal difference. It is not just that some people use the word 'God' to integrate and organize some of their experiences, while others are content to talk about 'Nature' or to use some other language. The difference is not only verbal, it is real, for only if certain patterns are really present is God-language justified. A pattern of order and regularity, for instance, would scarcely, at certain levels and in itself, be worthy to evoke God-language and all the overtones of meaning which such language brings along with it. But to this point we shall return.

In the meantime, we have to face the question: if God is not a being separate from the world, a gardener who comes from outside; and if he is not simply the world itself, or an adjective of the world and so world-dependent; then who or what can he possibly be? Are we simply deluding ourselves if we try to continue using God-language once we have moved away from the traditional model of classical theism?

It is necessary first of all to make a reservation. If God is real and if God-language is meaningful language, nevertheless this reality of God is unique and language about him cannot conform to the language we use about everyday situations in the world. There is, of course, a strong temptation to make God conform to everyday experience, and especially there is the tendency to talk about him in anthropomorphic ways, as, for instance, the gardener. Theologians have usually recognized the difficulties of God-language, in principle if not in practice, and they have acknowledged that their concepts must fall short of what they are trying to talk about, so that their language has always an oblique character. However, while the theologian admits that his language is incapable of making direct literal statements about God, he would hold that we can find concepts and images which light up something of the mystery of God, so that we are not reduced to complete silence concerning him. Thus when we take up the task of clarifying what we mean by 'God' and of saying how God is related to the world, the best we can do is to adduce certain concepts by way of analogues.

For my own part, I find that to conceive God as being, and his relation to the world as that of being to the beings, is very illuminating. It accords with a long theological tradition and derives new force from recent philosophies of being. But I am well aware that this language poses difficulties, especially for people of nominalist tendency, and that it needs to be supplemented by other ways of talking. Another possibility is to think of God's relation to the world as like that of a meaning to a process or series of events. In this sense, to believe in God is to believe in an ultimate context of meaning that gives sense to the world and is the opposite of chaos and absurdity.[7]

But I shall chiefly stress still another concept which seems particularly apposite to the foregoing discussions. May we think of God as *form*, and his relation to the world as analogous to that of form to matter? Immediately, however, I must make clearer what I intend by 'form' here. I certainly do not have in mind a Platonic form, if this is understood as eternal, timeless, unchanging. Much closer would be the notion of form found in Aristotelianism and Thomism, as, for instance, when it is said that the soul is the form of the body. In this case the form is, as it were, an active *Gestalt*, informing the body and expressing itself in and through the body. It would be in a somewhat analogous way that one might think of

God as the form of the world. Of course, this remains an analogy, and may not be pushed too far – and I must emphasize this point, since it tends to get overlooked, and what is offered as analogy is taken in full literalness. Obviously the physical world is very different from the body of a living creature – though it is worth noting, as David Hume did,[8] that the world is *more* like 'an organized body' than an artefact, and he drew from this the conclusion that the God–world relation is more plausibly understood in organic than in monarchical terms. Obviously, too, God, in the Christian understanding of him, is more than an immanent world-soul, for he not only informs the world but brings it into being, so that he is creative form. The ancient notion of world-soul, however, is not one to be despised as we seek to understand the intimacy of God's relation to the world. At any rate, within limits, the thought of God as creative, living form, a dynamic reality giving being, direction and intelligibility to the world, is a helpful one. Religious imagery has in fact often offered the picture of God as 'life' or 'spirit' and these are not substances or things of any sort but rather dynamic forms in something like the sense in which I have been using the expression.

To use the notion of the form of the world as an explanatory model for thinking about the God–world relation would presumably depart from the notion that God is completely independent of the world, or that his creation could be understood as in any sense an act of arbitrary will. We are acknowledging in fact that God is inseparable from the world or at least inconceivable apart from it, that he is not a gardener who may come and go but is rather the form of the garden, that which constitutes it a garden. Yet this is not to annex God to the world or to identify them in a pantheism. It is not to say either that it was *necessary* for God to create the world. I am inclined to agree with Vladimir Lossky that 'liberty and necessity are one, or, rather, can have no place, in God'.[9] But I think it could be said that it is of the very nature of a God of love, and of the very nature of a trinity one of whose persons is the outgoing Logos, to share the gift of existence with a creation. As the dynamic creative form, God is ontologically prior to the world, transcendent as well as immanent, but this is not incompatible with there always having been a world.

We must note too that when we talk of form, we must be intending something more than just the ordered regularities of physical nature if God-language is to be appropriate. To be sure, the order of the physical universe seems to raise some metaphysical question of its own, as Einstein recognized. But Ayer was correct when he wrote: 'If the sentence "God exists" entails no more than that certain types of phenomena occur in certain sequences, then to assert the existence of a God will be simply equivalent to asserting that there is the requisite regularity in nature; and no religious man would admit that this is all he intended to assert in asserting the existence of a God.'[10] The reason that no *religious* man would allow that this kind of form alone could properly be designated God is, of course, that whatever can be called God must be adorable. We have noted already that an ordered universe, though it may be awesome, is not in itself adorable. Hence to talk of God as the form of the world would imply that this form is to be discerned on the personal and historical level as well as on the merely physical. John Robinson has expressed the point by saying that the believer in God 'can trust the universe not only at the level of certain mathematical regularities, but at the level of utterly personal reliability'.[11] In this connection, Matthew Arnold's way of talking about God is worth pondering – 'the power not ourselves making for righteousness'.[12] This, in turn, seems close to the thought of God that finds expression in the Hebrew scriptures. It is the thought that there is active in history a form or directedness that by and large promotes righteousness and enhances the meaning and dignity of man's life. But, as the book of Job so forcibly recognizes, this does not happen in any simple and unambiguous way, so there can be no simple pantheistic identification of God with the world-process. He is the partly hidden, partly revealed dynamic form that is coming to expression in the process.

These remarks bring us back to the ambiguity of what we see in the world. It seems obvious that neither the theist nor the atheist (at least, among the great majority of human beings) reaches his stance as the result of a kind of calculus in which the connections or lack of connections supporting one view or the other are balanced against each other until opinion finally comes down on one side or the other. The truth is that the world always remains ambiguous, and although people can argue as long as they like, tracing their rival patterns, the case will never be established conclusively, one way or the other. Faith arises when the believer is so impressed by some particular limited area of reality that it becomes for him a paradigm for interpreting the whole and, so far as one can talk of proof or disproof in such matters, his paradigm will either prove itself or break down as he tries to extend it to wider areas of experience. For the Christian, the paradigm is constituted by Jesus

Christ. Thus, if we are to employ the concept of form as explained above, we may say that the Christian sees reality as christiform. We could also say he believes that the fundamental meaning (*logos*) of the universe is embodied in Christ, or that the clue to the nature of being is to be found in this particular being, Jesus Christ, who is one in being (*homoousios*) with the Father.

Incidentally, it tends to be overlooked that the atheist too is profoundly influenced by particular limited patterns, either in history or in his personal experience. These become paradigms for him – negative revelations, if you like. One may recall how such events as the Lisbon earthquake and, more recently, the tragedy of Auschwitz, have led some people to interpret the world as a whole to be godless.

In sum, then, we may say that God and the world are not identical, but they are much more intimately related to each other than much traditional theology has allowed. If we know God at all, it is in and through worldly realities – where else? He is prior to the world and transcendent, but the world is organic to him. We may call him the form of the world, the meaning of the world, the being of the beings, though recognizing that none of these concepts is adequate to the reality.

Notes

1. D. Pears, *Wittgenstein*, Collins 1971, p. 89.

2. R. G. Smith, *The Doctrine of God*, Collins 1970, pp. 22, 167.

3. S. Kierkegaard, *The Concept of Dread*, tr. W. Lowrie, Princeton University Press 1957, p. 79.

4. In John Wisdom, *Philosophy and Psychoanalysis*, Blackwell 1953, pp. 149-68.

5. Loc. cit., pp. 154-5.

6. Ibid.

7. See above, on being pp. 106ff., and on meaning, p. 93.

8. D. Hume, *Dialogues Concerning Natural Religion*, pp. 42-3.

9. V. Lossky, *The Mystical Theology of the Eastern Church*, James Clarke 1957, p. 45.

10. A. J. Ayer, *Language, Truth and Logic*, Gollancz 1946, p. 115.

11. J. A. T. Robinson, *Exploration into God*, SCM Press and Stanford University Press 1967, p. 68.

12. M. Arnold, *Literature and Dogma*, Smith, Elder & Co. 1876, p. 33.

11

The Nearer Side of God

The current concern to understand the relation of God to his creation in a more intimate way has coincided with an upsurge of interest in the Holy Spirit, to be seen not only in the rapid growth of the Pentecostalist sects but likewise in the rise of charismatic movements in the mainline denominations of Christendom. It may be that neglect of the doctrine of the Holy Spirit – a neglect which is universally acknowledged – has been one factor contributing to that sense of God's remoteness which has been an unhappy feature of the recent past. But the neglect is due also to the difficulty of forming any precise conception of Spirit. If anyone were to produce a neat definition of Spirit, it would be almost certain that he had missed the reality. The word stands for something or someone mysterious and even largely incomprehensible, yet so important and precious as may not be ignored. The fourth gospel declares, 'God is Spirit' (John 4.24). The Christian doctrine of God acknowledges the Holy Spirit as a coequal member of the Trinity. Spirit is associated too with man, and especially with those qualities which are most distinctively human and which we cherish most, freedom, love, truth and the like. It is in virtue of having spirit that man has some affinity to God and has even the possibility of being godlike. For the New Testament can speak of God as the 'Father of spirits' (Heb. 12.9) while the Apocrypha goes so far as to declare that God's 'immortal spirit is in all things' (Wisd. 12.1). But if spirit belongs to God and is associated with what is highest in man, we must not forget that there is a third possibility. In the Bible there is mention of evil spirits, and the early church was very much aware of them. Even today one encounters belief in the demonic, though for most sophisticated persons evil spirits have become at the most mere metaphors. Whatever one may think of the matter, the belief in evil spirits is a forceful reminder that that which is best and highest can become the worst when it is perverted. 'The spiritual hosts of wickedness in the heavenly places' (Eph. 6.12) may be mythological talk, but it vividly brings before us those dimensions of evil that seem to dwarf mankind and with which he seems unable to cope.

When one is confronted with a notion so difficult to grasp as that of Spirit, one must turn to analogies, images, pictures, models, whatever we may care to call them, in the hope of getting some illumination. Images and analogies do not describe in a literal or direct way, but they point us indirectly to the reality. We could say that they evoke rather than describe. Most of the present discussion will be devoted to passing in review a whole series of pictures or images that have been used for evoking an understanding of the Spirit of God. It will be something like an exercise along the lines advocated by Marshall McLuhan. We shall simply immerse ourselves in a whole sea of material that has been used in the Bible and in Christian thought to speak of the Spirit. As we let these different images impinge on our minds, we shall find that they evoke all kinds of new thoughts and open up insights into the reality of the Spirit. We shall see how amazingly rich and complex the Spirit is. As we are exposed to this range of suggestive imagery, we shall also be reflecting on it, trying to sort out the material and to bring some kind of theological order into it. Yet we must remember that the very notion of Spirit implies spontaneity and therefore elusiveness and even untidiness, so that if we were to attempt to systematize the doctrine of the Holy Spirit too strictly, we might end by stifling the reality of that same Spirit.

There are many images of the Spirit. There is the wind in its many moods. There is the subtle element of fire. There are the rain and the dew that fall upon the ground and make it bring forth. There is the dove. Perhaps these are the basic images, and already they bring before us a wealth of material.

The principal model or image for the elucidation of Spirit is the wind or breath, for in most languages the word used for Spirit is the word that literally meant wind or breath. In Hebrew the single word *ruach* had to do duty for both 'wind' and 'spirit' throughout the history of the language, and it is not always clear which of these meanings is intended. For instance, in the creation story, the Revised Standard Version translates: 'The Spirit of God was moving over the face of the waters.' But the New English Bible takes it more literally, and talks of 'a mighty wind that swept over the surface of the waters' (Gen. 1.2). It seems to me that it would be silly to argue about which is the correct interpretation. Both ideas were probably present in the mind of the writer, and in ancient times the dividing line between literal and symbolic was less definitely drawn than it is for us today.

Perhaps the first thing to be said in elucidation of the basic image of Spirit as the wind is to point out that this is a dynamic model. The wind is air in motion, and it seems to be the motion that is important for the evocation of Spirit. To believe in Spirit is to believe in a hidden activity in the world, an activity that lies deeper than the unceasing physical processes of nature. Ian Ramsey has written that 'discourse about the Spirit is a way of being articulate about God's initiating activity and our responsive activity'.[1] In this view, the Spirit is, first and foremost, God's way of acting in the world and in the affairs of men. No doubt many other things have to be said about the Holy Spirit, but it is a fundamental point to see the Spirit as God's activity in the world. Spirit, whether in God or in man, is active and dynamic. Spirit is activity. Because of this, we often find the notion of power (*dynamis*) associated with the Spirit in the New Testament. Jesus himself is said to have been anointed 'with the Holy Spirit and with power' (Acts 10.38); before his ascension, he promises his disciples, 'You shall receive power when the Holy Spirit has come upon you' (Acts 1.8); and Paul's prayer for the disciples is that 'by the power of the Holy Spirit, you may abound in hope' (Rom. 15.13). So the first point to bear in mind about the Spirit is this dynamic character: the Spirit is power, energy, activity, God at work in the creation.

A second point that strikes us when we think of the wind as an image of the Spirit is its elusiveness. We cannot grasp the wind, it slips through our fingers and escapes on all sides. We cannot see the wind or make it an object of inspection. If you ask, 'What is Spirit?' you cannot expect the same kind of answer as when you ask, let us say, 'What is copper?' Spirit is not a thing or an object within the world. Actually our minds – at least, in the West – seem to have a materialistic bent so that we tend to think in terms of things, and suspect that only what can be demonstrated to have thinghood is real, as if the solid existing thing were the criterion of reality. Sometimes Spirit has been visualized as if it were some kind of substance, no doubt very subtle but nevertheless thinglike. But if we try to think of Spirit as thinglike, however much differing from grosser bodies, we are in fact assimilating Spirit to the material world. The belief in Spirit as an elusive reality which cannot be pinned down, investigated and defined in the way that we are able to do with physical things, is intended precisely to say that there is more to the world than physical reality, more to it than can be grasped by our senses and our empirical modes of investigation. Spirit refers to a mysterious dimension of existence, stretching beyond the empirical and the manipulable. This does not mean that Spirit exists in a separate world, divorced from the everyday world. It is in the ordinary world that the spiritual dimension opens up, but as it does so, it reveals a depth of reality of which perhaps we had thitherto been unaware. We can never tell when such a disclosure or opening up will come to us. Certainly, we cannot arrange for it, though we can hold ourselves in readiness for it. 'The wind blows where it will', said Jesus to Nicodemus, 'and you hear the sound of it, but you do not know whence it comes or whither it goes; so it is with everyone who is born of the Spirit' (John 3.8). Thus the elusiveness of the wind points to the mystery of Spirit as the reality transcending the material world and yet immanent in it.

It is important to note that although the wind is invisible and elusive, it is audible – 'you hear the sound of it'. But the sound of the wind is an inarticulate sound. The wind sighs, it moans, it howls, it blusters, it whispers and so on. These are not accidental features of the model, and they suggest some important points about Spirit. Can we see a connection between the strange sounds of the wind and the groaning that Paul attributes to the Spirit? 'We know that the whole creation has been groaning in travail together until now; and not only the creation, but we ourselves, who have the first fruits of the Spirit, groan inwardly as we wait for adoption as sons ... Likewise the Spirit helps us in our weakness; for we do not know how to pray as we ought, but the Spirit himself intercedes for us with sighs too deep for words' (Rom. 8.22-6). We may notice also at this point that it is not only the divine Spirit who sighs, for in the phenomenon known as glossolalia or speaking with tongues, Spirit-filled disciples may give utterance to sounds which do not constitute articulate language but which may nonetheless be highly expressive.

What then is the meaning of those words of Paul about the Spirit's groaning and sighing, as if in travail? I think that a clue is provided by a remark of John Taylor, who says, 'There is more of Dionysus than Apollo in the Holy Spirit.'[2] This points to an essential distinction between the Spirit and the Logos. Both Spirit and Logos derive from the Father, from the primordial depth of Godhood. Of the Spirit, we say that he proceeds; of the Son or Logos, that he is begotten. Is this mere word-spinning? Let us admit that in the New Testament itself the Holy Spirit, the spirit of Jesus and even the risen Christ are not easily distinguished. Should the distinction between Spirit and Logos be abolished, so that we see both terms referring to what we might call the 'nearer side' of God, that is to say, God as he comes forth from his hiddenness? Cyril Richardson, for instance, claims that although Word and Spirit are distinguished in the New Testament, 'the logic would have been finally to identify them; if God himself was at work in Jesus of Nazareth ... then no distinction between the divine in Jesus and God's Spirit is really cogent'.[3] But it seems to me that this is to overlook the important distinction between the Logos as the rational articulate expression of the divine mind and Spirit as manifesting elements of the nonrational or numinous, which we might perhaps compare to the deep affective and conative elements in our own nature. The Spirit that is in travail with the creation is more of a *nisus* or striving than a *logos* or word. Of course, one must not press the distinction too far. The three persons of the triunity are inseparable, and no one of them exists or acts in isolation. Spirit and Logos complement each other. The Spirit not only brings to expression the loving striving of God, but leads into truth; while the Logos not only reveals truth but actualizes love. Nevertheless, we can distinguish, to revert to Taylor's language, the Dionysian character of Spirit from the Apollinian character of Logos.

Let us not underestimate the danger of the Dionysian. It reaches down into the very roots of our nature, and whoever would seek the Holy Spirit is, to change the image for a moment, ready to play with fire. Life in the Spirit can issue in the wilder forms of ecstatic and emotional experiences. That is why Spirit and Logos must go together. The sometimes frightening outbursts of spiritual energy in the primitive church made it necessary to 'test the spirits to see whether they are of God' (I John 4.1). The test of the spirits is Jesus Christ himself, the Logos and also the bearer of the Holy Spirit in the fulness of that Spirit. Whatever edifies the body of Christ and leads to the kind of life which he manifested can be recognized as the work of the Holy Spirit. Whatever does not obviously lead in that direction must be questioned. Especially anything that would injure community, such as the formation of a kind of spiritual élite through the cultivation of the more exotic spiritual gifts, would have to be regarded as a perversion. Such perversions, unfortunately, do tend to occur when the emotional and ecstatic elements get separated from the rational and ethical. On the other hand, it is dangerous to isolate the Apollinian. In the Western world, we have tended to suppress the emotional and to order our lives as far as possible in accordance with the rational and the pragmatic. But it may be that we impoverish life by causing to atrophy these emotional ecstatic depths. Worse still, if we seek to deny outlet to these depths of our nature, they may take revenge and issue in destructive forms. How was it that the most civilized and rational country in Europe, Germany, was suddenly seized with a dark nihilistic passion in the time of the Nazis? More generally, why has the West from time to time given vent to the most destructive aggression? At this point we again touch on the chilling phenomenon of the demonic and its links with the spiritual.

Returning to our model, we notice next the freedom and spontaneity of the wind. There is an unpredictability about it – the wind blows where it will. It is exactly so with the Spirit. We say that people are 'caught up' in the Spirit. There is no calculation about it, and we are impressed again with the essentially preconceptual character of Spirit and spiritual experience. The prophets, in both the Old and New Testaments, were men who were caught up in the Spirit and who spoke in ecstasy. Yet the picture is not one of disorder and confusion. Although the wind may gust around, it generally has direction. Indeed, in all parts of the world there are what we call 'prevailing' winds. Certainly the Spirit of God has direction. That *nisus* which is at work in the created order is striving toward the consummation of creation, toward fuller, more personal, more communal life for the creatures. It is for this reason that Jesus could promise his disciples: 'When the Spirit of truth is come, he will guide you into all truth' (John 16.13). The same gospel tells us that Christ is himself the truth, and we have noted that he is the criterion for testing whether any spiritual movement is indeed directed toward fuller life. So if the life of the Spirit is one of spontaneity, it nevertheless shows a consistent directedness toward the quality of life manifested in Christ. As Paul said in connection with the gifts of the Spirit, 'God is not a God of confusion, but of peace' (I Cor. 14.33). The life of the Spirit is to be lived in the tension of spontaneity and order.

This constant direction of the Spirit's activity toward the goal of a consummated creation is experienced by men as his striving with them. The Spirit is pervasive in the creation, not in the sense of a merely passive indwelling, but in the active sense that he is everywhere at work. In the words of an apocryphal writer, 'the Spirit of God has filled the world' (Wisd. 1.7). Therefore we cannot escape him and we have either to move with him or against him. 'Whither shall I go from thy Spirit? Or whither shall I flee from thy presence?' (Ps. 139.7). The answer is that there is nowhere to go from God's Spirit. Of the Spirit of God it might well be said that 'in him we live and move and have our being' (Acts 17.28). This particular saying, of course, was quoted from a Hellenistic poet for whom God was conceived as an immanent spirit. As men move with the Spirit of God, they experience his judgment. But the encounter, whether in grace or judgment, is personal. The Holy Spirit does not force us against our wills or overwhelm us, and to receive his gifts is to have one's freedom and personal being enhanced, not diminished.

The Holy Spirit, who pervades all things and who strives in all men who are willing to work with him, is thus seen to be also the unitive aspect of God's being. In the first place, the Spirit proceeds, he comes forth from God to move through all creation. But having penetrated the creation, he strives in it and with it to bring it into union with God. There is as it were a double movement of the Spirit – he proceeds and he returns. At this point it is again helpful to distinguish the Spirit and the Logos. The Word comes forth from the Father to create out of nothing a world of light, order and rationality. The Spirit penetrates deeply into the dark recesses of that world to lift it up from within, so to speak. To do justice to the full scope of the divine activity, we have to speak of three persons rather than two. Here I must again take issue with Cyril Richardson. He argues that the richness and complexity of a dynamic God demands at least two terms, or better still an indefinite number, but that 'three terms is an arbitrary way of conceiving the matter'.[4] Now I would not wish to plead for a literal threeness in God, but I would say that three is so far from being arbitrary that it is the first adequate stopping place in any attempt to express God's diversity in unity and unity in diversity. The unbroken unity of a monolithic God from whom had gone forth neither Word nor Spirit would be something less than a God who could be worshipped. If we move from stark unity to twoness or duality, then we are in very grave danger of introducing a split that cannot be bridged, and of ending up in some kind of Gnostic or Manichaean dualism in which both the world and its creative agent have been so far removed from the hidden God that a fundamental opposition is set up. We have to move on to threeness, to the completion of the circle, when the Spirit who has proceeded from the Godhead to work in the creation lifts that whole creation to God and, above all, builds the community of the Spirit among the finite spirits. This is his travail and his praying in us. The Spirit is the wind of God in the world but he is also the breath that gives life within man.

We have spent most of our space in a consideration of the image of the wind as a help to understanding Spirit, and that image is indeed the primary one. But there are others, and we shall look briefly at some of them that have been prominent in the Bible and in Christian theology.

One of these images is fire. In the account of the outpouring of the Holy Spirit at Pentecost, there is mention not only of 'the rush of a mighty wind' but also of 'tongues as of fire' (Acts 2.2-3). The symbolism of fire has, of course, much in common with the symbolism of the wind. Fire too is dynamic. It is, if anything, an even subtler and more elusive element than air. Fire has been almost a necessity to human life for something like four hundred thousand years, yet fire like wind can be fiercely destructive. Fire we connect with the passions and emotions, and not least we talk of the fire of love. But there is at least one new idea that the image of fire brings to our understanding of Spirit. Fire purifies. Isaiah speaks of 'a spirit of judgment and a spirit of burning' (Isa. 4.4). The refining of metals by fire is a common metaphor in the Bible for the purging of human life through judgment and suffering. We have indeed already seen that to struggle against the Spirit is to know judgment and is like going into the wind. But there is more to it, and perhaps the image of fire helps to elucidate this. No one can become a person or a spiritual being without knowing some adversity and without struggling against his own sinful tendencies. The work of the Holy Spirit has traditionally included sanctification, the making holy of human life. Part of that process of sanctification is the burning up of impurities in order that the spirit in man may emerge in its truly spiritual condition, and this happens through a spiritual discipline.

Another image that demands some attention is water. In the Old Testament God's coming is compared to the dew and the rain (Hos. 6.3; 14.4) and his Spirit to life-giving water (Isa. 44.3). But the image acquires a whole new range of meaning in the New Testament, where the Spirit is associated with the waters of baptism.

The Spirit descended in his fulness on Jesus Christ at his baptism (Mark 1.10) and in accounts of baptisms in the early church, the gift of the Holy Spirit was a normal accompaniment of the sacrament and an essential part of its meaning, though the gift might come upon the disciple before baptism or after, rather than at the precise moment of ministration (Cf. Acts 8.14ff.; 10.4ff.). This untidiness, by the way, illustrates the point about the freedom of the Spirit, though clearly it does not annul orderly procedures in the church. The waters of baptism, in turn, have been compared to the waters in the creation story, the waters over which the Spirit of God moved to bring a new creation out of the chaos. For baptism too is a new creation, the emergence of a new humanity, first in Christ and then in those who are joined to him. This image then draws attention to the creativity of the Spirit, his making new and his making alive. Of course, creation belongs to all three persons of the triunity, as do all the divine activities. What is especially characteristic of the Holy Spirit is his creation of new inward life, his awakening of the spirit in the human being so that he may set out on the way of sanctification.

Up till now, we have thought about three images of Spirit – wind, fire and water. It may strike us as an interesting fact that he seems to be represented under three of the four elements of ancient cosmology. Fire, air, water symbolize the being and the acts of Spirit, but what about earth? In biblical religion, earth and the deities of earth are kept very much in the background. No doubt this is a legacy from the days when the prophetic religion of Israel was struggling to differentiate itself from the pagan Canaanite cults – struggling even to survive the threat of being swallowed up in a syncretistic cult of chthonic spirits. Thus the gods and goddesses of the soil were held at a distance, and the fertility cults that went with them. The God of the Bible then tends to be very much a transcendent deity, and one also hears the complaint that he is very much a masculine deity, excluding any of the feminine characteristics of mother earth. I do not propose to attempt to revive the rejected earth imagery (though some theologians have thought of moving in this direction since the coming of the environmental crisis) but I would like to suggest that the Spirit introduces elements of the feminine into the Christian conception of God. That such elements should find a place is attested, I think, by the place given to the Blessed Virgin Mary in Christian devotion, but even the most enthusiastic mariologist who might have championed her role as *corredemptrix* would hardly have gone so far as to urge that she should be co-opted, as it were, into the Godhead, which, presumably, would have to be transformed from trinity to quaternity.

Proper attention to the doctrine of Spirit renders any such drastic theological innovations unnecessary. And first we have to take note of still another symbol or image of Spirit, namely, the dove. Ann Ulanov has drawn attention to the fact that the dove had two symbolic roles in the ancient world. Among Christians the dove was an image of the Holy Spirit, who had appeared in this form at the baptism of Jesus Christ (Mark 1.10). Among pagans, the dove was an emblem of Aphrodite, goddess of love. 'Iconographically,' writes Ann Ulanov, 'the dove is a messenger of the goddess and of the Holy Spirit. The messenger is properly feminine because what it does is to expose the dark mystery to the light of the world, just as the feminine modality lifts the material of the unconscious into the light of consciousness.'[5] Needless to say, this action never exhausts the mystery of the unconscious and the preconceptual. Many of the points we have made earlier will confirm this linking of Spirit with the feminine. There is the simple matter too that the Hebrew word for spirit, *ruach*, is of feminine gender. To be sure, this is a grammatical convention, but the genders of nouns have usually reflected something of the 'feel' that people have had for what these words signify, and the origins of gender can sometimes be traced back into mythology. We have seen that in *ruach* feeling rather than reason, intuition rather than inference, the Dionysian and orgiastic rather than the Appollinian and intellectual, are typical. Ann Ulanov makes the following remarks: 'In contrast to the goals of the masculine style of consciousness, goals of intellectual perfection, clear focus and specialization, the feminine style of consciousness moves towards completeness. The feminine style of spirit is to make progress on a downward going road, into the dark, into the roots of earth, into the unconscious.'[6] We can recognize in this something parallel to the proceeding forth of the divine Spirit into the depth of creation in order to travail there and to lift the creation up to God.

Of course, in other ways the Spirit has a masculine character. We have seen that he is symbolized as the rain that falls on the earth to make it spring, not as mother earth itself. Again, the Spirit has a masculine role in fecundating the Blessed Virgin at the annunciation. God has no sex, but transcends both sexes. But we should add that he transcends rather by inclusion and by bringing both roles to a higher level than by the exclusion of sheer sexlessness. As Carl Jung has made clear, every balanced human being likewise embraces both masculine and feminine elements, and the stereotypes that we commonly apply to the sexes have little applicability in concrete cases. Nevertheless, it is the idea of the Holy Spirit that most definitely expresses the feminine element in the Christian understanding of God, and this element certainly ought to find expression.

We have explored the images of Spirit mainly by letting them speak for themselves, so to say, that is, by letting them evoke associated images and ideas. We have correspondingly kept the attempts at theological conceptualization and systematization to a minimum. The result has been to let us see more clearly what I have called the 'nearer side' of God. It is a strange irony that God has so often been understood in terms of the 'farther side' – his transcendence, majesty, rationality, immutability, masculinity and so on. A renewal of the doctrine of the Holy Spirit would go far toward bringing a richer and more balanced understanding of God in his immanence, humility, accessibility, openness and love.

Notes

1. I. T. Ramsey, *Models for Divine Activity*, SCM Press 1973, p. 13.

2. J. V. Taylor, *The Go-Between God*, SCM Press 1972, p. 50.

3. C. C. Richardson, *The Doctrine of the Trinity*, Abingdon Press 1958, p. 48.

4. Op. cit., p. 113.

5. A. Ulanov, *The Feminine*, Northwestern University Press 1971, p. 325.

6. Ibid., p. 328.

12

The Problem of Natural Theology

The story of the decline and fall of natural theology is too well known to need any long telling. There was a time when most theologians and many philosophers believed that it is possible to demonstrate by rational argument the existence and beneficence of God, and some other matters of religious concern as well, such as the immortality of the soul. The proofs might be *a priori*, as in the case of St Anselm's famous ontological argument, or *a posteriori*, as in the case of St Thomas' equally famous five ways. But in any case it was supposed that one might begin from premises that would be accepted by any rational person, and go on from there to demonstrate by strict argument that the fundamental convictions of religion are true. Thus there was laid the foundation of a rational or natural theology, on which might be raised the superstructure of revealed theology. And clearly, revealed theology did derive support from this foundation of natural theology; for if it could indeed be demonstrated that there is a beneficent God and that man has an eternal destiny, then it would become almost inherently probable that this God would go on to bring to the human race a fuller, saving knowledge of himself, as revealed theology claims that he has done.

But along came modern philosophy, bringing with it the criticisms of Hume and Kant and their successors. The traditional arguments were shown to be defective at various points, and it began to seem as if man can have no certain knowledge of anything that transcends the world of natural phenomena. The traditional natural theology melted away under increasingly stringent philosophical criticism. Even at the beginning of the present century, when the Gifford Lectures on Natural Theology were still at their zenith, many of the most distinguished philosophers of the English-speaking world produced their most notable works in this field.

But today, many philosophers, even if they are not actually positivists, find plenty of interest in the problems of language and logic and would not dream of dealing with what in the past were deemed the great problems – God, freedom, immortality. Many theologians too have become convinced of the futility of natural theology, and they are left with revealed theology suspended somewhat perilously in mid-air, as it were, with its ancient support pulled out from beneath it.

It is true that there are still some philosophical theologians and a few theologically minded philosophers who are prepared to fight a rearguard action on the natural theology front, and sometimes to fight it very brilliantly. One thinks, for instance, of F. R. Tennant's attempted rehabilitation of the teleological argument which perhaps went beyond all previous statements in drawing attention to wide interlocking areas of phenomena that seem to manifest some purposeful direction; or of Austin Farrer's restatement of the cosmological argument with man himself as the primary datum; or of the continuing influence of Whitehead's philosophy, which, for all its elaboration and difficult terminology, presents an argument for the existence of God which is 'primarily the traditional one from the order of the universe to a ground of order';[1] or of Teilhard de Chardin's much acclaimed endeavour to argue from the empirical facts of terrestrial evolution to theistic conclusions; or, alongside all these empirical arguments, of the continued interest during recent years in the ontological argument.

These restatements are not to be lightly dismissed. Each of them succeeds at one point or another in overcoming some difficulty that had become apparent in some earlier formulation of natural theology. One would hesitate to say that there is a cumulative effect in these arguments, for if in fact there are flaws in them, then ten defective arguments are no more convincing than one. Yet it is impossible not to be impressed by the way in which able thinkers keep coming back to natural theology, and even to quite traditional formulations. Even so, it is hard for the modern mind not to entertain a lurking suspicion that there must be something wrong even in the most ingeniously devised natural theology. We have all to some extent been inculcated with the empirical spirit, and have great difficulty in seeing how one can argue from empirical data to conclusions about God, who is certainly not an empirical phenomenon. The authors of the modern restatements of natural theology are, for the most part, prepared to concede that they do not claim for their arguments the cogency that was once supposed to belong to the traditional proofs, but at most a measure of probability. However, in the popular mind at least, this modesty on the part of modern practitioners of natural theology has sometimes been interpreted as evidence of its failure. Thus, in spite of all efforts to rejuvenate it, natural theology continues to languish.

The whole position has been greatly aggravated by the fact that many theologians in the past few decades have frankly allied themselves with antimetaphysical philosophy in rejecting all natural theology as a mistaken endeavour. These theologians have welcomed the downfall of natural theology and happily occupy themselves with revealed theology alone. When one notes the changing attitudes to philosophy among theologians, one calls to mind Hume's jibe that so long as the philosopher is saying things that will support religious faith, the theologian will make him his ally; but that as soon as the philosopher begins to say things that are hostile to faith, the theologian suddenly remembers that all philosophy is merely the 'wisdom of this world' and can lend no support to that heavenly wisdom to which the theologian claims access through divine revelation. 'Sceptics in one age, dogmatists in another,' wrote Hume, 'whichever system best suits the purposes of these reverend gentlemen in giving them an ascendancy over mankind, they are sure to make it their favourite principle and established test.'[2] I hope that Hume was mistaken in the motive which he imputed, but he was correct in pointing to the theologians' changing fashions *vis-à-vis* rational inquiry.

Karl Barth has been the leading opponent of natural theology in recent times. One may recall his early debate with Brunner, in which he angrily rejected the possibility of any natural theology, even the very meagre kind which Brunner was willing to allow. When he was invited to give the Gifford Lectures on Natural Theology, Barth declared: 'I certainly see – with astonishment – that such a science as Lord Gifford had in mind does exist, but I do not see how it is possible for it to exist. I am convinced that so far as it has existed and still exists, it owes its existence to a radical error.'[3] Whatever other changes may have taken place in Barth's thought over the years, he remained consistent in this. There is no way from man to God, no way by which the human mind can rise to the knowledge of divine truth. This is not only because, as the antimetaphysical philosophers would also say, man is essentially limited in his powers of knowing; it is also, Barth claims, because of his fallen condition which has so perverted his intellect that any thought of God at which he might arrive could be nothing other than an idolatrous projection of his own reprobate mind. So the knowledge of God is found in revelation alone – and for Barth, this meant one specific revelation, that of the Bible and Christian faith, the revelation of Jesus Christ as the Word of God.

Up to a point one has to concede the strength of Barth's critique. Whatever may be thought about the sinfulness of man, there is no doubt about his radical finitude. It belongs to the very essence of human existence that it must be lived in ambiguity and risk. To demand the security of proof, of demonstrable answers to all the questions of life, is to reject the finitude of our existence, indeed, to reject our humanity and to seek the status of gods or angels. There is something pathological in this craving for certainty, whether it appears in the religious man who asks for unshakable proof of the truth of his beliefs, or in the positivist who refuses to give assent to anything that seems to him unverifiable. As finite beings, we cannot always have certain knowledge, and must be prepared to live in the conflicts of faith and doubt. Barth is correct too in stressing revelation, though he ought to have recognized the possibility of revelation outside of the biblical tradition. He is right in stressing revelation because the God of faith is known in a personal way and not as an inference from argument. If anything approaching certitude is possible in religious faith, it is engendered by communion with God. When we move from that to arguments about God, then, ironically enough, whatever certitude there may have been is shaken. The valid elements in Barth's critique were well expressed at a much earlier time by Kierkegaard when he wrote: 'With what industrious zeal, with what sacrifice of time, of diligence, of writing materials, the speculative philosophers in our time have laboured to get a strong and complete proof of the existence of God! But in the same degree that the excellence of the proof increases, certitude seems to decrease.'[4]

Yet what Kierkegaard and Barth seem to overlook is that to the best of our ability we must exercise our critical judgment upon our beliefs, so that whatever faith we hold will be a reasonable faith. Such a faith would not be one that could be rationally demonstrated – if it could, it would no longer be a faith – but it would be one that had been tested in the light of all the knowledge and experience we have at our disposal. If it is true that finitude is of the essence of our humanity, it is equally true that rationality belongs to it, and so our obligation as human beings is to be rational as well as to acknowledge the limitations of our knowledge. If we make the knowledge of God an isolated and arbitrary matter, given only in a specific revelation that is discontinuous with everything else that we know through either common sense or philosophy, this may be one way of rendering it invulnerable against the encroachments of secular thought, but it gives a security that is too dearly purchased, and that is in any case a false security. In the words of John E. Smith, 'A religious tradition which seeks to insulate itself from all connection with man's general experience and knowledge on the supposition that God is not to be measured by the wisdom of this world, not only shows impiety toward the divine creation but also runs the risk of losing its very life. The history of religion is filled with examples of causes lost because their proponents believed it possible to preserve their ancient wisdom free from all contaminating contact with insights derived from general experience and secular knowledge.'[5]

There is a further difficulty. There is something unnatural in the attempt to combine unreserved acceptance of a divine revelation with scepticism concerning the power of human reason to discover any truth about God. It is significant that one can think of a number of theologians who have tried to combine a sceptical positivistic outlook in philosophy with a fideistic type of belief in an absolute, divine revelation, and who sooner or later have found the tensions of such a double-think to be intolerable and have passed into open atheism – and have even found it something of a liberation. Most of the 'death of God' theologians began as Barthians, believing in an inaccessible God in whom we would have no grounds for believing apart from the Christian revelation. One of them, William Hamilton, has expressed the matter thus: 'It is a very short step, but a critical one, to move from the otherness of God to the absence of God.'[6]

So we are in something of a dilemma. We have to acknowledge the strength of the criticisms of natural theology, both those that come from philosophy and those that come from theology, and we acknowledge that only dubious success has attended those who have sought to rehabilitate the discipline. On the other hand, less attractive still is the alternative presented by the Barthians of abandoning natural theology altogether and contenting ourselves with a revelation that in its isolation is as odd as a rock in the sky. We cannot escape the challenge of seeking to revive natural theology or, rather, to construct a new natural theology. Biblical or revealed theology cannot be left standing on its own, or else it will drift more and more into remoteness from modern life. 'There is a great deal of talk', writes Howard Root, 'about biblical categories, as though to claim their existence made it unnecessary to ask whether they were adequate for whatever it is they are supposed to express.'[7] The sentence is quoted from an essay in which he shows that the sickness of natural theology is not just an academic concern but one of the factors that has contributed to making theology (and religious faith along with it) so utterly remote from and irrelevant to the secularized intelligence of our time.

The first step toward any reconstruction of natural theology is to get a clear idea of its basic function. At first glance, it might seem that its function is obvious. Surely the business of natural theology is to demonstrate the reality of those fundamental matters with which the theologian is concerned, that is to say, to prove the existence of God, the immortality of the soul, and whatever else may be deemed to be required as a prerequisite of revealed theology. But if this is the basic function, then we have to face all the objections already mentioned, both philosophical and theological, and we seem driven to reject natural theology.

It may be the case, however, that the obvious answer to the question about the function of natural theology is not the correct answer at all. Like so many answers that are claimed to be obvious or self-evident, this one may simply appear obvious because of long established assumptions which break down when we begin to examine them. The basic function of natural theology may be something quite different from devising a watertight proof, and the fact that our traditional natural theology has been formulated in terms of logical demonstration may be due only to the operation of certain historical and cultural factors in the West. We could say that the function of natural theology was to provide a connection between our ordinary everyday discourse about the world or even our scientific discourse on the one side, and theological discourse on the other. Significantly, in Root's essay the decay of natural theology was held to have led to the divorce of theology from everyday life, or at least to have been one factor in the separation. Certainly, natural theology began from premises that were supposed to be acceptable to all rational persons. To be sure, it then proceeded by way of a deductive inference which was claimed to be a proof. But the fact that there were flaws in the reasoning does not invalidate the whole undertaking. The way of natural theology that led from the empirical world to the world of theology has still to be explored, even if one relinquishes the ambition of a proof.

But is it enough to concede that although natural theology does not prove anything, it nevertheless provides a way from the everyday to the theological? Surely the real difficulty is that a gulf yawns between empirical matters of fact and those matters of which theology speaks and that no transition can be made from one to the other, whether it is called a proof or recognized for something much weaker. We seem to have two quite different language games or universes of discourse, with no point of connection. Nevertheless, they are supposed to be talking finally about the same reality – the reality in which we ourselves participate. The connection between the world of physical nature as revealed by the sciences to the problems of theology is, I think, very complicated and too often simplistic judgments are made. Theism is of quite a different order from a scientific hypothesis. It is more like a vision or a story that tries to account for the whole. Of course, the ordinary contingent happenings of the world start us off on the quest for such a vision. As one champion of natural theology, E. L. Mascall has written, this quest 'is closely linked with the capacity for contemplative wondering'.[8] One stage on the way to an overarching vision of reality is a philosophy of nature, an attempt to integrate the findings of the separate sciences into a conception of nature as a whole. The idea of a philosophy of nature was for a long time out of favour, but the global problems we are facing today seem to be driving us toward the construction of such a philosophy. Some scientists appear to believe that a philosophy of nature is possible, though clearly, like the sciences themselves, it would be provisional. J. Bronowski writes: 'In my view, we are in a better frame of mind today to conceive a natural philosophy than at any time in the last three hundred years.'[9] It would be through a philosophy of nature rather than directly that some connection might be established between the world revealed by the sciences and theology. Perhaps the most that natural theology would do would be to show the compatibility of the modern scientific understanding of the world with religious beliefs. This would be a much more modest enterprise than the traditional proofs, but it would be significant. In any case, much of the natural theology of the past was more modest than its critics have allowed – it neither claimed the finality of proof nor turned God into an object nor did many of the other things laid to its door. One of my own teachers who wrote a book on natural theology expressed his aim in very limited terms: 'I hope to show that there is room enough for both science and religion within our universe of experience.'[10]

I think the prospects for fulfilling this aim are brighter today than they were a hundred years ago. Both in the physical and in the biological sciences the picture that has emerged seems more readily reconcilable with the theistic vision than the picture that has been displaced. The nineteenth-century world of solid atoms all strictly determined in their movements has been succeeded by a view of the universe which is certainly much more complex but also more open. Similarly, the nineteenth-century view of evolution as unremitting struggle has been succeeded by a view which stresses symbiosis and interdependence. It is well expressed by J. Z. Young: 'All of us, animals, plants and bacteria, form one closely interlocked network of ecological relationships. It is easy to elevate these facts into a pretentious scheme of the whole living world as one "organism". Yet there is a sense in which this is true. It is difficult to exaggerate our interdependence.'[11] If God is a reality, then presumably it must be possible to learn something of his character from his creation, even if this can be done only indirectly. It would be more difficult to conceive of a philosophy of nature based on nineteenth-century science and compatible with theism than of a philosophy based on the science of the twentieth century.

A further point in the revival of natural theology is the desirability of making man himself the primary datum. It is true, of course, that much of the theology of the past few decades has been heavily weighted toward the doctrine of man. But much of this has come about through the influence of existentialist philosophy, and while that philosophy has offered many acute insights into man, its fault has often been that it has not related man to his environment. Indeed, in Sartre man and nature are so opposed to each other that his philosophy cannot escape dualism. Man is to be seen in the context of the nature out of which he has arisen as (to the extent of our knowledge) its most complex and astounding product. Presumably he affords a better clue to the nature of the universe than do atoms, stars or plants. A universe which brings forth persons is surely to be understood in ways not less than personal. It is proper, however, to notice that this consideration too must be modestly put forward. Whereas Teilhard de Chardin sees the evolutionary process directed toward the production of intelligent and personal beings, so that personal being is the clue to its nature, Jacques Monod takes a directly contrary view. According to him, 'The universe was not pregnant with life or the biosphere with man. Our number came up in the Monte Carlo game ... Man at last knows he is alone in the unfeeling immensity of the universe, out of which he emerged only by chance.'[12] Is there any way of deciding between these views? Actually, both of these thinkers have tried to leap too quickly from empirical data to sweeping metaphysical conclusions. Nevertheless, it is possible that there might be an empirical check. Let us suppose that as the exploration of the universe proceeds in the future, we discover that there are many races of personal beings scattered about, then it might begin to seem probable that the world is indeed a 'vale of soul-making' (Keats) or even a 'machine for making gods' (Bergson). But if we found nothing but empty silences, that might seem to support Monod. But in fact, the evidence will always be ambiguous, and this again reminds us that natural theology can do little more than show the compatibility of the world we know with a theistic belief.

Finally, on the approach that has been outlined here, the distinction between natural theology and revealed theology is no longer a sharp one. In particular, natural theology is not seen as a kind of preliminary that has to be carried out before revealed theology begins. Rather, it is an accompaniment of revealed theology, a critical reflection that keeps coming back from the assertions of faith to what we know about the world of the senses and seeks to relate and reconcile them.

Notes

1. J. B. Cobb, *A Christian Natural Theology*, Westminster Press 1965, p. 169.

2. David Hume, *Dialogues Concerning Natural Religion*, p. 14.

3. K. Barth, *The Knowledge of God and the Service of God*, tr. J. L. M. Haire and I. Henderson, Hodder & Stoughton 1938, p. 5.

4. S. Kierkegaard, *The Concept of Dread*, p. 125.

5. J. E. Smith, 'The Permanent Truth in the Idea of Natural Religion', *The Harvard Theological Review*, vol. liv, pp. 19, 196.

6. W. Hamilton, *The New Essence of Christianity*, Association Press 1966, p. 55.

7. 'Beginning All Over Again', *Soundings*, ed. A. R. Vidler, Cambridge University Press 1962, p. 12.

8. E. L. Mascall, *The Openness of Being*, Darton, Longman & Todd 1971, p. 141.

9. J. Bronowski, *The Ascent of Man*, Book Club Associates 1973, p. 15.

10. W. Fulton, *Nature and God*, T. & T. Clarke 1927, p. 4.

11. J. Z. Young, *An Introduction to the Study of Man*, Oxford University Press 1971, pp. 640-1.

12. J. Monod, *Chance and Necessity*, tr. A. Wainhouse, Collins 1972, pp. 137, 167.

13

Creation and Environment

It has been fashionable in recent years among some theologians to make much of the claim that Western science and technology owe their origins to biblical influences, and especially to the biblical doctrine of creation. Among Protestant writers, Harvey Cox has been one of the best-known proponents of this view. The Hebrew understanding of creation, he claims, 'separates nature from God'. Nature thus becomes 'disenchanted' and can be seen in a 'matter-of-fact' way. 'This disenchantment of the natural world provides an absolute precondition for the development of natural science' and 'makes nature itself available for man's use.'[1] Among Catholic theologians, Johannes Metz has put forward similar views. He writes: 'We could say that where there is no faith in a transcendent Creator, there is also no genuine secularization of the world and no genuine availability of this world to men.' He contrasts the Greek view in which God is a kind of immanent principle of the world and in which the world therefore retains some kind of numinous quality with the Hebrew view in which the world is entirely external to the creator God and therefore itself 'godless', pure world available for man's 'active disposing'.[2]

That there is a measure of truth in the position advocated by the theologians mentioned need not be denied. But their presentation of it is oversimplified and onesided. Furthermore, some disconcerting conclusions have been drawn from the claims which Cox, Metz and the others have been so anxious to press. It would not be unfair, perhaps, to suppose that at the time when these claims were being made the theologians concerned were hoping to re-establish the relevance to the contemporary world of the somewhat faded doctrine of creation and even to gain for it some reflection of the glamour that is popularly ascribed to science and technology. But in the meanwhile, serious questions have arisen about technology itself. Even in its peaceful applications it has revealed unsuspected ambiguities. In particular, it has already had such far-reaching effects on the environment that if present trends continue unchecked, man's very survival will be threatened through depletion of resources, overpopulation, pollution of various kinds, health hazards and so on. I do not propose to dwell on dismal matters with which we are all familiar, and I do not wish either to seem unduly pessimistic about the outcome, for man has surmounted many appalling difficulties in the past, and one may hope that he will continue to do the same in the future.

But one of the ironies of the new situation is that some secular writers have taken up the theological point that technology has its charter in the Bible, and, instead of reckoning this as a credit to the Bible and an illustration of its continuing relevance, have rather blamed biblical teaching and especially the doctrine of creation as major factors that have contributed to the misuse and consequent deterioration of the environment. Thus Lynn White, in an essay entitled 'The Historical Roots of Our Ecological Crisis' states that 'especially in its Western form, Christianity is the most anthropocentric religion the world has ever seen'. He points out that in the creation stories of the Bible, everything is planned explicitly for 'man's benefit and rule', and that 'it is God's will that man exploit nature'. As far as our ecological crisis is concerned, he thinks that 'Christianity bears a huge burden of guilt'.[3] It should be noted that White is not opposed to Christianity in a general way, and he calls for the renewal of the Franciscan elements in the Christian tradition to promote a better balance.

While Cox and Metz on the one hand and White on the other differ in their evaluation of the doctrine of creation, they are in agreement about its profound effects in shaping Western man's attitude toward nature – effects which continue to this day, even if an explicit acceptance of the doctrine of creation has been abandoned by large numbers of people. I believe they are correct in thinking that our practical everyday attitudes are influenced by deeply-lying convictions of a kind that may be called theological or metaphysical or ontological, and that these may continue to exert an influence in a culture even after they have ceased to be explicit. From this it would follow, however, that any lasting change in practical attitudes, such as might help us to cope better with the problems of environment in a technological age, must be correlated with a change in our deep convictions (perhaps barely conscious) about man and his relation to the world, for it is from these convictions that our motivations and evaluations proceed.

In saying this, I am agreeing with Lynn White that the problems arising from technology's impact on the environment cannot be solved *only* through the application of more and better technology. Certainly improved technology must be part of the answer, but to suppose that the problems of technology can themselves be solved purely by technology strikes me as not only superficial but illogical as well. Herbert Marcuse seems to be much nearer the mark when he declares that we need 'a new type of man, a different type of human being, with new needs, capable of finding a qualitatively different way of life, and of constructing a qualitatively different environment'.[4] But this seems to me to be virtually a religious demand, for a new type of man emerges only where there are fundamentally new evaluations, and those in turn spring from fundamental convictions of a theological or metaphysical kind. It is at this point that the theologian may make his contribution to the problem – a contribution no more important but surely no less important than those offered by the technologists in the various fields. The theologian will make his contribution by looking again at the Christian tradition, by inquiring at what points in the development of that tradition some elements in it came to be distorted through an exaggerated emphasis while others got lost, and by asking what latent resources remain in the tradition such as might respond to the needs of the present situation by introducing correctives and promoting the new attitudes required.

I have said that the doctrine found in Metz, Gogarten, Cox and other 'secular' theologians of recent times that the biblical doctrine of creation provided the charter for Western science and technology, though partially true, is oversimplified and onesided. This becomes apparent if we attend to a few facts which just do not fit the theory. The Hebrews themselves held to a doctrine of creation for several centuries, but they developed no science worth mentioning, and technologically they were inferior to most of the neighbouring peoples in the arts both of peace and war. The science of the ancient world (though admittedly it was different in important regards from modern science) arose among the Greeks for whom God was not a transcendent creator apart from the world, but rather he belonged to the cosmos or was an immanent world-soul. Again, although all Christians have accepted the doctrine of creation, science and technology have not developed equally among them. Early Christianity did not continue the rising science of Greece. Science and technology, as we know them today, are a relatively late development in Christendom, and even so they have arisen in Western rather than Eastern Christianity. So obviously some refinements and distinctions are needed if we are to disentangle the complicated influences that have been at work.

First of all, we may take note that the Hebrew tradition is itself a complex one. It is true that if we confine our attention to the creation stories, we read there of a divine *fiat* which brings into being a world quite external to God the creator. We read also that man is the primary end of the creation, and that he is commanded to subdue the earth. While man is at the centre of both creation stories, there is a remarkable difference between them. In the older story, the creation of man comes first, and he is then provided with a suitable environment. In the later and more sophisticated story, the environment seems to be accorded more importance, for it has to be prepared in successive stages over a period of time before man appears on the scene. As we go on through the Old Testament, however, we come upon other strains which, although never dominant, qualify both the transcendent and the anthropocentric emphases of the creation stories. A notable instance is the covenant which God makes with Noah after the flood. The covenant is made not only with Noah and his descendants, that is to say, with the human race; it is also 'with every living creature ... the birds, the cattle, and every beast of the earth' (Gen. 9.10). Again, while the Psalms typically celebrate the deeds of the Lord in the history of Israel, some of them frankly delight in the natural world and recognize God there. 'The heavens declare the glory of God ...' (Ps. 19.1). One commentator says about these words, almost in rebuke, that they 'come strangely from the pen of a Hebrew writer', and he claims that this psalm and others in similar vein have introduced non-Hebrew sources.[5] But surely we should be glad that these foreign elements (if they are foreign) have found a place in the Old Testament, thereby tempering the notes of transcendence and anthropocentricity that characterize the mainstream of Hebrew thought. Above all, there is the survival of priestly religion alongside the dominant prophetic religion of the Old Testament, and this priestly religion, though overshadowed, had its indispensable role. Prophetic religion stresses history against nature and upholds the transcendence and otherness of God. Priestly religion smacks rather of the earthy, the immanent, even the pagan. A contemporary Jewish scholar, Richard Rubenstein, writes: 'The priests of ancient Israel wisely never suffered Yahweh entirely to win his war with Baal, Astarte and Anath.'[6] Some elements of an earthy, immanent naturalism remained unexpunged in Hebrew religion, and perhaps they still survive at a deep unconscious level and we see a symptom of this in the incredible attachment of the Jews to the soil of Palestine after so many centuries of exile.

No doubt the dominant model for understanding the relation of God to the world in the Old Testament is what we may call the monarchical model. God is a self-sufficient and transcendent being who by an act of will creates the world external to himself. But, obscure and fragmentary though it may be, there are at least traces of an alternative model which we may call the organic model, a view in which God and the world are not so sharply separated.

With the rise of Christianity, the Hebrew heritage was speedily fused with contributions from Greek thought. The idea of God was profoundly affected by these new influences. Since Greek thought itself contained so many strains, it is difficult to say anything briefly without being guilty of serious oversimplification. We must remember too that its influence had already been felt in Jewish thought before the emergence of Christianity. It is certainly true that in some forms of Greek philosophy, especially the Platonist tradition, God was conceived as so utterly transcendent in his unchangeable perfection that he was beyond the bounds of speech or thought. In the Stoic tradition, on the other hand, God was an immanent world principle. But both views differed sharply from the monarchical model of the dominant Hebrew tradition. In the Greek conception, God, even in his transcendence, was a kind of cosmic absolute, and such a conception leans toward the organic rather than the monarchical model. The world itself might be conceived as eternal, and its relation to God understood in terms of emanation rather than making. Apparently the great Christian thinker Origen took over both of these ideas, though of course, his teaching was deemed to be heterodox. But even if most Christian thinkers did not go as far as Origen in these matters, the general result of the impact of Greek philosophy was to forge closer bonds between God and nature. An important role came to be assigned to natural theology and, even more significantly, to natural law. It was not indeed supposed that even God was subject to a natural law more ultimate than himself, but this law was nevertheless supposed to be inherent in the divine nature and not just a product of the divine will. As Paul Tillich has indicated, the impact of Greek rationalism on the early church forced it to raise the ontological questions hidden in the personalism of Hebrew religion.[7]

As a result, there took place a qualification of the monarchical idea of God and its accompanying anthropocentricity, and this meant in turn a higher estimate of nature and world. Perhaps it was the continuance of these ideas in Eastern Christianity which ensured the different attitude to nature that has prevailed there. And there are also affinities with the non-Christian religions of the east where, if there is an idea of God, he is usually conceived in terms of immanence and an organic relationship to the world.

However, our concern is with the attitudes that have arisen in the West. Long before the secular theologians of recent years had made their claim that science and technology have their origins in the biblical doctrine of creation and certainly long before there was any talk of an ecological crisis, philosopher Michael Foster had published an important article on 'The Christian Doctrine of Creation and the Rise of Modern Natural Science'.[8] Unlike Christian theologians who have tried to eliminate or minimize those elements in Christian teaching inherited from the Greeks in favour of what they would like to consider a purely biblical and revealed faith, Foster was quite clear that a balanced Christianity needs the contributions of the Greeks as well as that of the Hebrews. Concerning the Christian doctrine of creation, he wrote: 'The Christian doctrine on this, as on all other subjects, itself includes an element derived from Greek philosophy, and any doctrine from which all Greek elements are excluded is less than Christian.'[9] He was also clearer than some of the secularizing theologians that the rise of science required not only a doctrine of creation but, more importantly, a knowledge of mathematics. Obviously, we did not get that from the Bible, and perhaps the lack of it accounts for the absence of any science among the ancient Hebrews. But Foster's analysis also shows that from a very early time there was a drive within Christendom to rid Christian doctrine of Greek influence and to return to a pure biblicism, and especially the monarchical model of God. This drive, taking with it elements of Greek rationalism and combining them with an extreme Hebrew voluntarism, made possible, so it is claimed, the harnessing of science to technology and the transformation of the environment that has come about in the modern world. The ancient Greek science, by contrast, was pursued without much regard to its practical applications.

We see the attempt to expel Greek influences already at work in the late Middle Ages. Among the Scotists, natural law arising from the nature of God gave way to the conception of a law based purely on the will of God, while the Ockhamists rejected natural theology to rely on revelation alone. These tendencies reached their most extreme pitch in Calvinism. The sovereignty of God is the key stone of the Calvinist system and the monarchical model of God receives uncompromising expression. Everything happens by the divine will. The world itself is a product of the free act of God's will, and he might equally well have refrained from creating, so that in no sense is the world organic to God. There is a continuous line from Calvin to our time, to Barth, Gogarten, Brunner and finally the secular theologians who have pushed Barthianism to its conclusions. It was Brunner who gave one of the most extreme statements of that utter devaluation and profanation of the world which seems to follow from regarding it as a more or less arbitrary product of will. He put the statement in the form of two equations:

God minus the world = God
The world minus God = Zero

This may well be pure biblical theology, purged of all Greek influences. But it seems to me an acosmism, and possibly also expresses an unconscious will to power.

Concerning this doctrine that the world is the product of divine will and nothing in itself, Ludwig Feuerbach wrote: 'In the inmost depth of thy soul, thou wouldest rather there were no world, for where the world is, there is matter, and where there is matter, there is weight and resistance, space and time, limitation and necessity. Nevertheless, there *is* a world and there *is* matter. How dost thou escape from the dilemma of this contradiction? How dost thou expel the world from thy consciousness, that it may not disturb thee in the beatitude of the unlimited soul? Only by making the world itself a product of will, by giving it an arbitrary existence, always hovering between existence and non existence, always awaiting its annihilation.'[10] And if it is this acosmic or anti-cosmic attitude that has led us to exploit with recklessness and indifference the resources of the world and to subject science increasingly to the service of acquisitive ends, then White's accusation would stand – that Christianity, or at least one influential form of it, bears a huge burden of guilt for some of our present troubles.

The argument I have outlined might be compared at some points to the famous thesis of Weber connecting the rise of capitalism with Protestantism. Reinhold Niebuhr draws attention to a point of contact when he claims that 'the spirit of capitalism is the spirit of an irreverent exploitation of nature, conceived as a treasure house of riches which will guarantee everything which might be regarded as the good life'.[11] It might be added that in this particular regard, there seems to be no difference between capitalism and socialism.

Of course, it must be acknowledged that even in Western Christendom there have been other ways of understanding the meaning of the creation and these have conduced to better practical attitudes toward the natural world. I have mentioned already that White commends St Francis for his sense of affinity with the whole creation. A later example is Luther, who believed that because the world is God's creation, even the meanest objects in nature have some interest and dignity. To mention his own homely example, he says that God is present in a louse's belly. One might contrast this with the obvious contempt shown by Aristophanes for the alleged investigations by Socrates into such humble creatures as fleas and gnats: 'Thrice happy Socrates! It would not be difficult to succeed in a law suit, knowing so much about a gnat's guts!'[12] Karl Jaspers is a modern philosopher who has taken up the view that the Christian doctrine of creation has conferred upon everyday objects an interest which they did not have for the Greeks. But while there are some evidences to support this view, I fear that for the majority the doctrine of voluntary creation has led to depriving the world of intrinsic interest and to causing it to be seen primarily in a utilitarian way as an object for exploitation – a way in which the Greeks did not see it. Still another idea that has sometimes gained currency is that of stewardship. Belief in a creator, it is said, implies that the world is not placed at man's absolute disposal, for he is accountable to God. Unfortunately, however, the notion of a transcendent God who hands over the world to men can easily develop into a kind of deism in which this distant God who started things off has pretty well bowed himself out of the picture, and then there is not much validity left to the notion of stewardship. I think this has happened in some versions of secular theology which stress man's coming of age and his taking over the world – in Gogarten, for example.

Nevertheless, there are other possible ways of using the stewardship idea. Hugh Montefiore, one of the few Christian writers who has tried to face the theological issues raised by the ecological crisis, has rightly seen that 'what is needed is ... a redirection of inward attitudes'[13] and he believes that this might be achieved through a better awareness of our responsibility as stewards of creation. I believe that the idea of responsibility is of the greatest importance in this connection, but I have some doubt whether it can be adequately supported by a doctrine of stewardship, for in such a doctrine, it seems to me, the world is still considered as a piece of property and primarily from an anthropocentric viewpoint. Perhaps a better model is to be found in Heidegger's idea of man as the shepherd of being.

Least hopeful of all is still another attitude which sometimes clothes itself with religious phraseology – a kind of nostalgic, romantic, sentimental conservationism. This attitude is frequently hypocritical as well, as when Americans and Europeans who enjoy the affluence of technological civilization urge upon Africans or Asians the duty of keeping their forest lands in the unspoiled state in which God has created them. If this means a continuing marginal existence for the peoples of these lands except for the occasional crumbs that might fall from the picnic tables of vacationing tourists from the West, then the plea is likely to go unheard, and deservedly so.

In all parts of the world, science and technology will – if no unforeseen calamities occur – continue to advance, and so will the industrialization and urbanization that accompany them. I do not think we would have it otherwise, and even if we did, I do not think we could reverse the process, for these things have acquired a certain momentum. But it becomes increasingly important to control the process, to set limits to the exploitation of nature, to become sensitive to those points at which, in damaging his environment, man is also damaging himself, not only physically but mentally and spiritually as well. With technology as with so much else, we have still to learn the truth of that ancient piece of moral wisdom, *meden agan*, nothing too much.

We have, however, seen reason to believe that we shall not learn this truth unless there takes place a very profound change in our basic beliefs, so far as these shape our attitude toward the physical environment. As far as Christian theology is concerned, my thesis is that we need to move away somewhat from the monarchical model of God toward the organic model. The monarchical model is deeply entrenched in much traditional Christian language, including the language of liturgy, it is widespread in popular theology, and it is encouraged by those forms of biblical theology which try to exclude all philosophical influences and to found themselves on revelation alone. On the other hand, as the crisis in theism during recent years has shown, the monarchical model of God has become increasingly less credible to many people today. The organic model, by contrast, has gained ground in philosophical theology, and I think most philosophical versions of theism today, even those that proceed from very different schools, tend to the organic type. They seek to recover what was of value in the non-Hebraic elements of the Christian tradition, and especially the affinity between God and the world in opposition to the sharp separation of them. Of course, there is no attempt to isolate these elements. Rather, they have to be integrated into the mainstream of Christian thought on God, but when this happens, they profoundly qualify the monarchical model of God in the direction of the organic model.

If we go back to Brunner's two equations, mentioned earlier, organic theism has no difficulty in accepting one of them, namely, that without God, without the creative Spirit, the world ceases to exist. But it denies the other equation, namely, that without the world God is still God, as if quite unaffected in his majesty and self-sufficiency. For if God is indeed loving and creative Spirit, his creation cannot be a mere arbitrary product of will, so that he might either have created or not have created, or so that he would be unaffected by the absence of a creation. This does not mean that he *needs* to create, but that it is his nature *as God* to create. There is an analogy with natural law, which does not *bind* God but *flows from* him.

But what chiefly concerns us here is that the organic model of theism and of creation allows to the world a dignity and mystery that it could hardly have on the monarchical model. This means in turn that the world cannot be conceived from a narrowly anthropocentric viewpoint, as if it were provided solely for man's exploitation. If, as Christian theologians rethink the meaning of theism, the organic model becomes more influential and is allowed to qualify the monarchical model, then I think this will promote better attitudes toward the physical environment and will perhaps in some measure atone for excesses which in the past may have been encouraged by the exclusive dominance of the monarchical view. We shall learn better to relate to the world not only in manipulation but in appreciation. Regarding these two ways, manipulation and appreciation, Abraham Heschel has said: 'In the first way, man sees in what surrounds him things to be handled, forces to be managed, objects to be put to use. In the second way, he sees in what surrounds him things to be acknowledged, understood, valued or admired.'[14] Clearly we have to relate in both ways, and we have to search for the right balance between them.

But a final question remains to trouble us. Is it not too late for this theological rethinking to take place? I do not mean too late in the sense that the environmental crisis is so pressing that there is no time left for the reshaping of our attitudes before the day of reckoning arrives, though that, unfortunately, may be true. I mean rather that it may be too late for any theological model to have an influence because of the decline of theology and the secularization of our outlook. Is either a monarchical or an organic model of God's relation to the world of any relevance when many people have come to think of God himself as a projection of man? Possibly two answers can be given to this question. The first is that the theological understanding of these matters has still a considerable influence, perhaps more than is commonly supposed, and that in any case the theologian does have a duty to address himself to the problems vexing our time and to make what contribution he can from his resources. The second answer is that the position of the humanist may not be so very different, and that he too has to choose between different models. I think it would be true to say that there is a monarchical type of humanism, and there is an organic type. The monarchical type makes man the measure of all things and sets the world over against him as his object. This is the type which would maintain that the problem of technology and environment must be seen as itself a purely technological problem, or a series of such problems. The organic type of humanism is much more aware of man's affinity with the world and recognizes that he is part of something much bigger than he has yet understood and to which he owes a responsibility as yet undefined.

Since the theist believes that man is made in the image of God, then an organic type of theism and an organic type of humanism have some kinship. On the basis of this kinship, adherents of these different beliefs can work together to build up a better and more responsible attitude toward the environment, and so play some part in enabling man to survive the dangers which threaten him.[15]

Notes

1. H. G. Cox, *The Secular City*, Macmillan 1965, pp. 22-3.
2. J. Metz, *Theology of the World*, tr. W. Glen-Doepel, Herder & Herder 1969, pp. 65-6.
3. L. White, 'The Historical Roots of Our Ecological Crisis', *The Environmental Handbook*, ed. G. de Bell, Ballantine 1970, pp. 20-3.
4. H. Marcuse, 'Marxism and the New Humanity', *Marxism and Radical Religion*, ed. J. C. Raines and T. Dean, Temple University Press 1970, p. 7.
5. W. O. E. Oesterley, *The Psalms*, SPCK 1939, vol. i, p. 168.
6. R. Rubenstein, *After Auschwitz*, Bobbs-Merrill 1966, p. 124.
7. *Biblical Religion and the Search for Ultimate Reality*, Chicago University Press 1955, pp. 5ff.
8. In *Mind*, vol. xliii, 1934. Reprinted in *Creation: the Impact of an Idea*, ed. D. O'Connor and F. Oakley, Scribner 1969, pp. 29ff.
9. Loc. cit., p. 52.
10. L. Feuerbach, *The Essence of Christianity*, tr. George Eliot, Harper & Row 1957, p. 110.
11. Reinhold Niebuhr, *The Nature and Destiny of Man*, Nisbet 1941, vol. i, p. 21.
12. *The Clouds*, ll. 167-8.
13. H. Montefiore, *Can Man Survive?*, Collins 1970, p. 53.
14. A. J. Heschel, *Who Is Man?*, Stanford University Press 1965, p. 82.
15. This was my Inaugural Lecture after being installed as Lady Margaret Professor of Divinity in Oxford University, 1970.

PART THREE

Some Representative Modern Thinkers

14

Schleiermacher Reconsidered

The fortunes of Friedrich Daniel Ernst Schleiermacher (1768-1834) have been subject to many ups and downs since he first burst upon the theological world at the end of the eighteenth century. His message came at the right time to ensure that it got a sympathetic reception. It was the flood tide of the Romantic Movement, and in many fields men were awakening to the fact that there are in human existence dimensions of experience that tend to be under-valued and even ignored by a too narrow rationalism. It was Schleiermacher's destiny to bring about this awakening in the field of theology. Faith has foundations that are broader and deeper than the propositions in which we try to capture it. Whether the pro-positions in question are the orthodox creeds and confessions of faith or the abstract formulations of rationalistic philosophers, they are tenuous and even ghostly entities compared with the rich concrete experiences in which faith has its origin. Faith is an atti-tude of the whole man, not merely an assent of the mind. That Schleiermacher infused new life and interest into theology by taking actual experience as its primary datum rather than the propositions of either the Bible or natural theology, and that it could never be quite the same again, perhaps no one will deny. Whether or not one agrees with modern liberal theology, Schleiermacher must be acknowledged as the father of it, and all its major thrusts – experi-ential, humanistic, immanentist and so on are already to be found in his thought.

However, if Schleiermacher started off with the spirit of his time, he soon ran into criticism. Only a few years after the publi-cation of his famous *Reden*,[1] he was under fire from Hegel, who made some damaging comments and raised some questions that are still to the point. Hegel has been talking about 'the systematic development of truth in scientific form' and he contrasts this with another view which, he says, 'makes great pretensions and has gained widespread acceptance and conviction at the present time'. On this other view, the Absolute 'is not to be grasped in conceptual form, but felt, intuited; it is not its conception, but the feeling of it and intuition of it that are to have the say and find expression'. Hegel goes on to make the criticism that this exaltation of feeling blurs the distinctions which thought has so laboriously provided. And the question which he raises is whether we do not see here a turning away from the hard question of truth and falsity, which is, after all, the concern of the philosopher, in order to luxuriate in congenial experiences. 'What the Romantic approach wants from philosophy is not so much insight as edification.'[2]

But if Schleiermacher had his critics, he also had his admirers, and there were a great many of them in the later part of the nineteenth century and the early part of the twentieth. Among them was the philosopher Dilthey who wrote a *Leben Schleiermachers* and was specially interested in his work on hermeneutics. The Ritschlian school of theology, though it stressed action and willing rather than feeling, owed much to Schleiermacher and continued his anti-speculative bias. The kind of piety evident in the writings of Wilhelm Herrmann, Ritschlian teacher of both Barth and Bultmann, is surely close to the spirit of Schleiermacher. But perhaps the man who stood most directly in the succession was Rudolf Otto. He credits Schleiermacher with nothing less than the 'rediscovery of religion',[3] while his own great work, *The Idea of the Holy*, seems to me to take up where Schleiermacher left off and to bring new and penetrating insights into the mainsprings of religion.

Schleiermacher's fortunes, however, slipped once more. The theological renascence led by Karl Barth set its face against liberal Protestantism with its interest in religious experience. Religion itself was condemned as a work of man, and over against its subjective ponderings was set the objective truth of the divine Word. In a long essay on Schleiermacher, Barth does in fact criticize his theology for its subjectivism; it is a theology in which 'Christian pious self-awareness contemplates and describes itself'.[4] Yet in the same essay Barth generously acknowledges that 'the first place in the history of the theology of modern times belongs and always will belong to Schleiermacher, and he has no rival'. Barth has further acknowledged that it is by no means certain that we have got beyond Schleiermacher, and we may need to hear him again.

Perhaps the possibility to which Barth alluded is already upon us. Now that the Barthian period is itself in decline, there are signs that Schleiermacher's stock may be rising once more. Of course, it is hard to be sure about this. Part of the reawakened interest, such as the symposium which appeared in *The Scottish Journal of Theology*,[5] is due simply to the fact that the theological world has commemorated the two hundredth anniversary of the birth of this 'Church Father' of modern times. But there are symptoms that the renewed interest is not due only to pious acts of commemoration, and the purpose of the present 'reconsideration' is to ask what Schleiermacher may have to say that speaks to our contemporary problems in theology.

Obviously there is no simple answer to this question. Schleiermacher himself is a very complex figure, with many sides to his thought. It is no doubt true that he represents the Romantic Movement and that he laid great stress on feeling and inward experience, but this is only part of the truth about him, and even this is a very complex part of the truth, for what, after all, was the Romantic Movement and what is 'feeling', in Schleiermacher's sense? The rest of the truth is that Schleiermacher also had a metaphysic, though it was somewhat obscure; that he had a fairly well defined ethic; that he was sensitive in his theologizing to the claims of culture; and that he did pioneering work in hermeneutics.

Because there are these many strands in Schleiermacher's work, one would need to consider how each of them relates to the theological problematic of today, and whether any or all of them have contributions to make, or again, whether one can accept some things from Schleiermacher and reject others, or whether all the elements in his teaching are too closely bound together for particular insights to be separated out. His metaphysic (for undoubtedly he had a metaphysic, and perhaps everyone has at least an inchoate metaphysic) would not be likely to win wide acceptance nowadays. H. R. Mackintosh wrote of Schleiermacher's 'attenuated creed of idealistic monism',[6] and this is not an unfair description of the somewhat vague theism of one who was an admirer of Spinoza. Yet, in the recent debates about God, there has been a swing away from transcendence toward immanence, and to this extent Schleiermacher is in accord with our contemporary trend. His ethics are not likely to have much appeal today, being too Platonist in their orientation for an age as much preoccupied as ours is with the secular and the material. On the other hand, his awareness of the need to relate theology to culture is something that we need to reckon with as we move out of the Barthian period. Gerhard Spiegler, author of a book on Schleiermacher's cultural theology, remarks: 'We have rejected his problem solution, but his problem formulation is still ours. We are thus still truly his heirs.'[7] The relevance of Schleiermacher to the revived interest in hermeneutics is still more obvious, and Bultmann has paid tribute to his insights in this field.[8] Already Schleiermacher had made it clear that interpretation is not accomplished by applying only scientific rules ('grammatical interpretation') but implies a creative act on the part of the interpreter ('psychological interpretation'). In a way, however, this simply seems to say that no amount of hermeneutical study will ensure fruitful interpretation unless the interpreter has, in addition, a touch of genius.

One could spend a very long time investigating in detail each of these facets of Schleiermacher's thought, and their relation to where we stand in our several theological endeavours today. But I propose to go to the very centre of Schleiermacher's theology, to his much criticized 'Romanticism' and his stress on feeling and religion – all of them unpopular words in our time. Does this central area of Schleiermacher's thought have anything to say to us?

First of all, we have to face a difficult question. There can be little doubt that in much contemporary theology there is a powerful swing toward subjectivism. We live in a time when the intellectual difficulties of Christian faith have become very great. How do we talk intelligibly of God? What sense does it make to believe in Jesus Christ as the God-man? It is tempting in the face of these difficulties to reduce God to an idea in the mind or a norm of conduct, and to think of Christ as simply the paradigm of humanity. Could it be then that the renewed interest in Schleiermacher has come about through this subjectivizing tendency, and that some contemporary theologians are looking to him for an expression of Christianity so absorbed into the human consciousness that it becomes invulnerable to questions of fact, including ontological fact, if that is a permissible expression? At this point, it is salutary to remember that it was only a short road from Schleiermacher to Feuerbach, from talking about the God of experience to talking about the experience of God.

I quoted above the early objections which Hegel had raised against Schleiermacher, to the effect that philosophy was being asked to supply edification rather than seek truth. In our own time, voices are sometimes raised too, insisting that the *truth* of Christianity is a more fundamental problem than that of its relevance or its therapeutic effects. Donald MacKinnon, for instance, declares himself mistrustful of 'much that calls itself radical theology' on the ground that it does not face (and may even deliberately eliminate) the really radical questions of truth and falsity, but contents itself with dwelling on the experience of the Christian, 'suggesting that, in the end, even as the proper study of mankind is man, so Christian man finds his appropriate study in himself'.[9]

Although for my own part I favour the anthropological approach to theology, here criticized by MacKinnon, I agree with this particular criticism, and indeed I always have resisted those forms of experiential, existential and pragmatic theology which have tried to by-pass the ontological questions and which really end up by reducing theology to anthropology and Christology to Jesusology.

But I do believe that Schleiermacher can help us with this very problem of the truth of Christianity. Anyone in search of a subjectivized theology will not really get help from Schleiermacher, unless he is gravely misunderstood. The fact that Schleiermacher's theology has all the other characteristics mentioned above as well as what he says about feeling, shows that he was no mere subjectivizer or sentimentalist. But even when we confine our attention to his central ideas on religion and feeling, we can see these as having a significance that is far from subjective.

The problem is to determine the relation of feeling and thought in Schleiermacher. In his view, these are not sharply separated. Neither are they opposed, nor is thought swallowed up in feeling, so that the question of truth and falsity is abrogated. What he calls 'feeling' (*Gefühl*), he can also call 'immediate self-consciousness' (*Selbstbewusstsein*) and these are close to 'intuition' (*Anschauung*). In his early writing, he equates true religion with 'the sense and taste for the infinite', which is another related expression.[10] These various ways of speaking make it clear that for Schleiermacher feeling has definitely a cognitive element. Now this kind of feeling or intuition which is directed toward the infinite is not anything opposed to thought, but might be described as a leap beyond our thinking of particulars in an attempt to know things in their wholeness or totality. It is a kind of mystical vision, arising from a drive toward the whole or the infinite, a drive that is already within us and motivating our thought. According to Schleiermacher, 'true science is complete vision'.[11] The feeling of which he speaks is the leap by which our thinking seeks to transcend all particular objects of thought to reach toward that all-embracing unity which is reflected in all particulars and toward which man is already directed in the depth of his being. The essential unity of feeling and thought is expressed in a sentence reported to have been uttered by Schleiermacher on his deathbed, and noted down by his wife: 'I must think the deepest speculative thoughts, and they are to me completely at one with the most intimate religious sensations.'[12]

Whereas Schleiermacher talks in terms of feeling and of the 'sense and taste' that draws the human mind toward the infinite, we can bring his account of the matter into comparison with the intellectualist account given in the Aristotelian and Thomist tradition, and we find a remarkable parallel, even a convergence. Man's drive toward transcendence of any given state of himself was seen by Aristotle as the drive toward knowledge. 'All men by nature desire to know.'[13] In our time, a representative of transcendental Thomism, Bernard Lonergan, has finely expressed the matter thus: 'The specific drive of our nature is to understand, and, indeed, to understand everything, neither confusing the trees with the forest nor content to contemplate the forest without seeing all the trees. For the spirit of inquiry within us never calls a halt, never can be satisfied, until our intellects, united to God as body to soul, know *ipsum intelligere* and through that vision, though then knowing aught else is a trifle, contemplate the universe as well.'[14] Here the stress is explicitly on knowing and understanding, but the end is the same as that sought by Schleiermacher's 'sense and taste for the infinite'. There is a significant sentence in the book of Lonergan just quoted, in which he sets side by side the questions of the 'heart' and the 'mind' as exemplified by two great Christian thinkers: 'For Augustine, our *hearts* are restless until they rest in God; for Aquinas, not our hearts, but first and most our *minds*, are restless until they rest in seeing him.'[15]

Schleiermacher admittedly stressed feeling as the essence of religion, but he saw feeling (or intuition) as reaching in the same direction as thought, and then as completing thought's quest for 'complete vision' when one comes to the limits of thought. The Thomist stresses thought, but he does not believe that unaided human thought can attain to the vision which it seeks. In Gilson's words, 'the human intellect naturally desires an end that it cannot attain by merely natural means'.[16] In the case of both Schleiermacher and the Thomists, the human mind must break out (in obedience to its own inmost drive) beyond the bounds of everyday understanding toward the infinite, the other that for ever escapes the categories of our thought. Yet in both cases it is believed that the leap is made possible by an act of vision or intuition, granted by the other himself, for it is he who has implanted the drive toward himself in us.

But how can it be claimed that there is a vision or intuition of God, if we are also saying that he transcends the reach of our thought? What is this leap that is alleged to carry us beyond the limits of everyday understanding? I think that Schleiermacher is again helpful at this point, for he well understood the indirect and oblique character of our knowledge of God and our language about him. 'Dogmas', he wrote, 'are a knowledge about feeling, and in no way an immediate knowledge about the operations of the universe that give rise to the feelings.'[17] Again, 'Christian doctrines are accounts of the Christian religious affections set forth in speech.'[18] At first sight, these look like very subjectivizing statements. But are they really so? The feelings or affections are not themselves the final subject-matter of dogma – they point beyond themselves to God, to what Schleiermacher in his early work somewhat pantheistically calls 'operations of the universe'. The denial that we have *immediate* knowledge of these operations does not exclude – on the contrary, it implies – that we have *indirect* knowledge of them through the feelings they induce. It seems to me that this part of Schleiermacher's teaching provides an answer to Hegel's objection that, in Schleiermacher's theology, the Absolute 'is not to be grasped in conceptual form, but felt, intuited'. Unless one believes in the omnicompetence of reason, the Absolute cannot be grasped in conceptual form – if it could, it may be doubted if it would still be the Absolute. Schleiermacher is surely correct in making a more modest claim – that we see God only in a reflection, even in a riddle.

What Schleiermacher does not make sufficiently clear is the critical role of thought as over against feeling or intuition. It is not that he lacked the capacity for critical, analytical thought. For instance, his critique of the traditional Chalcedonian language of 'nature' and 'person' is quite brilliantly done, though finally I think it fails through a misunderstanding of the term *physis*.[19] But this is criticism of a particular doctrinal formulation, and it is a more radical kind of criticism that seems to be required and that Schleiermacher fails to offer. Even if we agree with him that an intuition or a mystical vision or something of the kind is necessary if the drive within thought itself is to be completed and we are to catch a glimpse of the whole, we must always ask whether the alleged intuition (which might almost be called a revelation) does really complete thought, or whether it is just a prejudice that we bring along when thought gives out. Clearly, thought cannot prove what goes beyond thought. Faith, just because it is faith, is vulnerable and not demonstrable. Yet one can at least consider whether the beliefs which the act of faith implies are more probable or less probable. Faith, if it is to escape the danger of becoming mere superstition, must be tested in every way by thought. Is this special experience or special dimension of experience from which faith arises consistent with our everyday experience of the world and our rational interpretation of it?

The reader may have noted that I have hardly used the expression, 'feeling of absolute dependence'. This famous phrase is used by Schleiermacher in his greatest work to designate the essence of religion,[20] but I have preferred to use such earlier and more affirmative expressions as 'sense and taste for the infinite'. The two expressions are actually complementary, but I have chosen the more affirmative one because I doubt whether the idea of 'absolute dependence' can have for us the force that it had even as recently as Schleiermacher's time. It is an almost ironic coincidence that in 1968, the bicentenary of Schleiermacher's birth and the occasion for the commemoration of his work, men for the first time broke out of the earth's field of gravity, circled the moon a quarter of a million miles out in space, and safely returned to earth. This spectacular event merely climaxed a process that has been going on since Schleiermacher's time. Man has more and more extended his control over the universe and is less and less at the mercy of the forces of nature. I do not think I am being presumptuous in saying that it is very hard for people today to experience a feeling of 'absolute dependence'. Contemporary theology is more likely to stress the responsibility of man and his vocation to be a co-worker with God in building the creation.

However, there is always the danger that this teaching gets distorted into the false belief that man is his own God or Absolute. It is just here that Schleiermacher's thought has its continuing relevance. In spite of the expression 'absolute dependence', his exposition of the idea by no means reduces man to a merely passive or servile role. The essence of the feeling of which he writes is expressed in an inimitable German polysyllable, *Sichselbstnichtsogesetzthaben*, which means that area of life which one has not disposed for oneself. The idea is not very different from what the existentialists have called the 'facticity' of existence. It also embraces the mystery of existence, its givenness and, I would add, its giftedness. It is man's awareness of the ultimate context of his existence.

'It is he that made us and not we ourselves' (Ps. 100.3). It is the *sensus numinis*. I have said that it is hard for man today to know the feeling of absolute dependence, but that is all the more reason why we should seek to experience the *sensus numinis* in a way appropriate to our time. Apart from the overworked and over-popularized expression, 'feeling of absolute dependence', Schleier-macher has many imporant things to tell us about the religious consciousness, that dimension of human existence in which we find ourselves related to ultimate and holy Being, and without which our humanity would be seriously diminished.

In our discussion of the *sensus numinis* and of absolute depend-ence, we have talked of man, meaning the human race in its solidarity, rather than of the experiences of individuals. This is entirely in line with Schleiermacher's thinking, for whatever roots it may ultimately have had in pietism, it is remarkably free from individualism. R. Richard Niebuhr, comparing Schleiermacher's description of religious experience with the descriptions offered by William James, is surely correct in judging the latter to be much more of an individualist than Schleiermacher. 'The American psychologist and philosopher has nothing of Schleiermacher's sense for social and historical relations', he writes.[21] This is surely a further point that would commend Schleiermacher to our attentions, for much of the criticism of the kind of mystical piety which he rep-resents has been directed against its alleged individualism. Can we learn something from Schleiermacher about the meaning of corporate religion?

I am suggesting that Schleiermacher may be able to some extent to do for us what Otto claims he did in his own time – help toward a rediscovery of religion. If the word 'religion' has become un-fashionable among some people today (the cultured despisers?) may this not be because those features which Schleiermacher stressed have been neglected – the concurrence of feeling and thought, the sense of mystery and the reverence which it generates, the sociality of human life in its ultimate context? If a 'religionless' Christianity wants to get rid of these things, then I would say that it is not only a sadly diminished Christianity but even a 'gutless' Christianity, for it lacks that 'visceral feel' by which we become aware that nothing less than the whole man is claimed by God in Christ.

Notes

1. *On Religion: Speeches to its Cultured Despisers*, tr. J. Oman, new edition, Harper & Row 1958.

2. G. W. F. Hegel, *The Phenomenology of Mind*, tr. J. B. Baillie, rev. edition, Allen & Unwin 1931, p. 70ff. Hegel, in accordance with his usual practice, does not actually name those he is criticizing. He probably had in mind not only Schleiermacher but others, such as Schlegel and Jacobi.

3. R. Otto, 'How Schleiermacher Rediscovered the Sensus Numinis', *Religious Essays*, tr. B. Lunn, Oxford University Press 1931, pp. 68-77.

4. K. Barth, *Protestant Thought*, tr. B. Cozens, Harper & Row 1959, p. 338.

5. Vol. xxi, 1968.

6. H. R. Mackintosh, *Types of Modern Theology*, Nisbet 1937, p. 100.

7. G. Spiegler, *The Eternal Covenant*, Harper & Row 1967, p. 187.

8. R. Bultmann, *Essays*, tr. J. C. G. Greig, SCM Press 1955, pp. 237ff.

9. D. M. MacKinnon, *Borderlands of Theology*, Lutterworth 1968, p. 31.

10. See F. Schleiermacher, *The Christian Faith*, tr. H. R. Mackintosh and J. S. Stewart, T. & T. Clark 1928, pp. 5ff. and *On Religion*, p. 39.

11. *On Religion*, ibid.

12. Quoted by Spiegler, op. cit., p 128

13. Aristotle, *Metaphysics*, Book A, 1.

14. B. Lonergan, *Verbum*, Darton, Longman & Todd 1968, p. 53.

15. Op. cit., p. 90.

16. E. Gilson, *The Spirit of Thomism*, Kenedy 1964, p. 57.

17. *On Religion*, p. 61.

18. *The Christian Faith*, p. 76.

19. Op. cit., p. 392.

20. Op. cit., pp. 12ff.

21. R. R. Niebuhr, *Schleiermacher on Christ and Religion*, Scribner 1964, p. 142.

15

Campbell on Atonement

John McLeod Campbell was a rather isolated figure in the development of modern theology, not easily related to any school or
movement and (though not through any choice of his own) working
for most of his life outside the ecclesiastical institution. But his
influence is growing rather than diminishing. He was a man ahead
of his times, and his ideas are relevant to current theological discussions. As we look back to the nineteenth century, it would be
difficult to dissent from the judgment of an historian of British
religious thought in that period, B. M. G. Reardon, that 'Campbell's
is the outstanding name in Scottish theology during the last
century'.[1]

Campbell is best known for the famous (or infamous) heresy
trial in which he was the central figure, but this essay
will be mainly concerned with his mature theology which did not
come to expression until a quarter of a century after the trial. But
it may be as well to begin by recalling in the barest outline the
events of his life. He was born in 1800, a son of the manse, and in
due course went to study for the ministry in the University of
Glasgow. He was inducted to the parish of Rhu on the Gare Loch,
and was a faithful pastor there for some five years. But his sermons
did not please everyone. Complaint was made to the ecclesiastical
authorities that his teachings were contrary to the Confession
of Faith accepted by the Church of Scotland. He was quoted as
having said, 'God loves every child of Adam with a love the measure
of which is the agony of his own Son', and, 'The person who knows
that Christ died for every human being is the person who is in a
condition to go forth to every human being and say, "Let there
be peace between you and God!"'[2] Such sentences clearly taught
an atonement or reconciliation available for all men, and contradicted the doctrine of the Confession that Christ died for the

elect only. The case came to the General Assembly of the Church in 1831, and after an all-night sitting, by a majority of 119 to 6, the Assembly found Campbell guilty of the charges and sentenced him to the heaviest penalty in its power – deposition from the sacred ministry.

This blow at the outset of a promising career might have crushed or at least embittered many a man. But not Campbell. For many years he laboured as pastor of an independent congregation in Glasgow. During these years his theology took shape, for he had become convinced that one could only assert the universality of the atonement if one rethought the whole doctrine and broke out of the categories in which it had been for so long expressed. The result was *The Nature of the Atonement*,[3] first published in 1856, and described by R. S. Franks as 'the most systematic and masterly book on the work of Christ produced by a British theologian in the nineteenth century'.[4] Campbell was recognized by the award of an honorary doctorate in divinity from his old university in 1868, but it was only after his death in 1872 that his work made its full impact on the church and was one factor in leading eventually to the modification of the form of assent to the Confession of Faith.

Let us return then to *The Nature of the Atonement*. On a cursory acquaintance, it is not a prepossessing book. The author's style is somewhat inelegant; he writes in long involved sentences which take time to disentangle. Again, there is some wearisome controversy with nineteenth-century Calvinist divines whose work and very names are now virtually forgotten. But what is most likely to turn away the modern reader is Campbell's use of the Bible in a way which is not possible for those who have been schooled in critical methods. The four gospels are quoted indiscriminately, and Campbell dwells especially on John's gospel which he accepts as accurately relating the words and deeds of Jesus. He sometimes ventures, in a way that few contemporary New Testament scholars would do, to reconstruct the intentions and inward life of Jesus on the basis of some reported utterances, such as the Lukan sayings from the cross, 'Father, forgive them for they know not what they do', and 'Into thy hands I commend my spirit' (Luke 23.34 and 46).

However, we have simply to accept that there are these less happy features in Campbell's work, and to bear in mind its nineteenth-century date. The merits of his work far outweigh the defects and give to it its continuing interest.

Confining ourselves still to the consideration of Campbell's general approach to theology, we may note four characteristic features.

First and most important, there is his consistent use of personal categories, as opposed to the legal categories in which the atonement had been traditionally discussed. 'We have here to do with *persons*,' he declares, 'the Father of spirits and his offspring. *These are to each other more than all things and all circumstances*.'[5] The use of the expression 'Father of spirits' for God in this quotation is very typical of Campbell. God is to be understood primarily under the image of father rather than that of judge. In his early days Campbell had rejected the idea of a limited atonement, but by now he had come to reject the whole underlying theology of atonement on which that idea of a limitation had rested. That Christ died for the elect only, was an idea that could enjoy whatever plausibility it acquired only if the atonement were expressed in legal categories, with God as judge, Christ as condemned and bearing the punishment due to mankind, as their substitute and with their sin imputed to him, while they are declared just through the imputation to them of Christ's righteousness. All of this is impersonal, and the relations among the parties concerned are impersonal. They are legal fictions. Moreover, when God is seen in the image of judge, the whole question is prejudiced, for God's justice is made primary and his love secondary. But if we begin with the idea of God as 'Father of spirits' and with the relation of Christ and indeed of all men ('his offspring') as filial, not only the idea of a limited atonement but the whole theology of penal substitution falls to the ground.

A second characteristic of Campbell's theology is his emphasis on what he calls the 'prospective' aspect of the atonement. Traditional theology had dwelt mainly on the retrospective aspect, on what Christ had done once for all, and on the benefits thereby procured for mankind. But Campbell makes the point that the aim of atonement is not just to deliver men from misery but to bring them to righteousness.[6] This can only happen if justification is not the legal imputation of righteousness but the beginning of a new life. This in turn is made possible by a participation in the life of Christ – in this connection, Campbell frequently alludes to the Johannine metaphor of the vine and its branches (John 15.1ff.). But the external categories employed in legal theories of the atonement do not allow for personal participation in the life of Christ. In particular, penal theories expressly exclude any possibility of sharing in the *suffering* of Christ, and since a sharing in Christ's suffering is important in Campbell's view, the impossibility of this on penal theories must be accounted one of his major reasons for rejecting them.[7]

A third point, obviously connected with the two already made, is Campbell's keen awareness of the true humanity of Christ. Theologians, he claims, have too often visualized the work of Christ as simply following out a prearranged plan. They have missed 'its character as a natural progress and development'.[8] Although Campbell considers the atonement both as the incarnate Christ's work on behalf of the Father toward us, and as his work in his humanity on our behalf toward the Father, it seems to be in the second of these ways of looking at it that he takes most interest. 'It is', he says, 'in the dealing of the Son with the Father on our behalf that the full light of the atonement shines on us.'[9] Christ's solidarity with the whole human race is stressed in many ways, though we shall see that the nature of this solidarity is one of the most difficult problems of Campbell's theology. Christology and anthropology are linked in his contention that there is a coincidence between Christ and conscience. It is conscience as well as the gospel that points us to the need for atonement, and atonement is understood because sin is seen to contradict the ideal of human excellence as well as the law of God. Yet we do not truly know 'what it is to be a man, what we possess in humanity', until we have seen humanity in Christ.[10]

My last general point about Campbell's way of theologizing is to draw attention to its intensely existential character. He could not be content with any *theory* of the atonement, however ingenious, because, as he says, the question of the atonement is nothing less than the question of Christianity itself.[11] He could also say: 'The answer to the question, "What am I to think? What am I to believe?" becomes one with the answer to the question, "What am I called to be?" '[12]

Let us now go to the heart of Campbell's theology of atonement. It had been suggested to him by some sentences of Jonathan Edwards, to the effect that the 'infinite punishment' due to the sin of the human race could be stayed only by 'either an equivalent punishment or an equivalent sorrow and repentance'. Edwards, in line with the classical Calvinist theology, did not pause to entertain seriously the second of these alternatives but represented Christ as suffering an 'equivalent punishment', so that his punishment could be reckoned in place of the punishment that was due to mankind because of sin. But Campbell takes up the other possibility. He claims that Christ's atoning work 'took the form of a perfect confession of our sins'. 'This confession ... must have been a perfect Amen in humanity to the judgment of God on the sin of man.'[13] This would be a response to God's condemnation of sin so perfect that one could say of it that it 'has all the elements of a perfect repentance in humanity for all the sin of man – a perfect sorrow, a perfect contrition, all the elements of such a repentance, and that in absolute perfection, all – excepting the personal consciousness of sin.'[14] And Campbell goes on to declare that there is more worth and atoning power in this perfect sorrow for sin than in all the penal woe imaginable.

This is a bold and imaginative theology of atonement, and it deserves more careful consideration than it has usually received. Too often, Campbell is praised for having broken out of the penal theology but is then said to have failed to offer a convincing affirmative theology in its place. Yet when we consider in depth all that is involved in this idea of a deep sorrow, repentance and contrition for the sins of mankind, this moral and spiritual expiation, we begin to see that it is a remarkably pregnant idea. It is obviously consistent with Campbell's intention of substituting personal for legal categories. Christ's perfect repentance in humanity and on behalf of humanity establishes a personal relation with the Father far more appropriate in dealing with one who is the 'Father of spirits' than any penal transaction could ever do. It is also very much in the spirit of the gospels. Campbell alludes to the obvious illustration – the case of the prodigal son who, having repented and confessed his sin, returns to the father and is received forthwith with joyful forgiveness, without any legal niceties or fictitious imputations of righteousness. As Campbell rightly says, his filial standing was not allowed to depend on any legal standing. On the other hand, Campbell's insistence on the pain and sorrow of Christ's confession of sin and its sacrificial character as a moral and spiritual expiation brings into his theology of atonement a sense of costliness which is lacking in the so-called 'moral influence' theories of atonement developed by liberal theologians who were also in revolt against the old penal theories.

But while Campbell's view has these obvious merits, it raises several difficult problems. I shall indicate what some of these are, and consider how one might respond to them.

The first problem is this: How could Christ make a perfect confession of sin and a perfect act of repentance if, as Campbell insists, he was himself sinless? Is there not something quite arti-

ficial in Campbell's theory at this point? He objected to the legal
fiction of the penal theory, whereby the sins of mankind were
imputed to Christ. But are we not still dealing in fictions when we
are asked to believe that Christ confessed and repented of sins
which he had not committed? A reviewer made this point at the
time when Campbell's book was first published. He quoted the
sentence which I have myself cited above, that here are 'all the
elements of a perfect repentance in humanity for all the sin of
man, all – excepting the personal consciousness of sin', and went
on to say; 'This exception, however, contains just the essential
element of the whole'.

It is certainly true that one can sorrow for the sins of others.
One may be very deeply grieved by them, and one may pray to
God that those who have committed these sins might turn from
them and be forgiven. But that one could confess them on behalf
of others or repent of them on behalf of others does not seem
possible. And if Christ were totally sinless in any case, could he
really enter into the penitent state of mind or make that turning
which seems to be of the essence of a true repentance?

To be sure, Campbell makes a point which seems to tell in the
opposite direction, namely, that *only* Christ in the purity of his
being could fully realize the weight and extent of human sin, and
so only he could make a full confession and repentance. But again
I think one would have to say that while Christ's sensitivity and
personal righteousness would enable him to perceive and to sorrow
for the sin of the human race in a uniquely profound way,
such sorrow could scarcely be called repentance. Thus Campbell
says that Christ 'has taken the nature and become the brother of
those whose sin he confesses before the Father, and feels concerning their sins what, as the Holy One of God, and as perfectly
loving God and man, he must feel'.[15] We may agree with Campbell
that no fiction is here being imputed to Christ. We have to do
with a deep, personal, perhaps almost infinite sorrow. And there
is something unique about it. As Kierkegaard had said; 'The only
one who innocently sorrowed over sinfulness was Christ'.[16] But
this sorrowing is not repentance. Yet if it is not repentance, what
becomes of Campbell's theology of atonement? His argument
had begun from the premise that atonement requires a perfect
repentance.

The only way out of the difficulty seems to be to recognize that
Christ's solidarity with the human race was such that he did indeed
participate even in the sinfulness of humanity and so was able

genuinely to repent of that sin and make an act of contrition. Campbell himself shrank from such a position, but the nettle has been grasped by several modern theologians. It is not necessary to deny the *personal* sinlessness of Jesus Christ, and if one were to identify him too closely with the fallen condition of man, then it would become very difficult to see how he could be a saviour or redeemer. But the corporate nature of sin is perhaps better understood now than it was in Campbell's time (though Schleiermacher had not neglected it). If Christ was truly man, then must he not, simply by living in human society, have in some ways participated in that disorientation of society which is corporate sin? For instance, he acknowledged the obligation to pay taxes to the Roman state (Mark 12.13ff.; Matt. 17.24ff.) and this means that in some measure there is a participation in the state and a condoning of its activities. To be truly in the human condition is inevitably to be involved in the moral ambiguities of that condition. Only a total drop-out from society could be immune from the contagion of corporate sin. But such total withdrawal is not possible, nor is it desirable; and certainly Jesus did not practise it. The whole notion of incarnation points to the reverse of withdrawal.

Without having to compromise the doctrine of the personal sinlessness of Jesus (though I would understand this in a dynamic and progressive way) I think that one can acknowledge his involvement in the corporate sin of humanity, and then the idea of his repentance in humanity and on behalf of humanity makes sense. And might one also hold that the perfect repentance of this one man was also a focal turning-point for humanity as a whole, the point at which a decisive atonement took place and a new humanity, centred in Jesus Christ, came into being?

I have said that Campbell himself shrank from the idea that Christ could in any way be involved in the sin of mankind. Yet his theory seems to require this, and there is one curious strand running through the book which seem to indicate that, even if it was only subconsciously, his mind was toying with the idea that in some real way Christ identified himself with human sin. I am referring to Campbell's fascination with some of Luther's teaching on the atonement, and especially with Luther's exegesis of St Paul's words that Christ 'was made sin for us' (II Cor. 5.21). Luther says this: 'In the selfsame person which is the highest, the greatest and the only sinner, there is also an everlasting and invincible righteousness; therefore these two do encounter together, the highest, the greatest and the only sin, and the highest, the greatest and the only righteousness. Here one of them must needs be overcome. The sin therefore of the whole world cometh upon righteousness with all might and main ... So in Christ all sin is vanquished, killed and buried, and righteousness remaineth a conqueror and reigneth for ever.'[17]

Campbell points out that Luther uses the strongest words to express the identification of Christ with our sins. 'This conception of Christ as the one man having present together in himself the sin of all other men and his own righteousness, Luther endeavours in all possible forms of speech to present as an *actual fact*. And, whatever difficulties the matter may have presented to Luther's own mind, or whatever difficulties his words may cause to us, attempting to attach to them a definite and consistent meaning, he leaves no room to doubt that what he sought to set forth he conceived as a reality and not as a legal fiction.' Almost immediately, however, Campbell feels constrained to add: 'But to think of Luther as really having any unworthy conceptions of Christ would be altogether erroneous.'[18]

Campbell keeps coming back to the theme. A few pages further on, we find him quoting some words of Luther about Christ's 'joining the company of the accursed, taking unto him their flesh and blood'. Again, Campbell says that Luther cannot mean here a mere imputation of sin but a reality. But once more Campbell himself draws back. 'Luther's words', he says, 'interpreted according to their plain grammatical meaning, the words by which he expressed Christ's relation to our sins, cannot be true.' Yet in the next sentence Campbell insists that nevertheless Luther's words had a meaning 'at once true and important'.[19] At this point one wonders whether he had read Luther's polemic against commentators who did not take words in their plain grammatical sense!

Much later in the book Campbell returns once more to Luther's ideas, and once more we find him both attracted and yet unable to go along because he could not admit that there could be any sin touching 'the Holy One of God'.[20] But if Campbell had been able to make the distinction between personal and corporate sin, he could have taken over Luther's ideas in a bolder way and greatly strengthened his own view of the atonement at one of its weakest points. For if we accept that a true incarnation must have meant a full solidarity of Christ with humanity, a 'joining himself to the company of the accursed', then it does become possible to think of Christ making a perfect confession and act of repentance for the sin which he had known from the inside, as it were. And it is surely possible to believe at the same time that this corporate sin which he had taken into himself was met there by an even more powerful personal righteousness so that a way was opened up out of sin and an atonement effected.

A second main problem in Campbell's teaching is related to the one we have just discussed in so far as it too has to do with Christ's relation to the human race. If we accept that an act of confession and repentance was possible for Christ on the ground of his participating in the corporate sin of mankind, we have still to ask how his repentance can avail for others. Repentance is such a deeply personal matter that again one must ask whether there is not some legal fiction here, in spite of all Campbell's inveighing against fictions

R. C. Moberly developed a theology of atonement that builds on some of Campbell's ideas but he made the criticism that in Campbell's teaching the confession and repentance of Christ are external to the rest of humanity. Moberly's own attempt to overcome the difficulty was to draw upon Hegel's philosophy, and he held that Christ's humanity was an 'inclusive humanity', a form of personal being which embraced all the individual personal beings of mankind. 'Christ consummated penitence ... not as a substitute, not even as a delegated representative, but as that inclusive total of true humanity of which men were potentially, and were to learn to become, a part.'[21] Now, I have always found it difficult to understand how one person can be included in another, and I believe that Moberly's theory at this point rests on a greater fiction than anything to be found in Campbell. Nevertheless, Moberly's criticism of Campbell needs to be taken seriously.

It may be agreed that Campbell does not deal with the question of how Christ's confession is related to the human race as clearly and explicitly as he might have done, and that at the time of writing the book he was not fully aware of the problem of individual and corporate being, though this problem was soon raised by his reviewers. In a note to the second edition of the book, however, he claims that he had unconsciously steered a middle course between the Scylla of an individualism that would cut men off from participation in Christ's confession and the Charybdis of a collectivism in which one's own personal being is merged in a more inclusive self.[22]

Campbell's understanding of how we participate in the perfect confession of Christ is closely related to his stress on the prospective aspect of the atonement, as not merely something accomplished in the past but as something still going on, and to his belief that justification is not a legal fiction but the beginning of a new life in the person justified. Christ is the representative man who confesses on behalf of all men in the sense that all may join themselves to him by faith and so participate in his confession. 'Our faith', writes Campbell, 'is the Amen of our individual spirits to that deep, multiform, all-embracing harmonious Amen of humanity in the person of the Son of God to the mind and heart of the Father in relation to man.'[23] Elsewhere he puts the matter thus: 'The confession of our sin in response to the divine condemnation of it, must, when offered to God on our behalf, have contemplated prospectively our own participation in that confession as an element in our actual redemption from sin.'[24] He also makes much of the idea of sharing in the suffering of Christ, where that suffering is understood chiefly as the pain occasioned by repentance and the contemplation of sin.

I believe that in such statements Campbell is showing (as he later claimed) the possibility of a way between individualism and collectivism, a way in which Christ's atoning confession can be for all men, yet without in any way swallowing up their personal identities. But it must be added that Campbell's views at this point are left weak and undeveloped because he offers no teaching about the church and the sacraments and the corporate life which they foster. This seems to me a more serious deficiency than the one of which Moberly complains, namely, Campbell's silence on the work of the Holy Spirit. It is also surprising, for Campbell is said to have had a strong sacramental sense.

I pass to a final problem. Is there, on Campbell's view of atonement, any necessity for the death of Christ? I do not clearly see that there is. Campbell gives priority to the incarnation over the atonement, and he rightly holds that Christ's atoning work must be seen as growing out of his life as a whole. But the real suffering of Christ, the real bearing of our sins, was his act of confession and repentance. If I may put it this way, Gethsemane rather than Calvary was, for Campbell, the climactic moment of the atonement. Christ's soul was 'very sorrowful, even to death', and he prayed that the Father might 'remove this cup' (Mark 14.34-36). What was the cup that Christ had to drink during those last hours of his life? Not primarily physical suffering. Campbell deplores all dwelling on the physical sufferings of Christ, though acknowledging that they were very real. Neither was it the Father's wrath that was contained in the cup, as the Calvinists had held, for the whole penal theory has been rejected. The bitterness of the cup, as Campbell seems to interpret it, was Christ's painful sorrowing for the sins of men encountered in their worst form, his experience of enmity as the response to love, and his making of these sins his own burden.[25]

Since his suffering then was primarily inward, a 'moral and spiritual expiation', the suffering of a perfect confession and act of contrition, what need was there of the outward suffering and death? Campbell seems to think of these as perfecting the atonement, the roots of which are already there in the incarnation and the whole life and ministry of Christ. The sufferings of the cross and passion, says Campbell, 'gave ultimate depth to his confession of our sins'.[26] This is very much in line with the primacy of the incarnation in his theology, and also with the Johannine tenor of his thought. In this connection, it is also to be noted that in spite of Campbell's many sensitive interpretations of the suffering of Christ and his attachment to Christ's true humanity, he insists that through it all the Son's consciousness of the Father remained unbroken.[27] 'Light' is one of the most frequently recurring words in Campbell's writing, but whether he deals adequately with darkness and death is open to question.

But his work stands as an original and profound meditation on its theme. He still has much to teach us, and opens up avenues that are still worth exploring.

Notes

1. B. M. G. Reardon, *From Coleridge to Gore*, Longman 1971, p. 404.

2. See J. G. Riddell, *The Calling of God*, St Andrew Press 1961, p. 46.

3. Quotations are from the fourth edition, James Clarke 1959.

4. R. S. Franks, *The Work of Christ*, Nelson 1962, p. 665.

5. Campbell, op. cit., p. 212.

6. Op. cit., p. 31.

7. Op. cit., p. 326.

8. Op. cit., p. 230.

9. Op. cit., p. 176.

10. Op. cit., pp. 13, 170.

11. Op. cit., p. 369.

12. Op. cit., p. 384.

13. Op. cit., pp. 135-6.

14. Op. cit., p. 137.
15. Op. cit., p. 146.
16. S. Kierkegaard, *The Concept of Dread*, p. 35.
17. M. Luther, *Commentary on the Epistle to the Galatians*, James Clarke 1953, pp. 272-3.
18. Campbell, op. cit., pp. 36-7.
19. Op. cit., p. 48.
20. Op. cit., p. 142.
21. R. C. Moberly, *Atonement and Personality*, John Murray 1901, pp. 282-3.
22. Campbell, op. cit., pp. 401-2.
23. Op. cit., p. 225.
24. Op. cit., p. 152.
25. Op. cit., p. 266.
26. Op. cit., p. 287.
27. Op. cit., p. 321.

16

Bultmann's Understanding of God

Bultmann has always had critics who have blamed him not for demythologizing the Christian gospel but for not carrying his demythologizing far enough. In the English-speaking world, Paul van Buren is one of the best known critics of Bultmann taking this line. He concedes that Bultmann's interpretation of the New Testament has met some of the modern objections directed against myth and miracle, but this interpretation still talks of God and sets forth the central message of the New Testament as God's gracious address to man. But, according to van Buren, it is this talk of God and God's acts that is the real stumbling-block for contemporary secular man.[1]

Bultmann, however, is quite clear in his determination to find the source of Christian faith in an act of God. He says explicitly that Christianity is not just the precursor of an existentialist philosophy, and that the Christian knows of an act of God whereby he is enabled to lay hold on authentic life.[2] Yet even if Bultmann is firm in his intention of relating his theology to God, to God's act and to God's address, his actual thought of God is very elusive. In the title of this chapter, I have deliberately avoided talking of Bultmann's 'idea' of God, or his 'conception' of God, for he shies away from any attempt at conceptualization. I have talked of his 'understanding' of God, but by this I do not mean an intellectual theory but a very existential type of understanding which is there only in that moment of experience when God touches a human life.

Our purpose is to seek some light on this understanding of God as we find it set forth in Bultmann's writings. It is characteristic of him to insist that in any talk of God, we are talking at the same time of ourselves, but his whole method of existential interpretation tends to stress the talking about ourselves, and clarifies this talk in terms of self-understanding. Of course, in self-understanding too, the expression 'understanding' is to be taken in an existential way. It is not a theory of the self. It is necessary, however, to do something to show how this talk of self can also be talk of the other whom we call God, and unless this is done, we may be left with the strong suspicion that, in spite of Bultmann's intentions, we are dealing *only* with self-understanding, and that the name 'God' is used simply as a mythological expression for a subjective ideal of human existence, much as Feuerbach had claimed.

Probably the most sustained attempt that has been made to delineate Bultmann's understanding of God is to be found in the work of the Finnish scholar, Esa Kivekäs. He claims that 'anyone who has examined Bultmann's thought of God during the different periods of his theological activity notices that his ways of expressing it vary'.[3] These variations are correlated by Kivekäs with five periods into which he divides Bultmann's work, from 1908 onward. These periods he names as follows: historico-critical, dialectic, hermeneutic, homiletic, synthetic. Of course, this notion of distinguishable successive periods in Bultmann's work is not to be taken too rigorously, and I should be inclined to say myself that the five types of material identified by Kivekäs, although they may be susceptible to some loose chronological ordering, do not so much characterize five distinct periods that can be clearly pointed out in the unfolding of Bultmann's thought, but are rather five tendencies that have been at work over the major part of his career. Perhaps all five tendencies have been present throughout most of Bultmann's productive life as a scholar and writer, though admittedly one or other of them may have predominated at one period or another.[4] At any rate, it is not my intention to try to trace the development of Bultmann's thought of God, in the manner of Kivekäs. Apart from anything else, there has been very little development, properly so-called. Bultmann appears to have been one of those scholars who makes up his mind on certain fundamental questions at the outset of his career, and pretty well stays with them later. Kivekäs himself is ready to acknowledge that even if there have been variations and transformations (*Wandlungen*) in the way in which Bultmann has expressed his understanding of God, there has been very little true development, and his final thought of God seems to be very close to the one which we can already discern in his early writings. The constancy in Bultmann's thinking which I am asserting here is something which has been noted also not only by Kivekäs but by such widely differing commentators on Bultmann as Helmut Thielicke and Schubert Ogden.

We shall now proceed to examine some passages on the subject of God, culled from writings of Bultmann coming from different periods. We shall find that there are some very constant elements that keep reappearing, but we shall also find changing ways of expressing them and, more than that, various hints and suggestions often left undeveloped, yet pointing to the possibility of a richer and fuller understanding of God than Bultmann's statements might normally seem to allow.

Let us begin with the relatively early work known in English as *Jesus and the Word*, and first published in German with the simple title *Jesus* in 1926. This book could probably be reckoned as both 'historico-critical' and 'dialectic' in Kivekäs' classification, for it reflects both the critical work of Bultmann that had already received fuller expression in the first edition of his *History of the Synoptic Tradition* (published in 1921) and also his involvement, along with Barth, Gogarten and others, in the revolt against the dominant liberal theology that was still entrenched in the University of Berlin and that had held the field in Germany for several decades. *Jesus and the Word* already yields statements that have proved to be fundamental in Bultmann's understanding of God. It is interesting to notice, however, that in this book he makes no direct assertions concerning God. He purports to be simply reporting what he believes to have been Jesus' understanding of God. Thus we read as follows: 'God, for Jesus, is the power that constrains man to decision, who confronts him in the demand for good, who determines his future. God, therefore, cannot be regarded objectively as a nature in himself, but only in the actual comprehension of his own existence can a man find God.' Again, he writes: 'For Jesus, God is not an object of thought or speculation. Jesus speaks of God only to claim that man is determined in his present existence through God's demand.'[5]

Both of these quotations are explicit in claiming to report Jesus' understanding of God, and they might even be supposed to do this in a quite detached and scientific way, without any reference to the beliefs of the author, who is merely recording a fact of history. But if one examines those writings in which Bultmann expresses his own understanding of God, then one finds that it is much the same as the view which he attributes to Jesus. Then, of course, one is faced with the problem of whether Bultmann's understanding of God has been determined by what he has found in the teaching of Jesus, or whether his interpretation of Jesus' teaching has been determined by a view of God which he already holds.

All the main points in Bultmann's understanding of God can be seen in an essay dating from 1931 and bearing the title, 'The Crisis in Belief'.[6] 'Belief in God', we are told, 'is *not a general truth* at my disposal and which I perceive and apply; on the contrary, it is what it is only as something continually perceived afresh and developing afresh.' Such belief is always self-involving and has to do with the decision of the 'moment'. It is 'never a question of knowledge gained by research and preservable as a possession, but is always one of the will and of responsiveness to the moment'. Yet while acknowledging that one can speak of God only in relation to those concrete situations where God's claim is laid upon us and when he acts upon us, Bultmann strongly denies that talk of God is *nothing more than* talk of ourselves. Christian faith claims that 'it hears a word which demands that it should recognize God as standing over against man'. The event of Jesus Christ and the word of the kerygma are experienced by the Christian as coming to him from beyond himself, and as liberating him from that sin that had hitherto made him impotent to respond to the demand of love. The dynamic, concrete, ethical awareness of God, of which Bultmann writes, is often explicitly contrasted by him with the knowledge of God that might be claimed either in connection with a metaphysical theory or with mystical experience. It seems to him that the claims of metaphysics and mysticism alike conflict with the temporal (almost moment-to-moment) character of finite human existence and perhaps also seem to be seeking a security which is not appropriate to this existence.

A later and somewhat more elaborate account of what it means to talk of God and his action is to be found in the writings of his hermeneutic period, especially in *Jesus Christ and Mythology* with a closely parallel account in *Kerygma and Myth*. Here again it is claimed that we cannot talk of God apart from talking of ourselves, but the subjectivizing tendency of such an interpretation of God-language is faced in a new way. 'If what we have said is correct, does it not follow that God's action is deprived of objective reality, that it is reduced to a purely subjective, psychological experience; that God exists only as an inner event in the soul, whereas faith has real meaning only if God exists outside the believer? Such objections are brought forward again and again, and the shades of Schleiermacher and Feuerbach are conjured up in this controversy.'[7] Here Bultmann is beginning to come to grips with the issue. He agrees that faith might be an illusion, and that no objective proof can be offered that the God experienced in faith is indeed an Other, standing over against man. There are not additional facts to which the believer has access or to which he can point in support of his conviction. He can only testify to this word that has addressed him in the critical decisive moment, and it is clear that Bultmann does not think that the believer should try to buttress his faith by looking for some confirmation beyond the moment. Yet, he wishes to maintain that although in one sense there must be risk and insecurity, in another the believer enjoys a certitude in his experience that an ultimate word or demand from beyond himself has come to him. The actual words or events which serve as vehicles for this ultimate or eschatological word can be seen as ordinary natural events, but the believer sees them as God's acts by 'the eye of faith'. Bultmann does not enlarge on this expression, but it would seem to mean that there takes place a perception of the event (or a hearing of the words) in depth, that is to say, in awareness of the connectedness, the relatedness, the ultimate implications of the event or word. It is through perceiving this texture of the event that one ascribes it to the agency of God; and this is not just something imposed or projected by our minds on the event, it really is part of the given that we encounter in the experience. This is my explanation rather than Bultmann's of what he means by the 'eye of faith', but it seems clear that he has in mind something of this sort.

However, he offers another consideration. His attempts to dissociate himself from any complete subjectivizing of God are carried further by the introduction in his demythologizing writings of a doctrine of analogy. To speak of an act of God, according to Bultmann, is not to use mythological language. The language here, he claims, is not mythological but analogical. And whereas myth gets demythologized, that is to say, translated into the language of human existence, presumably talk of an act of God, being analogy rather than mythology, cannot be reduced to language about the human existent. Unfortunately, Bultmann's doctrine of analogy is never spelled out, though this is astonishing when one considers how vital it is to the defence of his contention that the objective reality of God is not destroyed by his existential interpretation. From such hints as there are, it seems that for Bultmann the analogues are drawn from the experience of the human existent in contrast with the objectifying language of myth, which draws its images from the sensible world. But it is not entirely clear that this distinction can be consistently made, and it is not clear either what its full significance might be.

Kivekäs mentions a homiletic period, though in this case one is certainly not dealing with a period but with a type of literary and theological production. It is hard to know just how proper it may be to look to Bultmann's sermons for further elucidation of his understanding of God. It is true that his published sermons are, for the most part, models of exegetical and doctrinal preaching, and deserve the most serious attention. Yet it is also true (even if it is regrettable) that often a theologian will, in the confessional style of utterance that is appropriate to the sermon, permit himself to make affirmations that might not be wholly supported by the strictly reflective and critical findings that belong to his theology proper.

Here, for instance, is a passage from a sermon of Bultmann on the theme of the 'unknown God' mentioned in St Paul's speech on Mars' Hill. Bultmann has contrasted the way in which, as he believes, modern man exploits and takes possession of the divine, with the awe in face of reality evinced by those who sought even an unknown God. He goes on to say: 'God requires this of man, that he should not exploit the divine for the enhancement of his own human prestige and glory, but that he should submit to the Lord and give him the honour which is his due. Whosoever purposes to draw near to God must first pass through the dark valley of self-surrender. Only out of the valley of the shadow of death, where the self-will of man dies, shines the light of that plenitude of life which God bestows. And on what basis shall we dare to penetrate the darkness of this self-surrender? With what justification shall we allow ourselves to sink deep into this darkness, trusting that God's hand will enfold and keep us with gracious strength? For this reason alone, but really for this reason, namely, that the unknown God has made himself known to us in his word.'[8] Some new notes do seem to be struck in this way of speaking of God. The notions of drawing near to God and of passing through some kind of dark night are suggestive of the very mysticism of which Bultmann usually speaks in a negative or hostile way. Yet we should notice that even if what he says in this sermon could be regarded as having some affinity to mysticism (though not a close one), it is still tied very closely to the hearing of the word.

In another sermon, Bultmann speaks eloquently of the love of God, and asserts: 'This love of God is not a goal toward which we strive – who could ever attain it by striving? – but it is the power which already enclasps and enfolds us and to which our eyes have only to be opened.'[9] In this sermon, the demand of the moment is matched by the thought of the abiding presence of God's love and grace.

David Cairns, who has made a special study of Bultmann's sermons, offers this comment on the two which have just been quoted: 'These are fine, even splendid, passages of Christian preaching. But does Bultmann's theology give us any grounds for believing they are true?'[10] This is surely the vital question. Actually, Cairns comes to the conclusion that, in his sermons, Bultmann permits himself to make affirmations that go beyond what he is prepared to acknowledge in his theology. I would not say myself that what Bultmann has to say about God in his sermons is *incompatible* with his theology or with the understanding of God that we find there. But they certainly seem to fill out that thought considerably, and one wishes that he had at the same time developed a firmer theological basis for this kind of preaching about God.

The last piece of evidence we shall consider is an essay from late in Bultmann's career – 'The Idea of God and Modern Man',[11] written in 1963 in response to the debate concerning God that had broken out following the publication of J. A. T. Robinson's *Honest to God* and Gabriel Vahanian's *The Death of God*. It must be said frankly that this late essay is not among the best of Bultmann's writing. Much of it is taken up with cataloguing some of the ideas of God that have been expounded in recent years – in this sense, the essay is synthetic, to recall Kivekäs' expression. What principally emerges from the essay is the fact that Bultmann's understanding of God remains very much what it always has been, but perhaps he makes clearer here the kind of atheism that is opposed to his own form of faith, and what he takes to be the danger of this atheism. He follows Heidegger in believing that the period of Western thought after Nietzsche has been one in which the tendency toward subjectivism has taken over. In religion, this means that there is a loss of belief in any transcendence, and there comes about even a kind of nihilism, in which man becomes the sole author of values and the sole legislator of right and wrong. Here it may be recalled that even if the thought of God has sometimes been obscure in Bultmann's writings, he has always been critical of an absolutizing of human autonomy (*Eigenständigkeit*) where man sets up his own ultimates. This critique of an arrogant autonomy is just as clearly set forth in the strictly theological writings as in the sermons. And surely Bultmann had good reason to condemn the kind of nihilistic, arrogant, subjective will-to-power that he had witnessed when he lived through the period of Nazi ascendancy in Germany. He had seen the deadly fruits that are brought forth when man's ultimates are such immanent entities as blood and soil, and Bultmann had a very good record in standing up to Nazi pressures on church and university. It is against the background of such threats that Bultmann can again point to the importance of the God of whom he has spoken all along – the God who is known in the moment of decision as the transcendent demand, the eschatological word, the absolute claim, to which man cannot say no unless he would destroy his authentic self.

It is not surprising that after he has surveyed some of the perplexities that beset our contemporary attempts to think of God, we find Bultmann toward the end of the essay coming back to say again what he has said repeatedly for years: 'It remains to keep oneself open at any time for *the encounter with God in the world, in time*. It is not the acknowledgment of an image of God, be it ever so correct, that is real faith in God; rather, it is the readiness for the eternal to encounter us at any time in the present – at any time in the varying situations of life.'[12] It is as if in time and history there sometimes opens up an extra dimension, the transcendent or ultimate, or, as Bultmann would say in his own terminology, the eschatological, and in that moment we know the demand of the ultimate or possibly the grace of the ultimate, and it is in such a moment that we can speak of God.

Having before us some of the characteristics of Bultmann's understanding of God, let us now try to assess it. We begin with the strengths of this way of thinking of God, and they are considerable. The first and most obvious strength is simply that this is more than an *idea* of God. We have seen ample confirmation of my remark at the beginning of the discussion that there is a powerful existential character in everything Bultmann says about God. We are not confronted with the disjunction of a theoretical theism and a theoretical atheism, apart from any reference to what this means for human life. The second strength is the profoundly ethical character of Bultmann's understanding of God. To know God is to obey him, that is to say, to obey the demand of love and to be open to the neighbour. Indeed, God is virtually identified with the experience of the ultimate moral demand. There is certainly nothing sentimental about Bultmann's understanding of God, and it is at the furthest remove from any so-called 'wishful thinking'. Still a third strength, as Bultmann himself seems to believe, is that knowing the true God in his ultimacy is our only reliable safeguard against the distorting idolatries that arise from absolutizing one or more of the finite entities within the world.

Bultmann's account of God has a special relevance in the face of some of the criticisms that are from time to time nowadays levelled against belief in God. Certainly God, as Bultmann thinks of him, is not a problem solver for the immature, not a source of ethical or social complacency, not a cipher brought in to 'explain' things that we cannot understand otherwise. This God is much more like the God of the Hebrew prophets – a God who disturbs us and shakes us out of complacency, a God who drives us on beyond where we are by his demands for justice and mercy. This God, as Bultmann well says, so encounters us that he 'does not leave the "I" alone, the "I" that is encapsulated in its purposes and plans'. And more than this, 'he can encounter us where we do not expect it'.[13]

Yet, when we have conceded the undoubted strong points in Bultmann's thought of God, we have also to say that there are some weaknesses in it.

One weakness is that Bultmann's understanding of the relation between the believer and God is too 'situational'. God seems to act or speak or make himself known in certain discrete and more or less dramatic moments, but between times he is absent or at least quiescent. One can acknowledge that Bultmann's motive for talking in this way is a sound one, for he is constantly on his guard against any way of thinking or talking of God that might suggest we could take God into our possession or have him securely at our disposal. Faith in God and the knowledge of God have to be won ever anew.

But the defect of this account is that it does not sufficiently recognize the possibility of growth and deepening in the Christian life, through which there can develop a constant awareness of God's presence. The nearest parallel I can think of to Bultmann's 'God of the moments' is the theory of 'momentary deities', developed by H. Usener in his account of primitive religion and taken up by Ernst Cassirer. In this view, the earliest deities were fleeting forces, known in moments of intense encounter and then vanishing. Of such a momentary deity, Cassirer writes: 'In stark uniqueness and singleness it confronts us ... as something that exists only here and now, in one indivisible moment of experience, and for only one subject whom it overwhelms and holds in thrall.'[14] I do not think it would be unfair to say that this account of primitive religion could be applied almost unchanged to Bultmann's understanding of God. He too stresses the 'here and now' and above all, the concrete individual experience of the 'one subject'. But we ought not to isolate the 'here and now' of the encounter; rather, it becomes illuminating for a great many other moments that are more ambiguous. Furthermore, we are not restricted to an individualistic type of religion; rather, the experience of the 'one subject' is to be set in the history of a community of faith, and this supplies a continuity and depth that goes beyond the individual's own moments of encounter. Bultmann is also hampered by his almost exclusive preoccupation with the *word* as the mode by which God makes himself present. If he could allow more weight to mystical contemplation or to sacramental incorporation, he could hardly rest content with the 'God of the moments', and surely, in some of his sermons, we do see him breaking out of his self-imposed limitations.

A second weakness in Bultmann's understanding of God is perhaps more serious. I refer to his failure to give any satisfactory ontological account of the God concerning whom he speaks. His motive in omitting any such account is, once more, intelligible and, up to a point, valid. That motive is, of course, to avoid any kind of objectification of God, of making him a part of the world or another item of the same basic kind as those which we can enumerate within the world. Bultmann's fear of any such objectification leads him to set up what might be regarded as his own form of negative theology – a ban upon any metaphysical or ontological speculation about God.

It seems to me that if Bultmann is not content to think of God as just part of our experience and wishes to claim that God is a reality standing over against us (and we have seen that he does claim this), then he cannot avoid the ontological problem. There is no shortcut. Anyone who makes claims about what is real or unreal, about what is ultimate or less than ultimate, about what is or is not, has got into ontology, whether he likes it or not. Furthermore, I think it is possible to discuss the ontological status of God without getting into that illegitimate kind of objectification which Bultmann rightly fears. Let us agree that we cannot talk of God in abstraction or reach him through a purely intellectual speculation. We know him through his acting upon us, as Bultmann asserts. But this does not preclude the possibility, and even the necessity, of subsequent reflection on that moment of encounter, reflection that is phenomenological, analytic, critical as well as receptive. Such reflection weighs the experience, tries to discover its structure, compares it with other experiences, and seeks to lay bare the ontological conditions that would allow us to accept it as a valid experience of God. This kind of reflection is not opposed to faith. Rather, it is faith seeking to understand itself, it is theology. Bultmann's excessive devotion to the *sola fide* prevents him from following out the ontological inquiries that are implicit in the stance of faith itself, but some such inquiries are called for if Bultmann's understanding of God is to be elucidated and developed. Such ontological inquiry does not objectify God or force him into the categories of finitude, but clarifies and supports the claims of faith.

But in spite of these criticisms, one may readily acknowledge that Bultmann's writings yield an understanding of God that is very relevant to our time, on account of its biblical foundations and its spiritual maturity.

Notes

1. P. van Buren, *The Secular Meaning of the Gospel*, SCM Press 1963, pp. 57-79.

2. H-W. Bartsch (ed.), *Kerygma and Myth*, tr. R. H. Fuller, SPCK 1957, pp. 22-8.

3. E. Kivekäs, *Rudolf Bultmannin Teologinen Antropologia*, Suomalaisen Teologisen Kirjallisuusseuran 1967, p. 302.

4. For an account of Bultmann's early thinking and his relation to the early Barth, see J. D. Smart, *The Divided Mind of Modern Theology*, Westminster Press 1967.

5. R. Bultmann, *Jesus and the Word*, tr. L. P. Smith and E. H. Lantero, Scribner 1934, pp. 103, 151.

6. In *Essays*, tr. J. C. G. Greig, SCM Press 1955, pp. 1-21.

7. R. Bultmann, *Jesus Christ and Mythology*, Scribner 1958, and SCM Press 1960, p. 70.

8. R. Bultmann, *This World and Beyond*, tr. H. Knight, Scribner 1960, pp. 21-2.

9. Op. cit., p. 81.

10. D. Cairns, *A Gospel without Myth?*, SCM Press 1960, p. 182.

11. In *Translating Theology into the Modern Age*, ed. R. W. Funk, Harper & Row 1965, pp. 83-95.

12. Loc. cit., p. 94.

13. Ibid.

14. E. Cassirer, *Language and Myth*, tr. S. K. Langer, Dover Books 1946, p. 18.

17

Heidegger's Earlier and Later Work Compared

It is obvious to anyone who is acquainted with the work of Martin Heidegger that there is a very considerable difference between those works which belong to the earlier part of his career and those that come from later on. The earlier work of Heidegger, finding its classic expression in *Being and Time*, focussed upon the being of man and, in many ways, opened up new and important insights into the structure of our human existence. But that work broke off somewhat abruptly. As is well-known, the original plan of *Being and Time* was never completed. For twenty-five years successive editions of the book bore the description, 'First Half', but Heidegger finally deleted this description and acknowledged that the path he had originally chosen could not be followed out in the way he had first supposed possible. In the meanwhile, he had been writing many other works in which the centre of gravity of his thought seemed to have shifted, for in these works, and perhaps increasingly as time went on, not the being of man but simply being, the *transcendens* that is prior to any and every particular being, has become the major preoccupation of Heidegger's philosophy. This remains the case even in those late works where he seems to have turned from explicit discussion of being to the discussion of language, for language is, for Heidegger, the 'house of being'.

The relation between the earlier and the later work is a major topic of controversy among students of Heidegger's philosophy, and the question of this relation will provide the theme for this essay. The relation is usually described by the German word *Kehre*, an expression which Heidegger himself used about the reorienta-tion of his thought.[1] The dispute among Heidegger's commentators and students concerns the question of how radical this change in his thought has been, of whether there is a unitary philosophy that embraces what lies on both sides of the change, and whether the change was a constructive advance on Heidegger's part or a retreat from the insights that had been opened up in the earlier work. Very different opinions are held on all these matters.

The differences of opinion are apparent even in the way in which the word *Kehre* gets translated into English. Probably it is best translated simply as 'turning', and in ordinary German usage the word would perhaps refer most naturally to a turning in the road. Many writers, however, translate the word by the stronger term, 'reversal'. This is how it appears, for instance, in W. J. Richardson's extensive study, *Heidegger: Through Phenomenology to Thought*, and there is some justification for such a translation, for when Heidegger himself first used the word *Kehre* about his own thought, he was referring to an unwritten part of *Being and Time* that was to have been entitled 'Time and Being'. It should be noted, however, that this reversal was already envisaged in the original scheme of *Being and Time*. Some writers have gone so far as to equate Heidegger's *Kehre* with a 'conversion'. As an illustration of this point of view, I may mention Laszlo Versényi, whose book, *Heidegger, Being and Truth* talks freely of Heidegger's conversion.

But Heidegger himself tends to play down the extent of the turning and certainly rejects the interpretation of it as a conversion. While indeed he acknowledges that the path that he had originally mapped out for himself led into insuperable obstacles, he also claims that only by following that path was it possible to get into the problems treated in his later writings. In a letter to W. J. Richardson, he complains that those who have overdramatized the 'turning' in his thought have not made sufficient allowance for the fact that it takes time to think out the ramifications of a philosophy and that there is bound to be movement and development in the process.[2] After all, there are many philosophers whose later work differs quite markedly from their earlier – Wittgenstein and Sartre are contemporary examples – but this is accepted as belonging to their philosophical development.

More importantly, Heidegger has in his later writings given interpretations of *Being and Time* designed to show that there is no essential break in his philosophy. It must be admitted that these interpretations occasionally seem a little strained, and it may well be doubted whether, when he was writing *Being and Time*, the meanings which Heidegger now attributes to it were present in his mind. But this in itself would not be important for, as Heidegger says, all the implications of a philosophical position are not immediately obvious, and it may be only later that one sees the full (or fuller) meaning of what had been written earlier. Thus, although in *Being and Time* we meet the sentence, 'Of course, only as long as the human existent (*Dasein*) *is*, (that is to say, only as long as an understanding of being is ontically possible), "is there" being,'[3] and although this sentence might seem to imply a thoroughly man-centred philosophy that makes being dependent on our apprehension of it, Heidegger insists that this is not the case. In his later interpretation of the passage, he points out that the expression translated here ' "is there" being' represents the German ' *"gibt es" Sein*'; and he claims that the words *gibt es*, which admittedly appear in quotation marks in the original, are to be taken in the strictly literal sense as 'it gives'; and he adds that 'the "it" which here "gives" is being itself'.[4] In interpretations such as this, Heidegger tries to rebut the view that his early work was an existentialism of the humanist and sub-jectivist variety – similar, that is to say, to the existentialism of Sartre, from whose position Heidegger is explicitly dissociating himself in the passage quoted.

I shall maintain that Heidegger's own interpretation of the 'turning' is essentially correct, as against those commentators who have made too much of it. I believe it is possible to see definite lines of continuity, though this is not to deny that there are also new departures, and highly significant ones. However, I believe that the correct understanding of the 'turning' is not in terms of a fundamental reversal or conversion, but that it represents the working out of a dialectic that belongs to the very nature of Heidegger's problematic and of which he has been more or less aware from the beginning – though increasingly aware as he has gone along.

I have mentioned also the fact that different writers have passed very varied judgments on the change of direction in Heidegger's philosophizing. Generally speaking, I think that philosophers have been adverse in their criticism. A fairly typical view is expressed by Marjorie Grene, who writes: 'The later work is thin, ill-organized, in part even humdrum and dull. Being and Time, with all its weaknesses, has true philosophical power.'[5] Some philosophers have even suggested that the later writings, which profess to go 'beyond metaphysics' and to have a 'logic' of their own, have strayed so far into poetry and mysticism that they really amount to the abandonment of philosophy, properly so-called. On the other hand, some theologians have declared themselves appreciative of the later writings. Heinrich Ott, for instance, has seen in Heidegger's insistence on the priority of transcendent being and in the way this being gives itself to meditative thinking, something like a parallel to the theological idea of revelation, with its conviction that it is God who comes to man and grants to him the knowledge of himself.[6] But we must remember that the most fruitful theological application by far of Heidegger's teaching is still the work of Bultmann in his theories about the demythologizing and existential interpretation of the New Testament and that these theories rest entirely on the earlier work of Heidegger, as far as their philosophical content is concerned.

In accordance with my purpose of trying to show that Heidegger's philosophy, earlier and later, constitutes a unity, I shall agree neither with those who think of the turning as a deterioration, nor with those who suppose that after the turning Heidegger attained to profound insights hitherto hidden from him. If indeed the earlier and later works belong together, we cannot separate them or exalt the one at the expense of the other. Heidegger claims – and, I think, rightly – that we can appreciate the significance of his later work only if we have followed the path that is traced out in *Being and Time*. It is the fact that this path breaks off that presents us with the demand that we should look for other ways, and that enables us to appreciate the reasons that have led Heidegger to explore those other ways which we find in his later writings.

Let me now try to set out some of the main points of difference between the earlier and the later work. In the course of doing this, we shall be able to see both the contrasts and the considerations that point, in spite of the occasional sharpness of the contrasts, to the overarching unity of a dialectic that gathers them up. I shall mention five areas of contrast, though we shall find that one merges into another. Because of this overlapping, I shall deal with the first area in greater detail than will be necessary for the others.

1. The first contrast that comes to our attention is the one that has to do with existence and being. The early writings are preoccupied with existence, while the later writings have being for their theme. By 'existence', of course, Heidegger means human or

personal existence, the kind of being that belongs to man as the peculiar being who 'stands out' in an openness, so that he not only *is*, like all other beings, but is aware that he is. This means that he has his being and also other beings disclosed to him and therefore has the possibility, within limits, of shaping his own being and even the being of other persons and of nature. Heidegger's brilliant analysis of human existence or being-in-the-world is the achievement of his *magnum opus, Being and Time*. It is this achievement that has led him to be regarded as one of the leaders of existentialism. This too is the achievement that has principally impressed and influenced the philosophy of Sartre and other French existentialists, the New Testament theology of Bultmann, and the existential psychoanalysis of Binswanger and others.

In the later writings of Heidegger, however, it is no longer existence but being that occupies the centre of the discussion. But it must be confessed that we are not presented with an analysis of being that could be said to possess anything like the clarity and persuasiveness which belonged to the early analyses of existence. Much that is said concerning being is reminiscent of the *via negationis* in theology. Already in *Being and Time*, it had been said that being is a *transcendens*, a scholastic term which indicated that, together with unity, truth and a few other basic notions, being lies beyond the categories of thought and cannot be subsumed under any of them.[7] Being is said to be 'wholly other' to any particular being.[8] Again, being is described as the 'incomparable'.[9] Yet Heidegger is at the same time eager to maintain that being is not, as Nietzsche had said, a mere haze or empty word. The very fact that we continually make use of the verb 'to be' – and not merely as a logical operator – points to some understanding of being that, somehow, we already possess.[10] Furthermore, the fact that being has been consistently distinguished from other notions, such as becoming, appearing, thinking and even nothing, seems to point to some determinate content on the basis of which these distinctions have been made.[11] I believe it is true to say that in the later writings, enigmatic though they often are, Heidegger does sometimes succeed in lighting up something of the meaning of being. Yet this is always elusive and certainly never attains the clarity of his early existential analytic. But could it be otherwise? Could one do more than evoke being? The very point that being (*Sein, esse*) is not itself a being (*Seiendes, ens*) and is indeed wholly other to beings entails that one could never answer – at least, in any straightforward way – the question, 'What is being?' For this very question implies that being 'is' a 'what' or a 'something'.

The contrast of existence and being is therefore a fundamental one in Heidegger. Yet if we reflect on his handling of these matters, we shall see that the two contrasted themes do belong within a single philosophical framework. There are at least three reasons which support this interpretation.

First, from the very beginning of his philosophizing, Heidegger has been quite explicit that the object of his philosophical quest is nothing less than the question of being itself. This quest has occupied Heidegger from his student days. It was kindled in the year 1907, when he was eighteen years of age. At that time he had been given a writing of Franz Brentano on the manifold meaning of 'being' in Aristotle. This writing of Brentano's sets out from the saying of Aristotle, *to on legetai pollachos*. The most natural way to translate this sentence would be to render it, 'Being gets said in many ways', though Heidegger himself gives a typically loaded translation: 'A being becomes manifest (with respect to its being) in many ways.' At any rate, this set the problem for Heidegger's life-work. What is the meaning of being, this notion which, as it seems, we are continually using, whether explicitly or only implicitly? It is made perfectly clear on the opening page of *Being and Time* that this will not be primarily a treatise about human existence but an attempt to open up again the question of being. So we can say that from beginning to end Heidegger's philosophy has been held together by a single quest.

A second reason that leads us to assert the unity of Heidegger's thought through the transition from existence to being is the manner in which he considers human existence in *Being and Time*. The investigation of the structures of existence never becomes an end in itself, as it does in existentialism proper. Again, man is never considered to be 'the measure of all things', as he becomes in Sartre's equation of existentialism with humanism. On the contrary, we find Heidegger explicitly denying that it is his ambition to work out what he calls a 'philosophical anthropology'; he asserts instead that 'the analytic of the human existent (*Dasein*) remains wholly oriented toward the guiding task of working out the question of being'.[12] Heidegger does not even, except on rare occasions and usually when he is discussing some other philosopher's views, talk about man or humanity. He talks instead about *Dasein*, man in his ontological aspect, the one who is 'there' in the openness of his being. Man is the theme of the analytic only to the extent that he is the ontological being, the one who, in virtue of the very being that is his, raises the question of being in general. The investigation into human existence is conceived not as anthropology but as 'fundamental ontology', that is to say, a questioning of the foundations of the inquiry into being, in the being of that particular being for whom the meaning of being has become a problem. A striking confirmation of these remarks may be had from a circumstance to which Edward Robinson and I have drawn attention in our 'Translators' Preface' to *Being and Time*: that Heidegger has a remarkable predilection for impersonal language, even although he is describing human or personal existence. This very choice of language supports Heidegger's own contention that the anthropological question, as such, is kept at a distance throughout the argument of *Being and Time*.

A third reason for asserting the unity of Heidegger's philosophy as regards existence and being may be drawn from paying attention to what he says about the circularity of his procedure. The point is raised very early in *Being and Time* and the author returns to it in due course.[13] The circularity is this. In order to open up the question of being, it is proposed to explicate in its being that particular being which inquires about being. But how is it possible to do this, unless one is already assuming that the answer to the question of being is known? Heidegger's reply to this is that, although there is admittedly an element of circularity here, this is not the vicious circularity of a deductive argument which has already begged the question. It is rather the circularity that belongs to all interpretation – the 'hermeneutic circle', if we may call it such. Interpretation would be impossible unless we had some advance understanding of what was to be interpreted, but interpretation would be unnecessary unless there was something hidden that had to be brought to light. This kind of movement, which occurs in all interpretation whatsoever, is not so much a circularity as, to use Heidegger's expression, a remarkable 'relatedness back and forward'.[14] To the extent that the questions of existence and being are themselves involved in this hermeneutical reciprocity, each needs the other and neither can stand by itself. So we are again pointed to the underlying unity of Heidegger's work, and this is a further confirmation of my contention that the contrasting earlier and later phases are to be understood as the two sides of a massive dialectic.

We have spent a considerable time in bringing forward reasons for holding that in the first of our five areas of contrast in Heidegger, the one which has to do with the opposition of existence and being, we can best understand what is going on in terms of a dialectic that moves from existence toward being and then from being toward existence, but that is governed throughout by the unifying question of being. It will not be necessary for us to spend so long over the remaining four areas of contrast, and to the next of these we now turn.

2. This second area concerns the contrast between science and poetry as modes of discourse and ways of expressing truth. The discourse of the early writings is scientific. Strictly speaking, it is phenomenological. This means that it is scientific (*wissenschaftlich*) in the broad sense. Edmund Husserl, the father of phenomenology and the teacher to whom Heidegger dedicated *Being and Time*, believed that his phenomenological method afforded a strictly scientific way of approaching the problems of philosophy. He was convinced that 'the highest ideal represented in the modern age is the scientific ideal'.[15] Admittedly, he did not understand 'science' only in the sense of an empirical objectifying knowledge, but his descriptive method did aim at bringing to philosophy a way of thinking as rigorous as that of the natural sciences and at attaining a systematic and universally valid kind of knowledge that may properly be called 'scientific'. In *Being and Time*, Heidegger, although he freely adapts Husserl's phenomenology to his own purpose, nevertheless thinks of his procedure as 'scientific' as he presents an ordered account of his theme. In Thomas Langan's words, Heidegger succeeds in being concrete 'without sacrificing the coherence and methodicalness associated with traditional systematic philosophical analyses'.[16] But in the later writings, Heidegger's utterances are altogether more cryptic. His language at times becomes quasi-religious and mystical. In place of the thrust of a scientific method of investigation, there is rather the listening for what being may address to us. Again, whereas Heidegger began with man, the existent being to whom it belongs to ask questions and to pursue the ontological inquiry, he ends with man's submitting himself and his questions to being. Now it is not the investigator possessed of a scientific method of inquiry who penetrates to the mystery of being, but the poet who has the sensitivity to hear its words. Yet this too may be foreshadowed in *Being and Time*, where already Heidegger's interest in etymologies and the primordial meanings of words points to his later doctrine that language is the house or home of being, and that meaning –

at least, meaning on its deeper levels – is given to us rather than gained by us.

3. Closely connected with the contrast between science and poetry is a third one – that between calculative and primordial or essential thinking. Calculative thinking is the kind that is characteristic of science. This is active, investigative thought that aims at the mastery of things. It is the kind of thinking associated with the practical concerns that bulk so largely in the existential analytic presented in *Being and Time*, and we should not forget that the analytic there was explicitly concerned with 'everyday' existence. But the essential or primordial thinking of the later writings reverses the order. It is no longer governed by 'logic' in the ordinarily accepted sense of the term. It aims at overcoming the fragmentariness which characterizes the analytical thinking of science. This essential thinking is meditative in character. It is not so much something done by us as it is an 'occurrence of being' in us – and the word used here for 'occurrence' suggests a kind of lighting up, almost a revelation.[17] But here again I think we can trace the lines of development from *Being and Time*. In that book Heidegger manifested a profound interest in history. He gives a sketch of the 'repetitive' thinking of the historian who seeks to enter again into the experience of the historical figure.[18] Heidegger's own interpretations of the pre-Socratic philosophers may be regarded as examples of repetitive thinking. This may be considered as a kind of thinking which stands between calculative thinking and essential thinking. From this listening, repetitive thinking, it is only a step to the essential thinking which listens directly to the voice of being without the mediation of an historical agent.

As he moves increasingly in the direction of essential or meditative thinking, Heidegger becomes more critical both of science and of metaphysics, which is a kind of science in the broad sense of the term. Essential thinking lies beyond metaphysics. Yet Heidegger wishes to maintain that this essential thinking is still philosophy.

4. The contrast just discussed merges into a fourth one, which is connected with Heidegger's understanding of truth. All through his writings truth is understood as *aletheia*, literally understood as 'unhiddenness', and already in *Being and Time* he has rejected the common understanding of truth as the agreement of our propositions with some state of affairs in the world. Yet in the early writings the fundamental truth is the truth of existence. The *Dasein* that is disclosed to itself in its being is 'in the truth'. *Dasein* is

essentially 'discovering', that is to say, stripping away concealments so that unhiddenness or truth may take place. It is suggested
that the very laws of nature become true when they are 'discovered'
by *Dasein*.[19] But then, in an essay 'On the Essence of Truth',
we meet the kind of turning or even reversal with which we have
become familiar. Truth is now 'letting-be' (*Seinlassen*). It is something conferred on man in his overtness, and error and illusion
arise from the failure to 'let-be'.[20] The case of the artist is again
relevant to this situation, for the true artist lets the truth or disclosure take place, he lets us see things for what they really are.
But already in *Being and Time* the human existent was called the
'clearing' (*Lichtung*) in being, the place where being has become
transparent to itself.[21] This idea is further developed in later
writings, but from the beginning it suggests not only that *Dasein*
is the locus of truth but that it is the recipient of the truth that
belongs to being.

5. The last contrast concerns Heidegger's concept of the world.
In *Being and Time* there is a brilliant exposition of the world as
an instrumental system. Entities within the world are understood
and receive their meaning as they get incorporated into the system
and are made serviceable to *Dasein*, whose practical concerns are
what give unity to the whole.[22] In many ways, this looks like a
philosophy tailored to the needs of the technological age. Yet it is
precisely against this way of conceiving the world that the later
Heidegger has turned. Such a way of regarding the world is an
expression of the subjective will-to-power which, according to
Heidegger, has been for a long time the steadily emerging outlook
of the West. As against the early view of the instrumental world,
there is now set the thought of the world as possessing dimensions
that transcend human interest. The world is the place of inter-
section of four dimensions, which are designated by the poetic or
mythological terms: earth and sky, mortals and gods.[23] But once
more it is possible to see how this development was left open, if
not actually foreseen, in the early teaching. For even at that stage
the notion of the instrumental world was associated with the
everyday *Dasein*, that is to say, with the existent in his routine
concerns, where everything is levelled down by the preferences
and pressures of the collective mass, the 'they'. While indeed the
existential analytic takes its beginning from this everyday existing,
it is already implied that an authentic existence breaks out of
the everyday routines and affords better possibilities of understanding. Thus it is in the exceptional experiences of the artist,

the poet, the thinker and the mystic that the world in all its dimensions truly comes to light.

It cannot be denied that there is some exaggeration in the later Heidegger, and this has led some critics to claim that he has become anti-scientific and even unphilosophical. Unquestionably he has a bias against technology, though in this regard many of his criticisms are just, and cannot be dismissed as mere nostalgia for a simpler way of life. But his strictures on science (which he usually couples with technology) react excessively against his early admiration for the scientific (*wissenschaftlich*). His often quoted sentence, 'Science does not think',[24] was no doubt meant to shock and has to be read in context. But what he apparently fails to see is that the highly complex texture of scientific thinking is not by any means to be contained within his notion of calculative thinking. It would seem to me that the mental processes involved in scientific discovery, for instance, may not be so very far from what Heidegger would regard as essential or meditative thinking.

However, my concern here is not to attempt an evaluation of Heidegger's later philosophy or to judge whether he has swung too far in the new directions and would have done better to have paid more attention to some of his early insights. My aim has simply been to show that the early and late work belong together and that we best understand their relationship in terms of a dialectic, each complementing and correcting the other, but neither able to absorb the other or to be fused with it in a new synthesis. If there is the possibility of a philosophy of being, then perhaps it can only be done in some such way as Heidegger has himself followed. The way that starts off from particular beings, whether man himself or the beings of nature, comes to a place where the path breaks off, as the repeated failure of metaphysics has shown. Is there then another way, a way which can be called philosophical in so far as it still works with the language and concepts of philosophy, though it is also akin to the ways of the poet and mystic? Heidegger thinks that there is such a way, and that it leads to an 'overcoming of metaphysics' and to a thinking beyond metaphysics, yet a thinking that is still philosophical and still concerned with the question of being. We are left to judge whether he has been successful. But in order to make such a judgment, we must hold the two sides of his philosophy together in a dialectical tension, for neither the earlier nor the later thought can stand in isolation, and certainly neither can be judged without the other. In this philosophy, it is not a question of assessing 'results', but the way of thinking itself.

Let me in conclusion quote – with considerable abridgment – a passage from Heidegger summing up these matters very well: 'Every philosophical – that is, thoughtful – theory of the essence of man is *already in itself* a theory of the being of beings. Every theory of being is *already in itself* a theory of the essence of man. But neither theory can be obtained just by reversing the other ... No way of thought, not even the way of metaphysical thought, begins with the essence of man and goes from there over to being, nor does it, in reverse, begin with being and then return to man. Rather, every way of thinking is already *moving within* the total relation between being and the essence of man, or else it is not thinking at all.'[25] This, as it seems to me, is certainly a good description of Heidegger's own philosophical thinking and of the relation between its two major phases.

Notes

1. M. Heidegger, *Über den Humanismus*, Klostermann 1949, p. 17.

2. W. J. Richardson, *Heidegger: Through Phenomenology to Thought*, Nijhoff 1963, p. xvi.

3. M. Heidegger, *Being and Time*, tr. J. Macquarrie and E. S. Robinson, SCM Press and Harper & Row 1962, p. 255.

4. *Über den Humanismus*, p. 22.

5. M. Grene, *Martin Heidegger*, Bowes & Bowes 1957 p. 117.

6. H. Ott, *Denken und Sein*, Evangelischer Verlag 1959.

7. *Being and Time*, p. 62.

8. *Was ist Metaphysik?*, Klosterman ^{7}1955, p. 46.

9. *Einführung in die Metaphysik*, Niemeyer 1953, p. 60.

10. *Being and Time*, p. 23.

11. *Einführung in die Metaphysik*, pp. 71ff.

12. *Being and Time*, p. 38.

13. Op cit., pp. 27-8 and 193-5.

14. Op. cit., p. 28.

15. Q. Lauer, *Phenomenology: Its Genesis and Prospects*, Harper & Row 1965, pp. 11-12.

16. T. Langan, *The Meaning of Heidegger*, Columbia University Press 1959, p. 41, n. 46.

17. *Was ist Metaphysik?*, p. 47.

18. *Being and Time*, pp. 437ff.

19. Op. cit., pp. 262ff.

20. 'On the Essence of Truth', tr. R. F. C. Hull and A. Crick, in *Existence and Being*, ed. W. Brock, Regnery 1949, p. 305.

21. *Being and Time*, p. 171.

22. Op. cit. pp. 91ff.

23. Cf. *Vorträge und Aufsätze*, Neske 1954, pp. 145ff.

24. *What Is Called Thinking?*, tr. F. D. Wieck and J. G. Gray, Harper & Row 1968, p. 8.

25. Op. cit., pp. 79-80.

18

A Modern Scottish Theologian

In these days when churchmen in most countries are constantly bemoaning the shortage of candidates for the ministry, it is hard to believe that only a short generation ago the Scottish divinity halls were filled with students, many of them men of outstanding ability. New College, Edinburgh, was specially favoured, and in the decade before World War II it was the training ground for an extraordinary number of men who have since gone on to make their mark as theological professors and writers. Among the names that readily come to mind from that brilliant period are J. L. M. Haire, T. F. Torrance, J. K. S. Reid, Ronald Gregor Smith, John McIntyre – and, of course, Ian Henderson, the subject of this brief study. Though his work was hindered by ill-health and prematurely terminated by death, he made a contribution which puts him in the first rank of Scottish theologians of this century.

He was born in Edinburgh in 1910, but his upbringing was in the west of Scotland, and from an early age he took a keen interest in the Highlands and their tragic history. From Oban High School he went on to study philosophy at the University of Edinburgh, where his teachers were Norman Kemp Smith and A. E. Taylor. Then he proceeded to New College for his theological studies and came under the influence of two great theologians of those days, John Baillie and Hugh Ross Mackintosh. I believe it was Mackintosh who influenced him most. These were exciting times in theology, for the theological revolution initiated by Karl Barth was in vigorous progress. Thus it was natural for Henderson at the end of his New College studies to go for a time to the University of Basle to study under Barth. When Barth came to Scotland to give his Gifford Lectures, it was Ian Henderson and his friend James Haire (later Professor of Theology in Belfast) who acted as his translators and who were responsible for the published version of the lectures.[1] Although he became very critical of Barth's theological stance, Henderson always cherished a profound respect for him and frequently defended him against criticisms that were merely superficial or ill informed.

Henderson's own contribution to theology may be seen as threefold. In the first place, there was his important work on demythologizing and the existential interpretation of Christian faith. In this area, Henderson was a pioneer in the English-speaking world. It was he who recognized that Bultmann is important not only for New Testament studies but for systematic theology, and his acute evaluation of Bultmann remains significant. Secondly, Henderson was interested in the ethics of power. He realized that theology does not go on in a vacuum, but in the midst of human and political realities, and that it has to be related to these. I have mentioned already his early concern with the history of the High-lands and with the conflicts which led to the depopulation and impoverishment of that region, especially the 'clearances', when powerful but impecunious landowners drove the people from their homes and crofts to make way for more profitable sheep farms and deer forests. As a student and pastor, Henderson was living through the rise and fall of a still more terrifying concentration of unjust and destructive power, the Hitler regime, which he studied in considerable depth. His reflections on the ethics of power are less easy to define than his views on demythologizing, but they are just as essential to his total theology. Thirdly, there was his critique of the ecumenical movement. Henderson saw this movement not as an unmixed blessing but as an ambiguous phenomenon (for no movement in church or state is free from sin) and one replete with considerable dangers. His criticism made him very unpopular with the ecclesiastical establishment, and it may be conceded that some of his attacks were exaggerated. Still, as he wrote to me in 1967, 'Somebody had to write an explosive book before moderate criticism of the movement could have an effect'. I shall show that Henderson's critique was, on the whole, a just one, and that it was no isolated part of his work, for it followed logically from his two other theological interests – demythologizing and the ethics of power.

A clue to the character of Henderson's theology may be found in his understanding of himself as a child of the Enlightenment and a foe of Romanticism. He had a healthy respect for David Hume and admired the brilliance of Scottish society in the eighteenth century. As an inheritor of the Enlightenment, he could not rest content with myth or dogma, and it was the quest for intellectual integrity in theology that attracted him (whether justifiably or not) to Bultmann. 'Romantic', on the other hand, was a bad word with Henderson. He reserved it for superstitious and irrational loyalties and applied it, for instance, to the Oxford Movement. But no one is ever quite consistent. Henderson combined his respect for the Enlightenment with an admiration for Kierkegaard and existentialism, while his warm sympathy with Scottish nationalism had surely a considerable admixture of Romanticism.

For ten years Henderson served in the pastoral ministry, first in Fraserburgh and then in Kilmany, both parishes in the east of Scotland. Thus, when his first book appeared in 1948, it was the fruit of mature experience and reflection.

This book bore the title, *Can Two Walk Together?* More clearly indicative of its content was the explanatory subtitle, 'The Quest for a Secular Morality'. It deals with themes that are related to the second of Henderson's main theological interests, as I have listed them above. As the author himself noted, the book was concerned to raise questions rather than to answer them, and the questions are difficult indeed. They are questions that occupied him not only in this book but throughout his life. What is the foundation of morality? Can it be conceived in secular terms? What is the relation of belief to conduct? These questions are discussed not in abstraction but in intimate connection with the shattering events of those years – the rise of the Nazis, the ruthless repression of opposition, the staggering destruction and cruelty of war, the confused aftermath.

Henderson rejects the view that there is an independent secular morality operative among all men, irrespective of the dogmas which they hold. Even the so-called 'natural law' implies some supporting dogmas – that there is reason in every man, that there is a single criterion of action for all, and that there is a real community of all mankind. These dogmas are not explicitly Christian, but they are at least compatible with Christianity, perhaps even highly compatible. Henderson accepts Troeltsch's view that whereas the Atlantic nations (Britain, France and the United States) accept the dogmas of natural law, the Germans and Swiss reject them. On the one hand, we find Barth rejecting natural law in favour of a morality founded explicitly on Christian dogma; on the other hand, Hitler and the Nazis likewise rejected natural law, but they made the dogma of the superiority of the Nordic race the foundation for their morality – and, writes Henderson, 'once this single monstrous assumption is conceded, all the various steps in Hitler's theory and practice follow'.[2]

Dogmas, according to Henderson, cannot be proved. They are ultimate presuppositions. But he distinguishes between an inductive style of thinking which remains open to the possibility of revising dogma and is tolerant of other points of view, and a deductive style which is quite rigid in carrying through to their conclusion all the implications of the fundamental dogma. The first style is typical of the natural law mentality, the second is exemplified above all by the Nazis. The first is reasonable, the second is unreasonable and issues in the loveless misuse of power. But Henderson was too much of a realist to overrate the influence of reason in human affairs. He states bluntly that the natural law will be upheld not by an appeal to reason but by the power of those nations which believe in it.

To some, Henderson's analysis of the power struggle in World War II may seem to smack of what in those days was called Vansittartism, named after the British civil servant Lord Vansittart, who believed that there is an inherent aggressiveness in the German nation and that the Atlantic nations must take account of this in their dealings with Germany. I do not think that this was Henderson's view, for he was a great admirer of many things German. But he was always very much aware of the corrupting tendencies of power, and certainly his realism stuck far closer to the facts of the case than, let us say, the Romanticism of such men as the late Bishop Bell of Chichester.

There are in this early book many provocative sentences which show the way in which Henderson's thought was moving. He reveals himself as critical of Barth, and even more of the Barthians, who, in his words, 'seem to consider that their intellectual duty is to think the thoughts of Dr Barth instead of thinking for themselves'.[3] But, characteristically, he is also critical of those who refuse to take Barth seriously, and makes the point that Barth's grounding of morality on revealed dogma may have been the only appropriate response to the Nazi type of dogmatism. But any kind of dogmatism was abhorrent to Henderson. He praises the Scottish system of education with its respect for philosophy and its cultivation of the critical spirit. But his intellectualism is constantly tempered by a warm human concern and compassion. As an illustration of this, I may quote a remark in the book that 'unemployment is a *spiritual calamity* and not just an economic or social breakdown'.[4] Those who remember the years of the industrial depression in Scotland will appreciate the depth of understanding and feeling that lie behind these words.

It was in 1948, the year in which his book on ethics was published, that Ian Henderson was appointed Professor of Systematic Theology in the University of Glasgow, and he held this post for the remainder of his life. I first got to know him during the early years of his professorship, when I began my doctoral studies under his direction. He was at the height of his powers at that time, and working on what were then the frontiers of the theological enterprise – the problems of demythologizing raised by Bultmann. I was constantly amazed both by the extent of his knowledge and the acuteness of his critical judgment. But what was equally impressive was his enthusiasm for and his devotion to the theological task. He was a professor who really believed in his subject, and he imparted his zest to his students.

All of these qualities are apparent in his second book,[5] which comes from those years and sets forth the results of his studies of Bultmann. This, I believe, was the first book to introduce the controversy over demythologizing to the English-speaking world. A host of other writers have taken up the theme since that time, but Henderson's book, in spite of its brevity, already anticipated many of the issues that were to be more fully debated in the ensuing discussion.

The first two chapters of the book expound clearly and succinctly the essence of Bultmann's view and the philosophical concepts which underlie and articulate it. The exposition is scrupulously fair, but it is not hard to perceive that Henderson feels very strongly the attraction of Bultmann's proposal for demythologizing. Here perhaps he hoped to find a post-Enlightenment interpretation of Christian faith such as he had not found either in Barth or in that old-fashioned liberalism which Barth had so ruthlessly criticized. But Henderson's intellectual integrity held him back from any uncritical or merely superficial identification with Bultmann's position. To adapt his remark about the Barthians, it was clear that he did *not* think it his intellectual duty merely to think the thoughts of Dr Bultmann! So the two remaining chapters of the book are devoted to a searching analysis of two of the most debatable points in Bultmann's theology – the question of the historical Jesus, and the question of whether myth can be *wholly* translated into the language of human existence.

It was the first of these two questions which especially continued to engage Henderson's attention in the subsequent debates about demythologizing. A man so respectful toward the facts as he was could not rest content with teaching about Jesus which seemed to neglect a factual historical basis. In his lectures, he used to illustrate the point by reminding his hearers of the famous World War I recruiting poster showing a portrait of Lord Kitchener pointing his finger with the words: 'Your country needs you!' Would this poster have had the effect that it did if people had been aware that the *image* of Kitchener which the portrait conveyed was (as some have alleged) not at all commensurate with the *reality* of the man? Similarly, in the case of the Christian faith, does not its credibility entail a bond of continuity between the Jesus of history and the Christ proclaimed in the kerygma? Thus Henderson became interested in the so-called 'new quest' of the historical Jesus, and especially in the work of Bornkamm, Käsemann, Ebeling and Fuchs. He himself contributed an essay to an important German symposium on the theme.[6]

Bultmann himself, as is well-known, remained unswayed by the new questers and continued to claim that all the gospel needs to presuppose is the 'that' and not the 'what' – that is to say, the fact *that* he existed but not the question of *what* manner of person he was. But in his last published remarks on these matters in his little book, *Rudolf Bultmann*, Henderson rightly points out that one cannot really separate the 'that' and the 'what', and he claims that Bultmann himself assumes a good deal more knowledge of Jesus than his theory would seem to allow. However, although critical of Bultmann on this score, Henderson remained essentially close to him, and I think it may be fairly said that Bultmann continued to be, in his view, the most significant theologian of his day. 'Behind the negativities of Bultmann's position', wrote Henderson, 'lie his positive affirmations. If Bultmann is ready to surrender what he regards as the outworks, it is because he considers that the central citadel is intact.'[7]

In the last years of his life, Henderson's focus of interest shifted to the ecumenical movement and the problems raised by it. This may have surprised some, but it should not have done so, for he had always cherished a deep concern for the church. We have already noted that he served for a substantial period in the parish ministry. During his time as professor, he continued his interest in the church and identified himself with two parishes. First, while he lived near the university in Glasgow, he joined himself to a working-class congregation down by the shipyards.

Then, when deteriorating health compelled him to live out in the country, he took an active part in the parish of Campsie. He also served very acceptably for a term as Moderator of the Presbytery of Glasgow. It was therefore as one deeply involved in the life of the church and deeply caring for its well-being that he chose to become embroiled in the debates over the ecumenical question. As he saw it, the life and integrity of the church were being threatened by certain developments, and he felt challenged to speak out, even at the risk of unpopularity.

Incidentally, it is important not to make the mistake of supposing that Henderson's criticism of the ecumenical movement was a kind of by-product of his nationalism. Some people have claimed that this was the case, and they have made this an excuse for not taking Henderson's criticisms seriously. To be sure, nationalist motives were obviously present in some of his harsher utterances concerning Anglican 'imperialism' and also in his regrettable attack on the late James Pitt-Watson, who had been Moderator of the Church of Scotland at the time of the coronation of 1953 and had a part in that ceremony. But the main thrust of Henderson's argument about ecumenism is thoroughly theological and is entirely in accord with those interests which had shown themselves earlier in his career. His desire for intellectual integrity in theology, hitherto manifested in his work on demythologizing, now fused with his still earlier ethical critique of power to form the basis for his attack on what he regarded as a mistaken form of ecumenism. All who are active in ecumenical matters would do well to read and ponder what he has to say.

On the matter of intellectual integrity, Henderson had already written: 'One can hardly see much place for either Tillich or Bultmann in the one church that the ecumenical movement is exerting its immense pressure to bring about', and he gave as his reason for this judgment the fact that neither of these theologians was concerned 'to reproduce the views of ecclesiastical power groups' but were concerned simply with the pursuit of truth in theology.[8] In *Power without Glory*, the implied criticism of ecumenical theology is greatly developed. Here he makes the point that ecumenical language 'is designed not to describe but to conceal' and that it is 'a fiesta of double-think'.[9] Undoubtedly, this criticism justly applies to much that has come out of the ecumenical movement, especially from 'faith and order' groups and from commissions preparing 'plans of union'. Good theology is rarely, if ever, done by groups that are seeking a consensus at any price.

Admittedly, there can be a permissible vagueness and even ambiguity which simply recognizes that all theological positions are approximate. But there is also a language which conceals in order to evade, a language which does not explore open theological possibilities but rather manipulates the data in order to arrive at predetermined results. That there has been a good deal of this in the ecumenical movement cannot be denied, but it is utterly subversive of the theological task and can end only in the devaluation of Christian truth. All who care about theology and Christian truth should be grateful to Henderson for pointing this out so fearlessly.

The other side of Henderson's critique had to do with the temptations of power in the ecumenical movement. Most divisions in the church have in fact arisen in the quest for religious freedom. The idea of 'one church', in the sense of one organization, is an idea of the seventeenth century and is remote from our contemporary understanding of a pluralistic society. The tolerant 'natural law' mentality emerging from the Enlightenment is opposed to uniformity and to the concentration of power, whether civil or ecclesiastical. In spite of the protestations of ecumenists, it is clear that 'mergers' and 'organic unions' must lead to uniformity and power concentrations. Denominationalism may not be ideal, but at least, as Henderson points out, it is the only way that has so far been devised of protecting freedom, tolerance and legitimate diversity in religion.

Henderson was by no means opposed to ecumenism in the broad sense. Indeed, he welcomed, and was willing to learn from, contacts with all Christian groups. He especially welcomed the contacts between the Church of Scotland and the Roman Catholic Church, the first friendly intercourse between the two bodies since the Reformation. But he believed that such contacts become perverted when they are turned into theological manoeuvres or political bargaining aimed at so-called 'organic union'. He states bluntly that to try to achieve Christian unity 'by means of a series of mergers is so grotesquely superficial that in the end it can only exacerbate the problem, and has indeed already begun to do so'.[10] Events seem to be bearing out the truth of his remarks, as one 'scheme' after another runs into trouble and threatens to produce new divisions. It is time that those who concern themselves with ecumenical matters heeded Henderson's strictures and looked for a better way toward unity than 'mergers' – a better way that will allow far more room for freedom and diversity than has so far been envisaged. As I mentioned above, Henderson acknowledged that his own criticism had to be an extreme one, but his hope was that it would lead to a more moderate criticism that would produce constructive alternatives to those mistaken policies which he deplored.

Ian Henderson's many-sided theological work ended abruptly in Eastertide, 1969, when he died a few days before the publication of his last book, a collection of essays on those themes that lay near to his heart.[11] He has left an example of devotion to the theological task, of integrity, tolerance and courage, that should be inspiring for theologians of the future, both in Scotland and beyond.

Notes

1. K. Barth, *The Knowledge of God and the Service of God*, tr. J. L. M. Haire and I. Henderson, Hodder & Stoughton 1938.

2. I. Henderson, *Can Two Walk Together?*, Nisbet 1948, p. 14.

3. Op. cit., p. 22.

4. Op. cit., p. 85.

5. I. Henderson, *Myth in the New Testament*, SCM Press 1952.

6. *Der historische Jesus und der kerygmatische Christus*, ed. H. Ristow and K. Matthiae, Evangelischer Verlag 1960.

7. I. Henderson, *Rudolf Bultmann*, Lutterworth 1965, p. 47.

8. *Rudolf Bultmann*, p. 35.

9. I. Henderson, *Power without Glory*, Hodder & Stoughton 1967, p. 101.

10. Op. cit., p. 6.

11. I. Henderson, *Scotland: Kirk and People*, Lutterworth 1969.

19

Process and Faith:
An American Testimony

When Daniel Day Williams died in 1973, he was Roosevelt Professor of Systematic Theology in Union Theological Seminary, New York, and had been teaching there for almost twenty years. There are many reasons for the fame of Union Seminary – its magnificent library, its international connections, its location in the largest metropolitan area in the world, its freedom from outside control. But Union has been distinguished above all by a succession of outstanding scholars and teachers, and a high place among them belongs to Daniel Williams. He was a theologian of great intellectual ability, a Christian of real spiritual depth and, in addition, one of the ablest and most conscientious of teachers, especially at the graduate level.

The conjunction of intellect, conscientiousness and love, evident both in Williams' writings and in the man himself, may be illustrated from an incident that took place less than six months before his death. In conversation with him, I had occasion to quote some words from one of his books: 'It is the sheerest sentimentality to suppose that love can dispense with objective knowledge ... It is not loving concern alone which tells us what needs to be done.'[1] He at once replied: 'These are the most important sentences in the book.' I was not surprised by that reply, for these sentences do express something very central to Williams' understanding of Christianity. Conversely, though he was far from being a polemical theologian, he could not refrain from expressing his impatience with those Christian writers of recent years who have suggested that 'all you need is love', without providing any adequate analysis of the meaning of love or the grounds of love, and without betraying any awareness that frequently a great deal of hard thought is required to know what the demands of love in a given situation are.

Williams was born in 1910 in Denver, Colorado, under the shadow of the Rocky Mountains. After attending college in his native state, he went on to Chicago to study theology, and this was decisively formative for his whole subsequent career as a theologian. Chicago had long been a centre of a dynamic, empirical type of theology, with its roots in James, Bergson, Alexander and others. About the time when Williams was studying there, a new influence was making itself felt – that of Alfred North Whitehead. But although Whitehead's influence soon became dominant in Chicago, and although his is the name that first comes to mind when we think of 'process theology', the main lines of this type of thinking were already established.[2] The teachers who had most influence on Williams were the philosopher, Charles Hartshorne, and the theologian, Henry Nelson Wieman. Williams praises Hartshorne for his 'great logical skill and religious insight',[3] and for Wieman too he always cherished a profound respect.

For fifteen years before coming to New York, Williams himself taught theology in the Chicago Theological Seminary, and during that time became one of the acknowledged leaders of process theology. He also became a widely regarded authority on the philosophy of Whitehead. But he was never a narrow Whiteheadian. Bernard Meland writes: 'For Daniel Day Williams ... Whitehead's vision of reality forms a perspective within which theological reflection may be fruitfully pursued; but it is informed and supplemented and often critized by other perspectives, both within and without the organismic legacy of thought.' He also states that 'in his earlier years Williams was the most eclectic of the process group of empiricists in his selection of sources and perspectives, concerned that empirical theology be attentive to a broad canvas of alternatives within the theological tradition'.[4] For instance, Williams had a remarkable grasp of the teaching of St Augustine, and was always deeply influenced by it. Again, one has only to read his book, *What Present-Day Theologians Are Thinking*, to learn the breadth of his understanding and sympathies, so far as modern theology is concerned. His own remarks on the nature of theology make it clear also that he could not be accused (as some process theologians have been) of making the metaphysic of Whitehead determinative and then bringing in Christianity as supplementary material. He does indeed say that the function of theology 'is to meet the spirit of the times at the level of the deepest intellectual searching', but he says on the same page that theology 'lies under the judgment of the living and personal revelation of God'.[5] I think this is how he actually did his own theology, for when I read his major work, *The Spirit and Forms of Love*, although there are many references to Whitehead, Hartshorne, Wieman and other process thinkers, and although the background of that school of thought is discernible, I believe that most of the insights of the book come from Christian tradition and experience, and could have been available to someone who knew nothing of Whitehead.

In conversation, while ready to uphold the process view, he was never dogmatic or exclusive. I was his close colleague for eight years, and we often discussed theological questions. He used to argue, with considerable justification, that most existentialist approaches to theology fail to yield a theology of nature, and tend to evade the metaphysical issue about the ultimate significance of personal existence in the frame of reality. But he was quick to concede on the other hand that process thought is often less aware than existentialism of the tragic aspects of existence, and that its analysis of personal life is less subtle than that offered by existentialism. But traditions and points of view cannot easily be mixed, and perhaps they yield their best insights in dialogue rather than in an attempted synthesis. Dan Williams stayed with process thought, and his very moderation in the use of it has helped to exhibit its virtues.

There would not be much point in trying to present a summary of Williams' teaching over the whole field of theology, ethics and the philosophy of religion. Instead, I shall attempt to expound and evaluate his teaching on a single doctrine, albeit a very central one and in his eyes one essential to Christian faith – the doctrine of God. Possibly it is in this area that process thought has its most valuable contributions to make to Christian theology. Some process theologians have been at pains to stress the difference between their way of understanding theism and the classical doctrine, and their critics in turn have alleged that process theology offers a philosophical understanding of God that is independent of the Christian revelation and that is better described as panentheism than as theism proper. Although Williams was critical of some aspects of traditional theism, he always kept the biblical doctrine of God in mind and believed that his own teaching about God was thoroughly compatible with the biblical view. His courses of lectures on the doctrine of God were among his most popular offerings, but he never wrote a book on this subject, though it was in his mind to do so in the last two or three years of his life. However, since his book was not written, we have to gather his teaching on God from various writings.

In common with other process thinkers, whether philosophers or theologians, Williams claimed that the basic category for an understanding of reality is event rather than substance. So God is himself to be conceived as dynamic process, not as static substance. Williams quotes with approval a description of God by his old teacher Wieman, as 'that behaviour of the universe ... which preserves and increases to the maximum the total good of all human living where right adjustment is made'.[6] Similar ways of speaking of God, quoted from the same source, are 'the process of progressive integration', 'the creative event' and 'the growth of qualitative meaning'.[7] All the nouns here used of God – 'behaviour', 'process', 'event', 'growth' – are verbal nouns denoting movement and activity, not substance. Although Wieman's language tends to be impersonal, Williams' own version of theism is one in which God is conceived in terms both dynamic and personal. A person too is a dynamic reality, better conceived as an event or complex of events than as a substance.

Perhaps the main difficulty that many people are likely to encounter in such ways of speaking of God as we have just been quoting is not the dynamic character ascribed to God – after all, the God of the Bible is the 'living' God – but the apparent absorption of God into nature. Can we properly speak of God as 'that behaviour of the universe'? Is not this sheer naturalism, and inconsistent with any Christian theism?

Williams is not unduly upset by the charge of naturalism. He points out that 'naturalism' can mean various philosophical positions, and that 'it makes a great deal of difference whether or not you mean pre-twentieth century naturalism or contemporary naturalism'.[8] As representatives of the latter, he names Dewey, Alexander, Bergson, Wieman, Whitehead and Hartshorne, though acknowledging that some of those named might not have been too willing to have the term applied to them. The new naturalism, unlike that of earlier times, is not reductionist. 'Nature', according to Williams, includes human nature, the capacities and aspirations of the human spirit, and everything which is accessible to man as an experiencing being. 'So the naturalism in view here does not try to explain man in terms of purely material, mechanical or biological causes.' Williams likewise claims that the traditional contrast between nature and history is abolished if one takes a sufficiently inclusive view of nature. In the new naturalism, nature-history is seen as a continuous order. There is a direction common to both, for nature is no longer seen as cyclical but as having, like history, a linear movement.

These considerations lead Williams to affirm what he calls the 'one-order theory of the world'. This is opposed to the more traditional 'two-order theory', in which the supernatural is set over against the natural. Williams remarks: 'The term "supernaturalism" is now very rarely used in theology ... we are very hesitant about using the term "supernatural" precisely because we do not want to mean by this another realm, another set of causes, another order, to be added on to this one natural order with which we know we have to do.'[9]

Since, however, we have been assured that the new naturalism is not reductionist, then we must suppose that the realities once envisaged as supernatural are now accounted for in terms of a vastly enriched concept of the natural – and that they are still *realities*, not merely epiphenomena. Is there then any difference between a two-order theory of the world recognizing a supernatural and a natural order, and a one-order theory recognizing only a natural order but one with spiritual dimensions so that all that was ascribed to the supernatural is still secured for human experience? I think there is a difference, and it is this. In the one-order theory, the relation of God and the world must be conceived in far more intimate terms than it was on the two-order theory.

But when we raise the question of God's relation to the world, we strike on an area of Williams' philosophical theology which is not clear – and which he himself admits is not clear. Is God a reality distinct from nature, even when nature is conceived in the richest way? If he is, then has not the supernatural been restored? If he is not, then is he simply a 'behaviour of the universe', and is this an adequate conception of God? It should be noted that when Williams describes the enlarged non-reductionist understanding of nature, he does not go so far as to include God in it, but only 'the capacities and aspirations of the human spirit', as we have seen above. But he also makes it clear that his sympathies lie with those naturalist philosophers who speak of God (Whitehead and Hartshorne, who are 'naturalists' by Williams' definition) rather than with someone like Dewey, who does indeed have a conception of nature able to include 'the capacities and aspirations of the human spirit' but has no place for the ontological reality of God.

I think that if he had been quite consistent in his philosophical theology, Williams would have frankly included God as a dimension or mode of behaviour in that one-order reality which he can also call nature. He does in fact seem to hold that 'God and the world exist in a community of mutual action and passion' and that the mind-body relationship is a helpful analogy for understanding the God-world relationship.[10] Of course, on one view of the matter, 'mind' is simply a misleading word which designates the behaviour of the body – though such 'behaviourism' need not be understood in a reductionist way. But Daniel Williams' attachment to the distinctive Christian teaching about God was such that I do not think he would have bluntly subscribed to the view that God is the world's behaviour, even that very significant behaviour 'which preserves and increases to the maximum the total good'. As I noted in connection with his book on love, his theology, though it derives a general support from process philosophy, goes far beyond that philosophy in its Christian affirmations and bursts out of its categories.

However, the notion of the God-world relation as 'a community of mutual action and passion' is one that was very important for Williams' thought. To one as sensitive as he was both to love and suffering, the doctrine of a divine impassibility seemed quite unworthy of God, almost a blasphemy. Probably there was nothing in the whole corpus of Whitehead's writings that attracted Williams more than that famous description of God as 'the great companion, the fellow sufferer who understands'.[11] Suffering, Williams contended, is not something to be regarded as negative.[12] It is capable of transmutation, and leads into deeper selfhood, community and healing. But suffering does not only affect the community of human beings, for we form a community not only among ourselves but with God. 'I affirm', writes Williams, 'that God does suffer as he participates in the ongoing life of the society of being. His sharing in the world's suffering is the supreme instance of knowing, accepting and transforming in love the suffering which arises in the world. I am affirming the doctrine of the divine sensitivity. Without it, I can make no sense of the being of God.'[13] These words lie very close to the heart of his doctrine of God.

It will be clear from what has been said that the overwhelming emphasis in Williams' teaching about God was on immanence, participation, reciprocity, even suffering. Of course, he says from time to time that he does not mean to deny the transcendence of God or the hope in God's eventual triumph. But it is not always easy to see how these truths about the divine being can find a place in the structure of his general teaching. Nevertheless, in estimating what he says, we have also to remember that he is teaching against the background of a long continued stress on God's transcendence and majesty, and that whenever one sets out to correct an imbalance, it is almost inevitable that one should exaggerate on the other side.

A theologian for whom God and nature were so close is one for whom natural theology would be important. While Daniel Williams recognized the strength of the modern critique of traditional natural theology, he did not agree that the time has come to abandon it. But perhaps what he advocated would be better described as a 'theology of nature' than as 'natural theology' in the old sense. Though fully recognizing the difficulties and complexities encountered in an attempt to relate the statements of theology to those of the empirical sciences, he did believe that theology must take serious cognizance of the scientific picture of the world and consider how far that picture is consonant with theological assertions.

Daniel Day Williams will be remembered as one of the most sober and perceptive representatives of process theology. He has amply shown the strength of that theology, above all in what it has to teach us about the genuine sharing of God in the life of his world. I cannot believe that a doctrine of divine impassibility such as would represent God as unaffected by the sufferings of the creation can establish itself in the Christian Church again. God, if he is to be called God, must have that sensitivity which Williams ascribes to him. And this, in turn, may well mean that for an adequate understanding of God we have to deploy the concepts of modern philosophy – not necessarily process philosophy – rather than those we have inherited from the classical ages of Christian thought. But the dialectic of thinking about God is always a subtle one. God, if he is to be called God, must not only have that kind of participation in the world of which Williams wrote so persuasively, he must also have a measure of distinctness from the world and a measure of control over its destiny, and these truths do not come through very clearly. Process theology – and I suppose one can say this about most styles of theology – has its valid insights to offer, but, as Williams well realized, other ways of thinking are needed too if the riches of Christian truth are to be explored.

Notes

1. D. D. Williams, *The Spirit and Forms of Love*, Harper & Row 1969, p. 121.

2. Cf. Bernard Meland, 'The Empirical Tradition in Theology at Chicago', *The Future of Empirical Theology*, ed. B. Meland, Chicago University Press 1969, p. 33.

3. D. D. Williams, *What Present-Day Theologians are Thinking*, Harper & Row ³1967, p. 73.

4. Loc. cit., pp. 45-6.

5. *What Present-Day Theologians are Thinking*, p. 20.

6. D. D. Williams, 'Tradition and Experience in American Theology', *Religion in American Life*, ed. J. W. Smith and A. L. Jamison, Princeton University Press 1961, p. 466.

7. Ibid.

8. D. D. Williams, 'Christianity and Naturalism', *Union Seminary Quarterly Review*, vol. xii, 1957, p. 47.

9. Loc. cit., p. 50.

10. Loc. cit., p. 52.

11. A. N. Whitehead, *Process and Reality*, Cambridge University Press 1929, p. 497.

12. D. D. Williams, 'Suffering and Being in Empirical Theology', *The Future of Empirical Theology*, ed. B. Meland, Chicago University Press 1969, pp. 175ff.

13. Loc. cit., pp. 191-2.

20

Theologies of Hope:
A Critical Examination

Early in 1968 I was privileged to preside at a lecture given at
Union Theological Seminary, New York, by Jürgen Moltmann.
Ten minutes before the lecture was due to begin, the hall was
already filled with several hundred people and others were standing in the passages, so we decided to move to a larger auditorium.
No doubt the interest had been stimulated by a column in *The New
York Times* of the previous day, bearing the somewhat journalistic
heading, 'Death of God Gives Way to a Theology of Hope', and
giving a brief account of the young German theologian who had
embraced Christianity while a prisoner of war in Britain after
World War II. But surely more important was the drawing power
of the magic word 'hope'. After the depressing negativities of
so much recent theology – demythologizing, religionless Christianity, the praise of secularization, the death of God – a theology of
hope seemed to come as a new affirmation of Christian truth.
Does it offer the possibility of a renascence of Christian faith and
theology?

Along with Jürgen Moltmann must be counted Wolfhart
Pannenberg as another leader of this new school in German Protestantism. Close to both of them in many matters is the German
Roman Catholic theologian, Johannes Metz. But the influence
of the new ideas has spread far beyond Germany. There are
enthusiastic disciples of the theology of hope in the United States,
Carl E. Braaten being probably the best-known. Understandably,
the themes of hope and the future make a strong appeal to the
struggling peoples of the 'third world', and an articulate voice
from that quarter is that of the young Brazilian Protestant theologian, Rubem Alves. The literature is already so extensive that

I have thought it best in the title of this chapter to talk of 'theologies of hope' in the plural.

At first sight, the expression 'theology of hope' might seem to be no more than a tautology. Theology speaks of God, and hope is an essential constituent of the meaning of the word 'God'. To believe in God is to have a hopeful understanding of the world, to believe that history has some meaning and goal. However, when one speaks of a 'theology of hope' in the current sense, something more is implied. Every style of theology has its own distinctive perspective and makes some ideas basic in its interpretation of the meaning of Christian faith. The contemporary theologies of hope have adopted the *eschatological* perspective – indeed, they tend to identify theology with eschatology. Likewise, their basic interpretative concepts are those which have eschatological import – hope itself, resurrection, the future, the new and so on. As Moltmann expresses it, 'faith has the priority but hope the primacy'.[1]

But to acknowledge the eschatological perspective and the primacy of eschatological concepts in the theologies of hope does not yet sufficiently distinguish them. For has not eschatology been dominant in much of the theology of this century? At the beginning of the century, Weiss and Schweitzer had rediscovered eschatology as utterly pervasive of the New Testament. In his famous commentary on Romans, Barth uncompromisingly identified theology with eschatology. Then Bultmann too claimed that the New Testament teaching is cast in the mould of the eschatological mythology. If the importance of eschatology has been so widely recognized since the turn of the century, is there anything new or different about the stress on eschatology in the theologies of hope?

There is indeed. Although Schweitzer and Bultmann castigated the nineteenth-century liberals for ignoring eschatology, both of these scholars found it somewhat embarrassing themselves. They regarded eschatology as belonging to the intellectual outlook of the first century, and each of them in his own way demythologized it. While Barth did not demythologize, he gradually muted his early eschatological emphasis as he built up his dogmatic system. On the other hand, the new theologies of hope insist that we should take the eschatology of the New Testament with far more seriousness and even with a degree of literalness. It was not, they tell us, a temporary clothing for the gospel, which could then be disengaged from it. It was rather the very heart of the matter.

Pannenberg writes thus: 'One must be clear about the fact that when one discusses the truth of the apocalyptic expectation of a future judgment and a resurrection of the dead, one is dealing directly with the basis of the Christian faith. Why the man Jesus can be the ultimate revelation of God, why in him and only in him God is supposed to have appeared, remains incomprehensible apart from the horizon of the apocalyptic expectation.'[2]

This is a strong statement, opposed to any elimination or even demythologizing of eschatology. Pannenberg and Moltmann are in fact among Bultmann's bitterest critics. We may take note of two points in Pannenberg's statement just quoted: the assertion of the *future* character of the eschatological events, and the central place given to a concept of *resurrection*.

In locating the eschatological events in the future, the new theologians of hope are going counter to much of the interpretation of eschatology that was prevalent in the early part of the century, such as the realized eschatology of Dodd or Bultmann's view that any moment can become the eschatological moment if in it Christ arises in the soul of the believer. One might say that the theologies of hope go behind the teaching of the fourth gospel that now is the judgment and now we enter eternal life, to the synoptists' belief that these events lie in the future. In this respect we have a return to primitive Christianity. And the emphasis on the future is strong in all the theologians we have in mind – in Moltmann, Braaten and Alves, as well as in Pannenberg.

Let us notice, however, that it is not an otherworldly apocalypticism that these men teach but an historical future. In the thought of the Brazilian, Alves, this future is very much tied up with the aspiration of the poor nations for a better social and international order. On every other page of his book on the theology of hope, one meets, like a refrain, the expression 'a new tomorrow'. This new tomorrow is firmly located within history. 'Visions of the future not extracted from history cannot be called hope; they are forms of alienation.'[3] If this sounds somewhat Marxist, it should be added that Alves makes it clear that, as a Christian, he believes that history is shaped by God's action as well as man's. Furthermore, though the future he envisages is historical, it is by no means conceived in terms of material advancement alone. He has some sharp criticisms of technology as the supposed answer to the needs of the third world. He sees it in the role of 'bread and circuses', a new opiate designed to produce consumers of goods rather than creators of history and human values. 'Technology', he declares, 'creates a false man, a man who learns how to find happiness in what is given to him by the system. His soul is created as the image of what he can have.'[4]

It is interesting to contrast Alves' conception of the future with Braaten's. The latter too is concerned with a this-worldly historical future, but his understanding of it is derived from affluent techno-logical America. In such a society, planning has become a matter of major importance, and in both government and business there has arisen a new class of experts called by the uncouth name of 'futurologists' – men who by computers and other means seek to predict the conditions that will prevail at various times in the future. Braaten argues for a correlation between Christian eschatology and secular futurology. 'Today's Christians find they are not the only ones who dream dreams of a new and better future and are willing to work to usher it into existence. They find themselves mingling with utopians, futurists and other revolutionaries who live toward the future of a new world.'[5] But he adds (and this may well be an insuperable obstacle in the way of his proposed correlation) that a crucial difference between the two groups is that whereas for secular futurologists the future is to be reached by planning from where we are, the eschatology of Christians looks for God's kingdom to come to us (its advent). Moltmann too has, in a tentative way, investigated the relation between Christian hope and secular planning.[6]

The second idea which figured prominently in the statement quoted from Pannenberg was resurrection, and this is an idea important for the other champions of the theologies of hope also. Moltmann makes this blunt statement: 'Christianity stands or falls with the reality of the raising of Jesus from the dead by God.'[7] In talking of the 'reality' of this event, Moltmann makes it clear that it is to be understood as an event of history, and an event that happened in or to Jesus Christ, not merely in the disciples. Here again we are being invited to go behind the specula-tions of recent times – and especially demythologized versions of the resurrection – to a more 'objective' appraisal of the raising of Jesus from the dead. Likewise, the general resurrection of the dead as a future eschatological event is to be taken, not, it would seem, with full literalness, but certainly with a new seriousness as something more than a myth or metaphor.

There are, of course, many arguments favouring this position. Everyone is agreed that Christianity would never have come into existence unless the first disciples had been utterly convinced that God had raised Jesus from the dead. Also, it can be plausibly argued that one cannot identify the resurrection with what happened to the disciples, and that one is driven to posit a prior and independent event in Jesus himself. At the other end of the time-scale, what does Christian hope amount to, unless there is going to be some kind of restoration in which 'things which were cast down are being raised up, and things which had grown old are being made new, and all things are returning to perfection'?

Pannenberg's treatment of resurrection is especially interesting. As far as the resurrection of Christ is concerned, he claims that this was a truly historical event and not, as Bultmann suggests, a mythological construct for interpreting the meaning of the cross. He also challenges Bultmann's view that the empty tomb stories are later legends, invented to provide an 'objective' account of the resurrection to supplement the 'subjective' account of the appearances. Pannenberg believes that the empty tomb tradition is independent of the appearances tradition, and that these two traditions support one another as evidence for a real historical event of resurrection.[8] He has another argument relating to the idea of resurrection in general, and so one that relates the resurrection of Christ to the notion of a resurrection of the dead in the end-time. This argument is based on philosophical anthropology. The essence of man, it is claimed, is not fulfilled in his earthly existence, for there does not exist that ideal community in which such fulfilment would be possible. Thus 'it is inherent in man to hope beyond death, even as it is inherent in man to know about his own death'.[9] Whether or not Pannenberg's arguments are cogent, one must at least say that he has reopened the whole question of constructing an adequate theology of resurrection.

A further characteristic of the theologies of hope is their strongly social emphasis. The hope of which they speak is not the hope of the individual that he may be saved out of this naughty world, but a hope for the world itself. In this respect, the theologies of hope, like much other contemporary theology, have revolted against the excessive individualism that has been typical of so much Christian theology and piety, especially in the past few centuries. While this individualism has been very widely manifest, once again we may take Bultmann's eschatology as an illustration of it. For Bultmann not only demythologizes eschatology, he individualizes it. Rejecting the idea of an end to history, he interpreted the end rather as the death of the individual. Everyone lives in the face of an end, which is constituted by his own death. It is this fact that gives to every moment the possibility of becoming the eschatological moment of commitment in faith. But the theologies of hope repudiate this individualistic interpretation. For them, the end is an historical end in the future and one embracing all men, the resurrection of the dead or the kingdom of God. Certainly, in an age when we daily become more conscious of our interdependence, a new stress on the social dimension of Christianity is urgently needed.

Although this social interpretation is found in all the theologies of hope, it has been specially developed by Johannes Metz in his concept of a political theology. Such a theology he understands as a corrective to the private character of personalist interpretations of Christianity. The task of political theology is one of 'deprivatizing', to use his expression. 'This deprivatizing', he claims, 'is in a way as important as the programme of demythologizing.'[10] The promise, and so the hope, are given to mankind, to society. He points out that the peculiar form of the gospels makes them not biographies of a private individual but the proclamation of a public person.

The deprivatizing of the Christian hope brings it into relation to the social aspirations of the human race, and especially of the oppressed. Admittedly, there are serious dangers in the road which Metz indicates, and to turn Christianity into a political movement and nothing more would be disastrous. Metz himself shows considerable balance and sanity on these matters, and stresses that political theology is a corrective. He certainly does not suppose that individual commitment and devotion have become unimportant, as some enthusiasts nowadays have come to imagine. Nevertheless, Metz is recognizing that purely individual expressions of Christianity are inadequate in a world that becomes more and more institutionalized. And if Christ is indeed the Lord of all life, then it is correct to call for a deprivatizing of the gospel.

We have seen some of the main characteristics which, with variations from one writer to another, are to be found in the theologies of hope. We can now probe further into the underlying assumptions of these theologies – into their fundamental hermeneutic, so to speak, that gives to them their distinctive flavour. This hermeneutic has two roots – a biblical one and a philosophical one.

On the biblical side, developed especially by Moltmann, the basic categories are promise and fulfilment. This leads to a dynamic interpretation of biblical teaching. One is always on the way from the promise to its fulfilment, to the new which still lies ahead. Moltmann is especially critical of any 'epiphany' type of biblical interpretation, by which he seems to understand any interpretation which thinks of God as a static presence or as giving a finished revelation. God is always coming to his people from the future. God is described as 'the power of a qualitatively new future'[11] and seems indeed to be virtually identified with the expected resurrection of the dead. The life of the people of God, in turn, is to be understood in terms of pilgrimage, under such images as exodus or the march to the promised land, rather than as having settled in that land with an abiding temple in the midst.

On the philosophical side, Ernst Bloch is often mentioned as a major influence on the theologies of hope. But while indeed this verbose quasi-Marxist philosopher has made an impact on the theologians we are considering, it seems to me that the philosophical background is much broader. It is that whole important stream of philosophy that has flowed from Hegel through Feuerbach and Marx to such contemporary writers as Bloch and Marcuse. This stream offers an alternative to existentialism. Of the philosophers mentioned, it is Hegel who seems to be more important than the others. In Moltmann's *Theology of Hope*, Hegel rates thirty-four references as against seven for Bloch; in Pannenberg's *Jesus, God and Man*, Hegel is cited fourteen times as against a solitary mention of Bloch! We have to reckon with the possibility that after a long interval, the influence of Hegel may be coming back in theology. Certainly, the understanding of history found in both Moltmann and Pannenberg is, in many respects, quite Hegelian. The existentialist separation of fact and significance is rejected, and history itself is said to disclose a pattern which makes it revelation and the bearer of the *eschaton*. Likewise, Hegel's concept of the person as inseparable from the social context has had an obvious influence, especially with Pannenberg, who explicitly appeals to it.[12] However, I would like to repeat that the philosophical background of the theologies of hope is not to be found in any single philosopher, whether Hegel or Bloch. Hegel enjoys a certain pre-eminence because he was a far more powerful and original thinker than those who have followed him on the dialectical path. But the true background of the theologies of hope is that whole philosophical movement that may be called the Hegel-Marx-Bloch line, constituting a distinct alternative to what may be called the Kierkegaard-Heidegger-Bultmann line.

The theologies of hope obviously present us with an important development in modern Christian thought. Perhaps this is the most important new theological movement to emerge in the past two or three decades. These theologies are fresh, constructive, and, in many cases, very well argued. They are in some respects quite orthodox and biblical, while in others – especially in their social application – they are quite radical. It is obvious too that they have relevance to many of the concerns that are stirring the world today. However, they also display some characteristics that call for careful scrutiny and criticism.

I shall devote the remainder of my remarks to some critical comments and questions. Let us remember, however, that the positions being criticized may undergo further development, and also that criticisms which may apply to one of those whom I have loosely grouped as 'theologians of hope' may not apply to some of the others.

The first question is whether this whole movement does not involve us in a kind of remythologizing. Existential interpretation of eschatology at least made the subject intelligible by relating it to what we can experience in our existence here and now. Moltmann and Pannenberg are dissatisfied with the Bultmannian account of resurrection, whether the resurrection of Jesus or the resurrection of the dead generally, and they want to insist that in each case resurrection is a real historical happening in itself, whether in the past or in the future, and that this is to be distinguished from the existential experience of new life. But they also tell us that in using words like 'real' and 'historical', they do not mean 'literal'. What then do they mean? This remains almost completely vague. There is indeed some talk of 'transformation', but these theologians offer no philosophical conceptuality from which can be derived an understanding of resurrection that would offer a genuine alternative to Bultmann on the one side and mythology on the other. There are many questions to answer here. As Allan Galloway has remarked, 'What we have in Pannenberg is the outline of a philosophical and theological task that has still to be done, rather than a finished result.'[13] The same could be said even more forcibly about Moltmann.

A second question concerns the ideas of history implicit in the theologies of hope. We have seen reason to believe that a speculative scheme of history is presupposed here, and there seems to be a corresponding disregard of the canons accepted by the ordinary secular historian. Bultmann and many other New

Testament scholars have believed that the critical methods of the historian must be applied quite rigorously to the New Testament, and they have also believed that this can be done without destroying the basis of faith. Moltmann, on the other hand, is very critical of what he calls the 'positivist' historian. This comes out very clearly in his cavalier treatment of the principle of historical analogy. It was Troeltsch who formulated this principle as a canon of historical method. The principle states that a report of a past event will be more or less probable to the extent that we can point to analogous events in our own present experience. Since Bultmann interprets the resurrection of Christ existentially in terms of his appearances to the disciples and their experience of a new life in Christ, he has no problem in pointing to analogous experiences today. Christ still encounters men, they still respond in faith, and so he can say that any moment has the possibility of being the eschatological moment, the moment of rising into a new life. For Moltmann, however, the resurrection is a reality independent of what happened to the disciples, and is, moreover, an historical reality. But then he has to concede that there are no analogies in present experience. The resurrection is said to have been an event 'without parallel'. But how then can it be an historical event? Moltmann is sufficiently respectful toward the principle of historical analogy not just to dismiss it out of hand. He argues that although there is no present analogy, there will be one in what is to come – the resurrection of the dead in the future.[14] The difficulty that he finds himself in is obvious. It is on the basis of the resurrection of Christ in the past that he looks for a resurrection of the dead in the future; yet it will only be this future resurrection of the dead that will supply the analogy giving us reason to believe in the report of a resurrection in the past – or will enable us to understand what could be meant by such a report! There has been resurrection and there will be resurrection, but alas! there is no resurrection now. But how can past and future be used to verify each other, without any reference to the present, which is alone directly accessible to us? One is reminded of what the queen said to Alice in *Through the Looking-Glass*: 'The rule is, jam tomorrow and jam yesterday – but never jam today.' Unfortunately, if there is never jam today, we cannot even know what jam is, still less have any confidence that it either has been or will be available.

This leads to a further critical question, concerning the obsession with the future which seems to be characteristic of the theologies under consideration. We have noted that 'epiphany' is a bad word with Moltmann. An entire tradition of Christian theology and spirituality, centring on what John Baillie called 'the sense of the presence of God', is thus summarily dismissed. With me, let me confess, 'epiphany' is a good word. If there were no present epiphanies of God among the ambiguities of the world, how could we have any beliefs about his actions in the past or in the future?[15]

God is Lord of the present as well as of the future, though we may certainly hope that his Lordship will one day be more fully manifested. But he is assuredly more than a God of promise. The category of promise introduces considerable difficulties into theology. What do we mean by this somewhat mythological expression, 'promise of God'? How does one recognize such a promise? How does one know when it is fulfilled? The theologians of hope sometimes tell us that God's promises are fulfilled in ways different from what we expect. Does this simply mean that the promises are so indefinite that almost anything can be regarded as fulfilling them? Here we seem to be faced with a problem similar to the problem of falsifiability. If everything that happens is taken to be a fulfilment of the promise (albeit a fulfilment different from what was expected), then has not the notion of promise become completely jejune? These difficulties have been felt by Pannenberg, who has given up the 'promise-fulfilment' schema of Moltmann for what he calls 'the history of the transmission of tradition'.[16]

It is worth noting that Rubem Alves is much more aware of the danger of dwelling excessively on the future than are the German founders of the theology of hope. Alves criticizes the coming God of the future as a new kind of docetism. But just as importantly, he points to the dangerous practical consequences of an obsession with the future. Moltmann believes that only if we recognize the godlessness of the present will we be incited to seek the future of God. But Alves (who has probably acquired in Brazil a firsthand knowledge of revolutionaries and utopians) writes: 'The revolutionary absolves man from inhumanity and brutality in the present because this is the time which does not count – only the future matters.'[17] We are thereby reminded of the temptation not to care for the present, because everything and everyone is sacrificed for a (possibly illusory) future. Of course, one may learn the same lesson from Camus.

A further question concerns the rescuing of genuine Christian hope from mere optimism. This seems very difficult if one follows those theologians who advocate the correlation of Christian eschatology with secular planning and futurology. One would have to be very careful not to turn God into the patron saint of a technological society, or identify his kingdom with the attainment of universal affluence. To be sure, a this-worldly emphasis and concern are needed to correct the otherworldliness of much traditional Christian eschatology. But hope for the coming of God's kingdom still remains essentially distinct from an optimistic belief in the modern planners' ability to deliver the good life. Again, it is Alves who shows most balance in this matter, reminding us that human dignity is more important than the consumption of goods – though he would not, of course, deny that human dignity itself requires a floor of material well-being.

These criticisms are not meant to detract from the real merits of the theologies of hope, and especially their determined effort to break out of the individualism that has affected not only eschatology but much else in Christian theology. Perhaps further dialogue between these theologies and other schools of thought will lead to new insights and more adequate ways of understanding Christian truth in our time.

Notes

1. J. Moltmann, *Theology of Hope,* tr. J. W. Leitch, SCM Press and Harper & Row 1967, p. 20.

2. W. Pannenberg, *Jesus, God and Man*, tr. L. L. Wilkins and D. A. Priebe, SCM Press 1968, pp. 82-3.

3. R. Alves, *A Theology of Human Hope*, Corpus Books 1969, p. 102.

4. Op. cit., p. 23.

5. C. E. Braaten, *The Future of God*, Harper & Row 1969, pp. 26-7.

6. J. Moltmann, *Hope and Planning*, tr. M. Clarkson, SCM Press and Harper & Row 1971, pp. 178ff.

7. *Theology of Hope*, p. 165.

8. *Jesus, God and Man*, p. 105.

9. W. Pannenberg, *What Is Man?*, tr. D. A. Priebe, Fortress Press 1970, p. 44. Cf. *Jesus, God and Man*, p. 85.

10. J. Metz, *Theology of the World*, tr. W. Glen-Doepel, Herder & Herder 1969, p. 110.

11. *Hope and Planning*, p. 51.

12. *Jesus, God and Man*, p. 182.

13. A. D. Galloway, *Wolfhart Pannenberg*, Allen & Unwin 1973, p. 131.

14. *Theology of Hope*, p. 180.

15. These points are more fully discussed in my essay, 'Eschatology and Time', *The Future of Man*, ed. F. Herzog, Herder & Herder 1970.

16. W. Pannenberg, *Basic Questions in Theology*, tr. G. H. Keim, SCM Press 1970, vol. i, p. xvii.

17. *A Theology of Human Hope*, p. 155.

INDEX

Index

Alexander, Samuel, 111
Altizer, T. J. J., 52, 54, 62f.
Alves, R., 221, 223f., 230
Anselm, St, 132
Apostles' Creed, 24
Aquinas, St Thomas, 8, 23, 106f., 132, 162
Aristophanes, 149
Aristotle, 75, 162, 196
Arnold, Matthew, 119
Atheism, 88ff., 94ff., 115, 120, 136
Atonement, 167ff.
Augustine, St, 162, 214
Austin, J. L., 18
Ayer, A. J., 38, 119

Baillie, J., 94f., 204, 230
Barr, James, 80
Barth, Karl, 8, 10, 67, 70, 134f., 148, 158, 181, 204ff., 222
Being, 11f., 32, 58, 90f., 106f., 117, 191, 193ff.
Berdyaev, N., 37
Berger, P., 18, 54
Bergson, H., 111
Bloch, E., 63, 227
Bonhoeffer, D., 21f.
Bornkamm, G., 209
Braaten, C. E., 56, 221, 223f.
Bradley, F. H., 26
Brentano, F., 196
Bronowski, J., 138
Brown, R., 34
Brunner, E., 134, 148, 151
Buber, Martin, 64, 102
Bultmann, Rudolf, 11, 67, 70, 81,
160 179ff., 194, 205f., 208f., 222, 225, 227
Buri, F., 93

Cairns, D., 185
Campbell, J. McLeod, 45f., 51, 167ff.
Camus, A., 88, 230
Chadwick, H., 34
Chalcedonian Definition, 25, 38
Cone, J. H., 54
Cosmological Argument, 133
Cox, H., 142f.
Creation, 11, 113, 142ff., 151

Daniélou, Jean Cardinal, 97
Demythologizing, 70, 88, 183, 205, 208, 222ff.
Descartes, R., 28, 39
Dewey, J., 105, 217
Dipolarity, 113
Dodd, C. H., 223
Dualism, 110f., 127f., 139

Ebeling, G., 23, 209
Ecumenical Movement, 205, 209ff.
Edwards, J., 170f.
Epiphany, 227, 230
Eschatology, 65, 67, 139, 186, 222f., 228, 231
Existentialism, 31, 95, 139, 179f., 193, 196, 199, 215, 227f.

Faith, 9, 11, 15, 18, 30, 45f., 90f., 119, 135, 164, 189, 222
Farrer, A., 91, 133

75 76 77 10 9 8 7 6 5 4 3 2 1